Grammar Explorer
TEACHER'S GUIDE

Daphne Mackey & Kristin Sherman

Australia • Brazil • Japan • Korea • Mexico • Singapore • Spain • United Kingdom • United States

Grammar Explorer Teacher's Guide 1
Daphne Mackey and Kristin Sherman

Publisher: Sherrise Roehr

Executive Editor: Laura Le Dréan

Managing Editor: Eve Einselen Yu

Development Editor: Kasia McNabb

Associate Development Editor: Alayna Cohen

Assistant Editor: Vanessa Richards

Senior Technology Product Manager: Scott Rule

Director of Global Marketing: Ian Martin

Marketing Manager: Lindsey Miller

Sr. Director, ELT & World Languages: Michael Burggren

Production Manager: Daisy Sosa

Content Project Manager: Andrea Bobotas

Senior Print Buyer: Mary Beth Hennebury

Cover Designer: 3CD, Chicago

Cover Image: George F. Herben/National Geographic Creative

Compositor: Cenveo® Publisher Services

© 2015 National Geographic Learning, a part of Cengage Learning

ALL RIGHTS RESERVED. No part of this work covered by the copyright herein may be reproduced, transmitted, stored, or used in any form or by any means graphic, electronic, or mechanical, including but not limited to photocopying, recording, scanning, digitizing, taping, Web distribution, information networks, or information storage and retrieval systems, except as permitted under Section 107 or 108 of the 1976 United States Copyright Act, or applicable copyright law of another jurisdiction, without the prior written permission of the publisher.

> For product information and technology assistance, contact us at
> **Cengage Learning Customer & Sales Support,**
> **1-800-354-9706**
>
> For permission to use material from this text or product, submit all requests online at **www.cengage.com/permissions**.
> Further permissions questions can be e-mailed to **permissionrequest@cengage.com**.

Teacher's Guide 1: 978-1-111-35091-8

National Geographic Learning
20 Channel Center Street
Boston, MA 02210
USA

Cengage Learning is a leading provider of customized learning solutions with office locations around the globe, including Singapore, the United Kingdom, Australia, Mexico, Brazil and Japan.

Cengage Learning products are represented in Canada by Nelson Education, Ltd.

Visit National Geographic Learning online at **ngl.cengage.com**

Visit our corporate website at **www.cengage.com**

Printed in the United States of America
Print Number: 01   Print Year: 2014

CONTENTS

From the Series Editors iv

Series Components v

General Guide to Teaching a Unit 2

Unit-Specific Teaching Tips and Answer Keys 9

    Unit 1 9

    Unit 2 20

    Unit 3 31

    Unit 4 43

    Unit 5 52

    Unit 6 61

    Unit 7 70

    Unit 8 79

    Unit 9 90

    Unit 10 100

    Unit 11 111

    Unit 12 120

    Unit 13 130

    Unit 14 140

Audio Scripts A1

FROM THE SERIES EDITORS

Message from the Series Editors

As the series editors, we are pleased to introduce the exciting new *Grammar Explorer* series. Throughout the process of developing these materials, our goal has been to provide students and teachers with a solid and thorough grammar experience that is easy for teachers and engaging for learners.

We do not take the word *explorer* lightly. We want to provide students and teachers with fascinating global content that acknowledges the incredibly diverse world we live in. This content allows students to explore the world and discuss their roles in it through meaningful communication. Students also explore language. They encounter the grammar in rich listening, speaking, reading, and writing activities that focus on a wide variety of topics—from science and innovation to ancient history. Students develop communicative skills that will serve them beyond the classroom.

Rob Jenkins and Staci Johnson

Introduction to *Grammar Explorer*

Grammar Explorer is a three-level grammar series starting at high-beginning and moving through low-advanced. Each unit of *Grammar Explorer* has two to four well-structured lessons that introduce and practice the target grammar gradually, with control and *without* overwhelming students.

Each *Grammar Explorer* lesson will captivate students with its content and engage them with a series of thought-provoking activities. The lesson starts with a short high-interest text where students *discover* the grammar. It continues with controlled practice of the target grammar point, and gradually moves toward open-ended speaking and/or writing activities.

Students learn, construct meaning, and practice using **all four skills**, with the goal of communicating fluently while using the target grammar accurately and appropriately. Each activity serves a purpose and provides a step in the path to student success. Furthermore, the series assists teachers by providing well-thought-out lessons that make teaching and learning both more effective *and* more fun.

Why does *Grammar Explorer* work?

Real-World Content

Relevant up-to-date topics and photos capture students' attention and bring learning to life. Students immediately have a reason to communicate on themes that reflect the world they live in. Grammar discovered through interesting content, as it is throughout *Grammar Explorer*, provides a common starting place for all learners and eventually leads seamlessly to application.

Integrated Skills in Controlled Lessons

Every unit of *Grammar Explorer* provides numerous opportunities to read, write, listen, and speak. Charts are simple and do not provide more information than a student can grasp at one time. After warming up with the *Explore* section, students do the controlled practice in *Learn* to ensure that they have a sufficient understanding of the structure before moving on to more open-ended and communicative activities in *Practice*.

Application of Knowledge

Each lesson and unit in *Grammar Explorer* ends with an application exercise. Teachers everywhere know that students not only need to master rules but also try out those rules by speaking and writing on their own. Carefully designed application exercises aim to help students gain the confidence they need to successfully transfer what they have learned to real life. Application exercises ask students to **critically think** about a variety of topics, **synthesize** information they have learned in a lesson or unit, and **use English** to discuss and communicate their ideas.

Flexible Learning

1. **Flipped Classrooms:** The readings, controlled practice activities, and listening activities can be assigned as out-of-class work, allowing teachers to focus on interactive and productive activities in class, while students work at their own pace at home.

2. **Blended or Online:** The Online Workbook and interactive eBook provide options for teaching a blended or fully online course.

SERIES COMPONENTS

Grammar Explorer components support a variety of classrooms, including traditional, flipped, blended, and online.

For the Student

Student Book

Also available in:
- split editions
- eBooks

Audio CD

Students can listen to:
- all *Explore* readings
- all listening activities
- all pronunciation activities

eBook

eBooks give learners fully integrated online, downloadable, and mobile access to their programs. With eBooks you can:
- complete and save activities
- listen to embedded audio
- search for keywords or phrases
- skip to any section with a functional table of contents
- highlight text and make notes
- view on devices running Mac®, Windows®, iOS™, and Android™

Online Workbook

The Online Workbook has both teacher-led and self-study options and includes:
- extensive additional practice of grammar in each lesson
- review exercises, including a "Unit Challenge" game
- interactive, automatically-graded activities
- independent practice for self-study, or results reported to instructor in MyELT
- additional listening practice
- additional pronunciation practice

For the Teacher

Teacher's Guide

In addition to presenting a general guide for teaching a unit, the Teacher's Guide provides:
- detailed teaching notes and background information for each unit
- suggestions for online activities to engage students with lesson themes
- extension activities and alternative writing exercises
- tips for flipped classrooms: activities can be assigned as homework, allowing teachers to focus on interactive activities in class
- answer keys and audio scripts

Teacher's eResource

The Teacher's eResource can be used as a reference and a Classroom Presentation Tool. With the Teacher's eResource, instructors can:
- project the Student Book pages and reveal answers
- challenge students to provide new example sentences in customizable grammar charts
- play embedded audio in the classroom
- reference the complete Teacher's Guide in an electronic version

Assessment CD-ROM with ExamView®

Assessment CD-ROM with ExamView® is an easy-to-use test generating program that:
- provides pre-made test questions for every unit
- allows teachers to customize their tests or create quizzes in as little as three minutes

GENERAL GUIDE TO TEACHING A UNIT

Unit Opener

Each unit begins with an engaging National Geographic photo, the unit theme, and a list of the lessons and target grammar structures.

Using the Photo

- Direct students' attention to the photo and the photo caption. Ask them level-appropriate questions such as: *Who are the people? What do you see? Where is this? What is the theme of the unit? What does the photo say about the theme?*
- Ask students to write three questions about the photo. Then, if they have Internet access or are previewing at home, see if they can find answers to their questions online or in another reference.
- Read the Unit-Specific Teaching Tips to find background notes on the photo and theme-specific questions to ask.

Using the Table of Contents

- Draw students' attention to the table of contents in the box on the lower right. You may want to check their previous knowledge of the grammar by asking them: *Which grammar do you already know? What is an example?* Write any examples on the board and ask other students if they are correct. Don't provide any explanation at this point. This is a good way to get a sense of where your students are.
- If the grammar is new or if you want to be sure they understand the grammar-related language, you can preview the grammar terms that students will see in the unit. For your convenience, the Unit-Specific Teaching Tips provide a list of grammar terms and definitions for each unit. Also be sure to tell students to refer to the Glossary of Grammar Terms in the back of their Student Book any time they are unsure of a grammatical term.

Orienting Students to the Unit Theme

- Tell students to flip through the unit for one minute, looking at the pictures and reading any titles and captions. Then, ask students what they think the unit will be about and have them write their three guesses on a piece of paper. After they discuss their ideas with a group for two minutes, ask each group for their "best" answer.
- For three- or four-lesson units, tell students to flip through and look at the *Explore* readings at the beginning of each lesson in the unit. Ask them to rank the readings in order of interest. If possible, they can explain why.

Lessons

Each unit has two to four lessons.

- See the Unit-Specific Teaching Tips for student learning outcomes (SLOs) for each lesson. The **SLOs** help you and your students see more concretely what they will learn, or have learned. Write or project the SLOs on the board before you begin a new lesson and after you finish a lesson or a unit.

EXPLORE

1 READ.

This section provides a model reading in one of many genres, including magazine articles, websites, conversations, blog posts, radio shows, and others.

- Have students skim the text quickly and call out any words they don't understand. Write them on the board and, as a group, define each one using an example sentence or a drawing. **Option:** On the board, write only those words you feel are necessary for students to know. See if a student can provide a definition or an example sentence for each. Write your students' correct definitions or example sentences on the board. Write your own if they do not have any.
- See the Unit-Specific Teaching Tips for "Be the Expert," which provides background information on the content and often includes ideas on how to use the information in class.
- Play the audio as students follow along silently. Try stopping at the end of each paragraph and asking students comprehension questions.
- Play the audio again or have students read in pairs. Reading more than once will help students become more familiar with the content, vocabulary, and grammar.

Photo Tips: In addition to the unit opener, the Student Book features many photos. Some illustrate the text, while others provide context for listening activities.
- Direct students' attention to a photo and use it to illustrate any vocabulary.
- Use photos to recycle target grammar from previous lessons or units.
- Be sure to draw students' attention to captions as these will provide additional important information and provide context for the exercise.

General Reading Tips

The reading activities provide students with grammar in context, help them expand their vocabulary, and engage them with interesting content. While the Unit-Specific Teaching Tips offer information for individual passages, for further expansion and exploitation, you can also:
- have students create additional comprehension items about the passage;
- have students do paired readings of the passage to practice oral fluency;
- photocopy and cut up the passage into pieces for students to put in order, jigsaw-style:
  1. Cut reading passage into three or four parts. If it's a conversation, consider cutting after each line or group of lines.
  2. Put students into groups of three or four (See *Tips for Grouping* on page 6) and give each student one part of the text.
  3. Students read their part and learn the general ideas. Then, they tell their groupmates what is in their part.
  4. As a group, they decide which part is first, second, and so on. This can be a good opportunity to point out discourse markers such as topic sentences, introductions, and conclusions.

General Vocabulary Tips

Both the reading passages and the audio inputs expose students to vocabulary that may be unfamiliar to them. Incorporating the following techniques into the classroom will help students acquire language better and develop study habits that will help them outside and beyond the classroom.
- Suggest that students keep a vocabulary notebook and add unfamiliar words as well as definitions and sentences. Tell them to write down sentences they hear or find online. This will help them see the common collocations and grammar patterns that often occur with certain words.
- Facilitate dictionary skills by having students look up new words.
- Help students acquire these words by suggesting that they practice them in speaking and writing activities.
- At lower levels, encourage students to make flashcards and practice them in pairs. Be sure to tell them to focus on commonly used words as opposed to highly specialized words. For beginners, for example, the word *mangrove* is not as important as *forest*.

Front

```
explore (verb)
/ɛksplôr/
```

Back

```
Translation: (students
first language)

Collocation: explore a
place/a topic/ideas

Other forms:
explorer (noun, person)
exploration (noun, idea)
```

GENERAL GUIDE TO TEACHING A UNIT

2 CHECK.

This section provides short comprehension questions about the reading.

- Have students complete the activity individually before checking their answers with a partner.
- For higher-level students or early finishers, write additional questions on the board to complete, or have them write their own additional questions.

3 DISCOVER.

These section activities guide students from noticing the target structure in the reading to identifying information about the structure. Exercise **A** generally provides a noticing exercise, and exercise **B** elicits rules or shows students important level-appropriate aspects of the form or function of the grammar.

- Have students complete exercise **A** alone or for more interactivity and support, in pairs.
- Have students complete exercise **B** individually. This will help them learn to notice patterns and infer rules. Then, provide an opportunity for peer or class discussion to clarify the usage of the grammar and explain or elicit rules.
- See the Unit-Specific Teaching Tips for ideas to help bridge the *Explore* section to the grammar charts in *Learn*.

FLIP IT!

Have students do the *Explore* section of a lesson at home.

1. Preview the reading in class and ask students to look at the photo and title and make predictions about the content.
2. Pre-teach unfamiliar vocabulary.
3. Students read and complete the *Explore* exercises at home.
4. Students compare their answers to exercises **2** and **3** with a partner as soon as they get to class.
5. Allow students to discuss any questions they have about the grammar. Encourage other students to explain the rule.

LEARN

Grammar Charts

- See the Unit-Specific Teaching Tips for information specific to the grammar in a unit and for ideas for presenting the grammar in class.

Presentation of Model Structures

Option 1: Read the sentences in the chart and have students repeat. If the chart poses questions and answers, call on students and ask the questions, eliciting the appropriate responses.

Option 2: Call on students to read the sentences in the chart. Ask questions to check comprehension (e.g., *What form of* be *do we use with* he? *What form of the main verb do we use in a question? What part of speech is this word/phrase?*).

Practice of Model Structures

Option 1: Write the parts of the sentence on different cards or sentence strips and have students come to the board and put them in order.

Option 2: Draw the outline of the grammar chart on the board or project the customizable chart in the Teacher's eResource. Include the grammar labels (e.g., *Noun, Verb, . . .*), but do not include the example sentences. Have students provide new examples sentences of their own.

Option 3: As in Option 2, provide the model structure, but with a new example filled in and the grammar labels missing. Have students choose or tell you the correct label for each part of the sentence.

Presentation of the Notes/Rules Chart

Option 1: Have students read the notes silently (or at home). Ask them to tell a partner another example sentence. Then, have some students write more examples sentences on the board. Answer any questions.

Option 2: With partners, ask students to cover the rule/note side of the notes chart and first read the examples, noticing the bold words. See if students can tell you the rule. Then, read the rule together and check.

Practice of the Notes/Rules Chart

Option 1: Either to review or as a follow up to home study, project the notes on the board and have students write examples of their own.

Option 2: Provide examples and have students identify the rule from their chart in their book.

> **BE A GRAMMAR EXPLORER!**
>
> Let students know that language and its rules are always changing. They may hear examples of language that there are no rules for, and they may find that native speakers often disagree on what is "correct." Encourage them to notice the language and explore it outside of their textbooks. Try the following.
> - Have a grammar *Show and Tell*. Tell students to find examples of the grammar they are studying and bring it to class. Let students figure out the grammar rule, if there is one. Guide them when necessary to a relevant chart. This can bring to light many unusual usages that they will not find rules for.
> - Have students keep a grammar journal, noting examples that they find in the real world.

General Tips for Controlled Activities
- Have students compare their answers in pairs before asking for the answers from individual students. This will help reduce anxiety and give students the confidence to speak.
- Use the Teacher's eResource to project the exercise with answers on the board and let students check their own work. You can also write answers as students say them, or ask students to come up and write the answers.
- When calling on students to check answers or demonstrate the language, be sure to surprise them by calling names randomly. This will keep them more focused on the task since they are never sure who will be next.
- Avoid letting stronger or more talkative students dominate the class. Check names as you call on them, so you are sure that everyone has a chance to participate.

PRACTICE

LISTEN Activities
- Set the context, provide background and cultural notes, and pre-teach essential vocabulary. You may want to write the vocabulary on the board. Instead of pre-teaching, elicit possible meanings of the words after students listen once.
- Play the audio once from beginning to end so that students have a chance to listen for overall comprehension. They should be able to get the gist of the input in one listening. If you are reading the script, read with expression and at a natural pace. Do not slow down or overarticulate. You can also photocopy the audio script and have students read along chorally.
- Play the audio again as students complete the task. You may want to stop at intervals to give students time to answer questions.

General Listening Activity Tips
- Before any listening, have students read through the items so that they know what to listen for.
- In many exercises, you can have students predict correct answers before they listen and check.
- The audio provides another kind of language input for students. Many students are intimidated by listening, so you may need to provide extra scaffolding. Allow students to listen to the audio first to achieve a more authentic experience. Then, if students have difficulty, let them read the audio script.

SPEAK Activities
- After students work with a partner and you monitor their work, call on a few students to model for the class, addressing any common errors.
- With free speaking that asks students to offer their own ideas, allow them to work with a partner. After a set amount of time (5–8 minutes), call on two or three pairs of students to share their ideas and/or tell the class about their partners.

General Speaking Activity Tips
- Model any controlled speaking activity. Ask a student to be your partner and demonstrate the first item to the class. Have students repeat any language they may need before they begin.
- Walk around and monitor students during any group activity. Help individual students with pronunciation or other aspects of their speaking as you walk around.

GENERAL GUIDE TO TEACHING A UNIT

WRITE Activities
- If students completed the activity for homework, put them in pairs to exchange work and provide feedback.
- As with freer speaking activities, call on students to share their ideas and/or tell the class about their partner's ideas.
- You may want to collect writing samples to use as an informal assessment. To help, have students exchange papers with a partner and provide feedback.

FLIP IT!
Have students complete the writing tasks at home. If you have a class website, blog, or LMS, let students post their work. Ask students to read each other's work and leave at least one positive comment and one comment that suggests an improvement.

EDIT Activities
- Display the corrected sentences on the board or with a projector, using the Teacher's eResource. Give students the opportunity to ask questions and discuss the corrections.
- You may want to display the EDIT activity without the answers and correct the errors as students say them or let students correct them on their own.

General Tip for Error Correction
If a student makes an error either in writing on the board or in a spoken exercise, be sure to give them a chance to correct themselves. Indicate that it is wrong with a facial expression or gesture of some kind. Give the student or her classmates a chance to identify and correct the error.

APPLY Activities
- To make the activity more interactive or to provide extra scaffolding for students, have them work in pairs or small groups to generate ideas and/or gather information.
- Students produce language in spoken or written form. After students have completed this part, provide an opportunity for them to share their work by speaking or reading to the class, a small group, or a new partner.
- Facilitate any interaction by encouraging students to get up and talk to five new classmates.

General Tips for Grouping
- To assure that students do not only talk to their friends, try assigning them to a different partner each time by using different techniques:
- Prepare cards from a deck with two of each type of card, e.g., aces, ones, twos, . . . (depending on the number of students). Hand them out and have students find their match.
- Try pairing lower-level students with higher-level students. Read their names and indicate where they should sit.
- For small groups (three to four students are best), tell students to count off in threes or fours (for classes of 12–21 students). Then, ask all number ones to raise their hands; then twos, threes, etc. Point to a part of the room and tell each group where to sit.

Review the Grammar
This section always includes an activity that combines the grammar from the lessons in a unit, a listening activity, and an editing activity. It can be used for assessment purposes by you or as a self-assessment for the students.

FLIP IT!
Have students do the controlled activities, EDIT, and LISTEN as an out-of-class assignment to allow them time to go back and review the unit as necessary.

Note: Students need the audio in order to complete the LISTEN exercise. They can find this on the Student Companion Site at NGL.Cengage.com/GrammarExplorer

Connect the Grammar to Writing
Students first read and identify the grammar in a model. Then, they analyze the organization/content of the model text. After they brainstorm and organize their ideas, they write their own piece of writing. Students focus both on accurate usage of the target grammar and a new writing strategy or skill. The Writing Focus boxes are designed to build on each other throughout each book, giving students a toolbox for writing by the end of the series.

1 READ & NOTICE THE GRAMMAR.

> **FLIP IT!**
>
> Students can do the READ & NOTICE THE GRAMMAR activities at home. Then, let them check answers with a partner and brainstorm ideas for their own writing when they come to class.

- If you do this activity in class, have students preview the three parts of the activity.
- Have students read the text silently or follow along as you read it aloud. Put students in pairs to discuss answers to the grammar noticing activity.
- Have students read the Grammar Focus box and complete the task in exercise **B**.
- Have students compare the information in the graphic organizers in exercise **C** with a partner.
- Or project the graphic organizers, using the Teacher's eResource, and have students fill it in together. Discuss as a class, eliciting any corrections from students.

2 BEFORE YOU WRITE.

- After explaining the activity, provide students with enough time to generate ideas. Don't rush this part of the writing process. **Option:** Have students share their ideas in pairs or small groups. Encourage them to ask each other questions to clarify and get more information.
- Walk around the room to provide help as needed. **Option:** Have students generate ideas as an out-of-class assignment, and then share their ideas in the next class.
- See the Unit-Specific Teaching Tips for an alternative writing option that can be used for additional in-class writing or homework.

3 WRITE.

- Go over the instructions and the Writing Focus box. Have students complete the assignment in class or at home.
- See the Unit-Specific Teaching Tips for more activity ideas for practicing the Writing Focus box in class.

4 SELF ASSESS.

- Go over the checklist. Have students use the checklist to edit their own work. You may want to have students exchange their writing and use the checklist to edit each other's work and provide feedback.

> **FLIP IT!**
>
> Have students complete WRITE at home. If you have a class website, blog, or LMS, let students post their work. Ask students to read each other's work and leave at least one positive comment and one comment that suggests an improvement, or use the checklist and have students evaluate their own or each other's work in class.

Assessment

Grammar Explorer provides four different types of assessment:

1. **Formative Assessment within the Unit**

   Formative assessment is used to determine how learning is going and whether or not more explanation, practice, and general help are needed before continuing. The LEARN activities after the charts, the final exercises before the APPLY, and the Review the Grammar activities can serve as the formative assessment.

2. **Review the Grammar**

   By monitoring student success in these end-of-unit activities, instructors can determine if students are prepared to go on to the writing section; they can determine how much students have learned and what their problem areas might be.

3. **Connect the Grammar to Writing**

   This end-of-unit writing is another type of assessment. It will show your students' progress with the grammar of the current unit and all previous units. A rubric is a good way to evaluate students' work. Share the rubric with students before they write. You may want to start with a simple rubric, and then with each new unit add a writing focus and/or grammar review point from a previous unit or units. See page 8 for an example rubric.

4. **Assessment CD-ROM with ExamView[R]**

   - Create custom tests and quizzes. Teachers can choose the test questions they want and/or add their own items.
   - Can be used to create tests for various purposes that include:
     - creating a unit pretest to see what students already know;
     - creating a summative final test;
     - creating additional practice activities in the form of a quiz.

GENERAL GUIDE TO TEACHING A UNIT

Rubric to Assess Writing

Standard	3	2	1	0
Student writing is clear and easy to understand.	Writing is clear and requires little or no inferences.	Writing is somewhat clear and requires some inferences.	Writing is more unclear than clear and requires many inferences.	Writing does not relate to the assignment or is completely unclear.
Student uses [grammar points here] correctly.	90–100 percent of the time.	70–89 percent of the time.	Less than 70 percent but more than once or twice.	Rarely if ever.
[Writing Focus for the unit; add each new writing focus as you progress through the book.]	90–100 percent of the time.	70–89 percent of the time.	Less than 70 percent, but more than once or twice.	Rarely if ever.
[Add your own focus.]	90–100 percent of the time.	70–89 percent of the time.	Less than 70 percent, but more than once or twice.	Rarely if ever.

UNIT 1 People
The Verb *Be*

Unit Opener

Photo: Ask students for their ideas about the photo. Point and ask questions (e.g., *Who are the people? Where are they?*).

Location: Uttar Pradesh is a state in India bordering Nepal. Ask a student to locate India or Uttar Pradesh on a map.

Theme: This unit talks about people and their lives in different parts of the world. Ask students to look at the photos on pages 12 and 28. Ask, *Where are the people in these photos? Where is she? Where is he?*

Page	Lesson	Grammar	Examples
4	1	Simple Present of *Be*: Affirmative Statements; Contractions with *Be*	I **am** from Italy. Megan**'s** from Canada.
11	2	*Be* + Singular/Plural Noun; Simple Present of *Be*: Negative Statements	South Africa **is a country**. You and Sam **are engineers**. They**'re**/They **are not** from China.
21	3	Descriptive Adjectives	They are **late**. She is an **interesting** person.
28	4	Possessive Adjectives; Possessive Nouns	**My** name is Manik. The **student's** last name is Ming.
35	Review the Grammar		
38	Connect the Grammar to Writing		

Unit Grammar Terms

adjective: a word that describes or modifies a noun or pronoun.
➢ She is **friendly**.
➢ Brazil is a **huge** country.

affirmative statement: a sentence that does not have a verb in the negative form.
➢ My uncle **is** tall.

negative statement: A statement that has a verb in the negative form (*not*).
➢ I **don't have** any sisters.
➢ She **doesn't drink** coffee.

noun: a word that names a person, a place, or a thing.
➢ They're **students**.
➢ It's an excellent **hospital**.

possessive adjective: an adjective that shows ownership or relationship (*my, your, his, her, its, our, their*). It is used with a noun.
➢ **My** car is green.
➢ **Your** keys are on the table.

possessive noun: a noun that shows ownership or a relationship.
➢ **Leo's** apartment is large.
➢ The **girls'** books are on the table.

pronoun: a word that takes the place of a noun or refers to a noun.
➢ The teacher is sick today. **He** has a cold.

subject: the noun or pronoun that is the topic of a sentence.
➢ **Patricia** is a doctor.
➢ **They** are from Iceland.

LESSON 1	Simple Present of *Be*; Contractions with *Be*
Student Learning Outcomes	• **Read** about greetings around the world. • **Listen** and fill out name cards. • **Complete** a name card. • **Find** and **edit** errors with subjects and simple present of *be*. • **Introduce** yourself and classmates using appropriate greetings. • **Write** a paragraph about yourself using subject + *be*.
Lesson Vocabulary	(v.) bow (n.) classmate (n.) custom (v. & n.) kiss (n.) city (n.) country (n.) greeting (v.) shake (hands)

EXPLORE

1 READ, page 4   20 min.

- Have students look at the photo. Read the caption and model the Thai greeting with a student, saying "Hello" with your palms together, straight up and down.
- To introduce or review these words before reading, pantomime *bow, shake hands, hug,* and *kiss* (point to each cheek).
- Say the names of other countries from the reading (*Japan, France, Germany, Italy*) and see if students can pantomime the greeting from that country. Then read or listen to the text to check answers.
- If students in your class are from different countries, have them teach each other how to greet properly in their countries, using sentences from the reading: *My name is . . . In [country], we . . .*

Be the Expert

- Different countries have different greetings. For example, in Arabic countries people often offer *As-salaam alaykum* (Peace be upon you) as a greeting, and respond with *Alaykum as-salaam* (Upon you be peace).
- People in Arabic and other countries use their right hands to shake hands. People in many countries feel the left hand is dirty.

2 CHECK, page 4   10 min.

Marie is from France.   Martin and Greta are from Germany.
David is from Italy.
Miyo is from Japan.   Aran is from Thailand.

- **Tip:** Ask higher-level students to give answers in complete sentences. Ask lower-level students to give you just the name and country.

- **Tip:** For higher-level students, a good first day activity is exercise **13** on page 10.

3 DISCOVER, page 4   10 min.

1. is   2. 'm   3. 're; are

- **Tip:** To prepare students for the chart in LEARN, write these sentences in chart form, but leave the verb and top row blank. Tell students to write the missing words in their notebooks. Then complete the chart by asking students to write or say the missing words. Finally, write the headings *Subject, Be* in the top row.

Subject	Be	
I	am	from [country].
He/She/It	is	from France.
We/You/They	are	from Japan.

LEARN

Chart 1.1, page 6   15 min.

- **Note 5:** To practice subjects with nouns connected by *and*, select two students and have them begin a sentence: *Jean and Misha are . . .* Let the class finish if they are able, or you can complete the sentence . . . *students/tall/happy/smiling.*

4 page 6   10 min.

1. Hello. (My name) is Miyo.
2. (Marie and Jean) are from France.
3. (I) am from New York.
4. (Chile) is a country.
5. (We) are students.

10   THE VERB *BE*

6. (Jim and Alex) are teachers.
7. (I) am Japanese.
8. (You) are from Thailand.

5 page 7   5 min.

1. am   6. is
2. are   7. are
3. is   8. am
4. is   9. are
5. are   10. is

- **Expansion Tip:** Project or show photos of famous people. Have students tell a partner a sentence about the person. Then have pairs share answers with the class. *They are from China. She is from Brazil.*

6 SPEAK, page 7   5 min.

- **Expansion Tip:** Teach students the phrase *Nice to meet you.* Model a conversation of introduction with a student. Then have students walk around the classroom for two minutes saying, "*Hello. My name is . . .*" to classmates they don't know.

Chart 1.2, page 7   10 min.

- **Note:** Some students may believe that contractions are too informal. Assure them that we use contractions a lot. Tell them that everyone uses contractions in speaking, even presidents. If a student says the full form, say the contraction back with a little emphasis to let them know it's appropriate.

7 page 8   5 min.

1. She's   5. You're
2. They're   6. It's
3. We're   7. He's
4. I'm   8. They're

- **Expansion Tip:** If you have students from different countries, ask a volunteer to stand. Tell other students to use the language in exercise 7 to talk about the student. (e.g., *Jun is from Korea. He's Korean.*)

8 page 8   10 min.

1. A: 's; 'm
   B: 's; 'm
2. A: 'm
   B: 's
   A: 're; 'm
3. A: 're
   B: 're; 'm
   A: 're
   A: 'm

PRACTICE

9 page 8   10 min.

1. is; She's   6. are; They're
2. are; We're   7. is; He's
3. 'm; I'm   8. are; You're
4. is; She's   9. is; I'm
5. is; He's   10. is; It's

10 page 9   15 min.

1. name's   6. Feng's
2. I'm   7. are
3. I'm   8. Diego's
4. are   9. She's
5. 's   10. are

- **Alternative Writing & Speaking:** Give students five minutes to write the paragraph in exercise **10**, but tell them to change the information so it's about themselves and their class. Ask a volunteer or two to read their paragraph aloud.

11 LISTEN & SPEAK, page 9   15 min.

A
Adele Silva	Anna Rossi	Nick Clark
Recife	Rome	Boston
Brazil	Italy	U.S.A.

12 EDIT, page 10   10 min.

My name **is** Adele Silva. **I'm** from Recife. **It's** a city in Brazil. **I'm** a student in Boston. **It's** a city in the United States. **It's** in Massachusetts.

13 WRITE & SPEAK, page 10   15 min.

> **REAL ENGLISH, page 10**
>
> Before students do exercise **C**, read the box (or ask a student to read it). Then model using *This is . . .* to introduce a student in class.

- **Tip:** This is a good activity to do on the first day of class with higher-level students.

14 SPEAK, page 10   15 min.

- **Tip:** This is another good activity to do on the first day of class with higher-level students.

15 APPLY, page 10   10 min.

- **Tip:** If your students have mastered talking about themselves, have them create a chart similar to the one in exercise **10** with famous people they know about. Then have them share their information with other students.

UNIT 1   LESSON 1   11

LESSON 2	Be + Singular Noun; Be + Plural Noun			
Student Learning Outcomes	• **Read** about adventurers and animals in Africa. • **Listen** and **practice** pronunciation of *-s/-es* endings. • **Write** descriptive information about people. • **Find** and **edit** errors with singular and plural nouns, *a/an*, and negatives. • **Speak** in a group about categorizing words. • **Describe** people using *be (not)* + nouns. • **Write** statements about your classmates using *be (not)* + nouns.			
Lesson Vocabulary	(n.) animal (n.) author	(n.) continent (n.) filmmaker	(n.) island (n.) photographer	(n.) profession (n.) river

EXPLORE

1 READ, page 11   20 min.

- Before reading, read the caption and use the photo to preview the vocabulary *animal, filmmaker, photographer,* and *camera.* Pantomime the difference between *photographer* and *filmmaker*.
- As you listen, point to Africa, Botswana, and Johannesburg on the globe.

Be the Expert

National Geographic supports people who research and explore the world. Dereck and Beverly Joubert are two of National Geographic's many explorers. They have been exploring, filming, and writing about Africa for over 25 years and have won many awards. You can learn more about them and other explorers on their website. Search *National Geographic Explorers.*

2 CHECK, page 12   5 min.

1. a   2. b   3. a   4. b   5. a

3 DISCOVER, page 12   5 min.

A 1. an   2. a   3. a

B Rule 1 is correct.

- **Tip:** Say a few words. Have students identify whether they are singular or plural. Hold up one finger or many fingers as nonverbal cues.

LEARN

Chart 1.3, page 13   10 min.

- **Note 1:** Many languages do not use articles. It's helpful to consistently use a nonverbal cue to signify that an article should be used when correcting this mistake.

- **Note 2:** To help students remember the vowels, give them a visual cue. Draw a face with *a* and *e* as eyes, *i* as the nose, *o* as the face, and *u* as the mouth.
- **Notes 1, 2 & 3:** Ask students to use *a* or *an* with additional examples (e.g., class, book, Canada, exercise, photo, app, Dereck, etc.).

REAL ENGLISH , page 13

On the board, write *Vowel sound?* and list *university, you, hour,* and *house.* Pronounce and ask students to tell you if the word begins with the sound of a vowel. Read the *Real English* box. Then elicit and write *a* or *an* before each word in the list.

4 page 13   5 min.

1. a   5. a   9. a
2. an   6. a   10. an
3. a   7. an   11. a
4. an   8. a   12. an

5 page 14   10 min.

1. Beverly is a photographer.
2. A leopard is an animal.
3. Africa is a continent.
4. Harvard is a university.
5. She is a professor.
6. He is a student.
7. You are an engineer.
8. Photography is a profession.
9. Carmen is an author.
10. It is an article.

Chart 1.4, page 14   10 min.

- **Note 1:** Some languages do not have a plural marker for nouns such as *-s*.

6 page 15 — 5 min.

1. are explorers
2. are women
3. are animals
4. are universities
5. are students
6. are classes
7. are countries
8. are continents
9. are cities
10. are languages

7 PRONUNCIATION, page 15 — 20 min.

- **Tip:** Demonstrate the difference between voiced and voiceless sounds by having students put their hands on their throats and pronounce the example words.

A
1. /z/
2. /s/
3. /əz/
4. /z/
5. /əz/
6. /z/
7. /z/
8. /s/
9. /əz/
10. /z/
11. /z/
12. /z/

Chart 1.5, page 16 — 10 min.

- **Tip:** Give students oral practice with more examples to change from affirmative to negative: *You're teachers. I'm a student. Yun is from Canada.*

8 page 16 — 15 min.

1. No, he isn't/he's not a photographer. He's a filmmaker.
2. No, they aren't/they're not from Botswana. They're from South Africa.
3. No, they aren't/they're not brothers. They're friends.
4. No, it isn't/it's not a book. It's a film.
5. No, he isn't/he's not a teacher. He's a student.
6. No, they aren't/they're not from Brazil. They're from Portugal.
7. No, she isn't/she's not a doctor. She's an engineer.
8. No, she's not/she isn't an author. She's an artist.
9. No, she isn't/she's not Canadian. She's French.
10. No, it isn't/it's not a country. It's a city.
11. No, it isn't/it's not an ocean. It's a river.
12. No, it isn't/it's not a city. It's a country.
13. No, they aren't/they're not countries. They're continents.
14. No, they aren't/they're not countries. They're nationalities.

PRACTICE

9 page 18 — 10 min.

1. Korea isn't/Korea's not a city.
2. Nora and I aren't explorers.
3. Seoul and Tokyo aren't countries.
4. Nick isn't/Nick's not Brazilian.
5. I'm not a teacher.
6. You aren't/You're not from Mexico.
7. She isn't/She's not a filmmaker.
8. We aren't/We're not actors.
9. He isn't/He's not from Japan.
10. It isn't/It's not a film.

10 EDIT, page 18 — 10 min.

1. Madrid, London, and Prague are ~~city~~ cities.
2. Europe ~~aren't~~ isn't a country. It's a continent.
3. Iceland and Ireland ~~is~~ are islands. Water is all around them.
4. The Rhine is a river in Europe. It's in Germany.
5. Correct
6. The Atlantic isn't a river. It's an ocean.
7. Correct
8. Lisbon isn't in Spain. It's in Portugal.

11 SPEAK, page 19 — 15 min.

1. desk
2. banana
3. Rome
4. book
5. India
6. notebook
7. Romania
8. Tokyo

12 SPEAK, LISTEN & WRITE, page 19 — 25 min.

B 1. doctor 2. musicians 3. professor
C 1. Brazil 2. England 3. China
E
1. Larissa isn't/Larissa's not from England. She's from Brazil.
2. Chu Ying's not/Chu Ying isn't a doctor. He's a professor.
3. Jude and Liz aren't professors. They're musicians.
4. Jude's not/Jude isn't from China. He's from England.
5. Liz isn't a professor. She's a musician.
6. Chu Ying is from China.
7. Larissa isn't/Larissa's not a musician. She's a doctor.
8. Liz isn't from Brazil. She's from England.

- **Alternative Listening & Writing:** Dictate three false affirmative sentences about yourself. Have students (1) write the sentences, (2) change them from affirmative to negative, and (3) change them from first person "I" to the third person.

13 APPLY, page 20 — 20 min.

- **Tip:** Follow up by having students write two true sentences and one false sentence about themselves. Other students have to guess which one is false and correct it.

LESSON 3 Descriptive Adjectives

Student Learning Outcomes	• **Read** descriptions of people with interesting lives. • **Identify** adjectives in sentences. • **Find** and **edit** errors with adjectives and *a/an*. • **Read** a job description, **listen** to people describe themselves, and **analyze** people's qualifications. • **Describe** yourself using adjectives. • **Write** a description of a classmate.
Lesson Vocabulary	(adj.) brave (adj.) difficult (adj.) huge (adj.) noisy (adj.) clean (adj.) funny (adj.) late (adj.) young

EXPLORE

1 READ, page 21   15 min.

- Write or say sentences with *be* and adjectives about the photos on pages 21 and 22. Ask, *What do you think—true or false? The man isn't happy. The bear is huge. This photo is funny.* Then explain that the bears are famous. They're actors in movies, and the men are their trainers.

Be the Expert

- The animal trainers in this story live in Utah, in the United States. For more information about them, see Doug Seus's website (Search keywords: *Doug Seus* or *Bart the Bear.*) Students may find interesting the list of movies these trainers and animals worked in.
- Ask students for other examples of animals in movies. Ask if they are dangerous or friendly.

2 CHECK, page 22   10 min.

Adjective	Tank	Doug
brave		✓
kind		✓
famous	✓	
patient		✓
friendly	✓	
huge	✓	
gentle	✓	
heavy	✓	

- **Tip:** Ask higher-level students to give answers in complete sentences. For lower-level students, say the adjective and have students say *Tank* or *Doug*.

3 DISCOVER, page 22   10 min.

A 1. huge; heavy

2. brave

3. dangerous; difficult; fun

4. patient; kind

- **Tip:** After students fill in the sentences, ask them to look at the sentences and find nouns and pronouns. Tell students that all the words they filled in are called adjectives.

B 1. True   2. True

- **Tip:** To prepare students for the chart in LEARN, write two sentences on the board: *Doug is brave. He is a brave man.* Ask students to identify the adjectives and underline them. Draw arrows to show the words the adjectives describe.

LEARN

Chart 1.6, page 23   10 min.

- To practice sentences with adjectives, ask students to agree or disagree with statements (e.g., *English is easy. I am not a good student. The room is small.*)

> **REAL ENGLISH,** page 23
>
> Ask students to find sentences about Doug or Tank in the reading that use two adjectives with *and*.

4 page 23 — 5 min.

1. It is an <u>interesting</u> article.
2. Tank is <u>famous</u>.
3. Doug is <u>brave</u>.
4. They are <u>friendly</u>.
5. He is an <u>excellent</u> teacher.
6. Canada is a <u>huge</u> country.
7. She is <u>funny</u>.
8. Sandra is <u>young</u>.
9. I am <u>late</u>.
10. You are <u>kind</u>.

5 page 24 — 10 min.

1. Sandra is an amazing artist.
2. Bears are big.
3. I am happy.
4. Akira Kurosawa is a famous filmmaker.
5. David is a good engineer.
6. My phone is new.
7. Rome is an interesting city.
8. We are tired.
9. Chinese is a difficult language.
10. I am an excellent student.

- **Tip:** Write opposite adjectives on the board: *small/huge, happy/sad, easy/difficult*, and have students complete sentences such as *Tokyo is . . . , I am . . . , English is . . . .*

PRACTICE

6 page 24 — 15 min.

Answers will vary. Possible answers:

1. Our teacher is friendly.
2. My classmates are serious students.
3. This exercise is easy.
4. We are smart.
5. I am quiet.
6. My friends are nice people.
7. English is a difficult language.
8. This classroom is clean.
9. This building is big.
10. My hometown is small.

- **Expansion Tip:** Have students find opposite adjectives in the box. Ask them to write true or false sentences (on paper or on the board). Have other students make the sentences true.

7 EDIT, page 25 — 10 min.

This is **a** photograph of a Sherpa climber on Mount Everest. It's **an** amazing photo. Mount Everest is **a** beautiful mountain, but it's dangerous. Fura Gyaljen is **a** Sherpa climber. He is strong. His job is difficult and dangerous. Sherpa climbers are ~~braves~~ **brave** people.

8 SPEAK, LISTEN & WRITE, page 26 — 20 min.

- **Tip:** Read the job advertisement. Ask, *Who is Keiko? What does she want?* Preview any unfamiliar words in the vocabulary list, e.g., *experienced, retired,* and *helpful*.

A Answers will vary.

B Kevin: funny, smart

Liz: hardworking, patient

Jane: retired, patient, helpful

C Kevin is funny. He is smart.

Liz is hardworking. She is patient.

Jane is retired. She is patient.

9 SPEAK & WRITE, page 27 — 20 min.

Answers will vary.

> **REAL ENGLISH, page 27**
>
> We only use *both* for two, and we don't use it in the negative. Give some additional examples of *both*: *You and I are **both** in class. We are **both** happy today. **Both** students are late.* Have students write additional sentences using *both*.

10 APPLY, page 27 — 15 min.

Answers will vary.

LESSON 4	**Possessive Adjectives; Possessive Nouns**
Student Learning Outcomes	• **Read** about a group of people in Norway and their way of life. • **Refer** to people, things, or places using possessive adjectives. • **Find** and **edit** errors with possessive nouns and adjectives. • **Listen** and **complete** information about the relationships in a family. • **Describe** people and relationships in your family. • **Write** about your family using possessive nouns and adjectives.
Lesson Vocabulary	(n.) brother (n.) daughter (n.) mother (n.) son (n.) children (n.) father (n.) sister (n.) wife

EXPLORE

1 READ, page 28   20 min.

- Use the photos to show the meaning of *reindeer herder*.

Be the Expert

The Sami are an indigenous group of people who live in Scandinavia in the Arctic. There are about 70,000 Sami in the world, and few of them still live this traditional lifestyle. In the old days, they used to follow reindeer herds on foot or on skis. Now they use all-terrain vehicles (ATVs).

- After reading, ask students about indigenous people in their countries.

2 CHECK, page 29   5 min.

   1. F   2. F   3. T   4. T

- **Tip:** Ask higher-level students to correct the false sentences.

3 DISCOVER, page 29   5 min.

A 1. Her
    2. his
    3. their; their

B *Her* refers to Ingrid, or Gaup's wife. *His* refers to Gaup. *Their* refers to the Gaups.

- **Tip:** For lower-level students, point to the possessive adjectives and ask, *What does this mean? Who is her?* etc. Then tell students that these words are called possessive adjectives. For higher-level students, list the subject pronouns and ask them to tell you the possessive adjectives.

LEARN

Chart 1.7, page 30   10 min.

- **Note 1:** You can emphasize this point by showing the contrast between subject pronouns and possessive adjectives in the example sentences in the chart.

4 page 30   10 min.

  1. They; Their   8. You; Your
  2. We; our   9. She; Her
  3. He; his   10. I; My
  4. You; Your   11. He; His
  5. I; My   12. They; Their
  6. We; Our   13. You; Your
  7. She; Her   14. It; Its

Chart 1.8, page 31   10 min.

- **Notes 1 & 2:** Students sometimes get confused about the difference between a plural noun and a possessive noun. To show the difference, write sentences on the board, leaving a blank for the verbs, e.g., *The student's book ___ on the desk. The student's books ___ on the desk.*

5 page 31   5 min.

  1. Ken's   5. girl's
  2. doctor's   6. mother's
  3. father's   7. children's
  4. sons'   8. Italy's

6 page 31   5 min.

  1. Aileen's   4. roommates'
  2. women's; men's   5. husband's
  3. Kim's   6. children's

- **Expansion Tip:** Have students point to objects on each other's desks and make the possessives of their classmates' names, e.g., *Lena's book. Ken's jacket.*

PRACTICE

7 page 32   10 min.

  1. His job is dangerous.
  2. Her children are herder's, too.
  3. Their company is successful.
  4. Their grandfather is famous.
  5. Her office is huge.
  6. His house is beautiful.
  7. Her grandmother is 89 years old.
  8. Its rooms are small.

8 EDIT, page 32   10 min.

Teresa Pereira is from Portugal. She's Portuguese. Óbidos is ~~his~~ her hometown. Her ~~father~~ father's name is Antonio, and her mother's name is Fatima. They are teachers. ~~Teresas~~ Teresa's brother is an engineer. ~~He~~ His name is Pedro. His ~~wife~~ wife's name is Luisa. She's a doctor. ~~They~~ Their children's names are Rui and Eduardo.

- **Expansion Tip:** Give a short dictation about your family. After students write and correct it, have them change "I" to "My teacher" and make the rest of the changes in possessive adjectives.

9 SPEAK & WRITE, page 33   20 min.

B 1. Their; Their   6. her
       2. Sara's   7. Ana's
       3. His   8. Ana's; her
       4. Her   9. his
       5. his; Renata's   10. her

C *Answers will vary. Possible answers:*

  Camila: Camila is Pedro's wife. She's Sara's mother.
  Mario: Mario is Sara's husband. He's Diego's brother-in-law.
  Carlos: Carlos is Sofia's brother. He's Mario's nephew.

10 LISTEN & SPEAK, page 34   15 min.

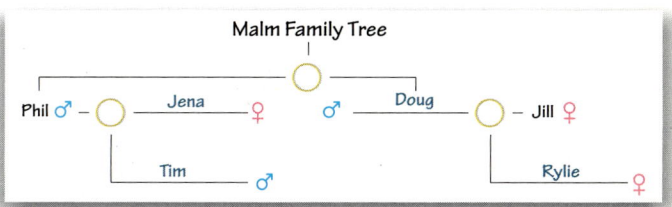

- **TIP:** There is a photo of this family on the National Geographic website.

11 APPLY, page 34   15 min.

Answers will vary.

- **Expansion Tip:** Have students compare family sizes (e.g., *Alex's family is large. My family is small.*). Discuss typical family size in your students' countries.

Review the Grammar — UNIT 1

1 page 35 — 10 min.
1. I'm Pat.
2. My name is Jim.
3. She is Pat's sister.
4. We are Carl's parents.
5. Ken's brother is tall.
6. My job isn't dangerous.
7. My friend is an interesting person.
8. It's an easy exercise.

2 LISTEN, page 35 — 20 min.
1. I'm a teacher.
2. He's my brother.
3. It isn't an easy job.
4. My friend's name is Jim.
5. Our parents aren't happy.
6. She's a serious person.
7. Your new shoes are nice.
8. Our homework isn't difficult.

3 WRITE & SPEAK, page 35 — 15 min.
A Answers will vary.

4 page 36 — 15 min.
1. Ed's not funny. He's serious.
2. You aren't/You're not late. You're early.
3. My car isn't/My car's not old. It's new.
4. She isn't/She's not from Mexico. She's from Chile.
5. They aren't/They're not engineers. They're explorers.
6. I'm not a photographer. I'm a student.
7. We aren't/We're not lazy students. We're hardworking students.
8. My mother's father isn't my uncle. He's my grandfather.

5 page 36 — 10 min.
Answers will vary. Possible answers:
1. Lions and bears are dangerous animals.
2. You and I are good students.
3. Tokyo isn't a small city.
4. Geometry and Biology 101 aren't difficult classes.
5. French isn't an easy language.
6. Actor and artist are interesting professions.
7. Belgium and Costa Rica aren't large countries.
8. Antarctica isn't a warm continent.

6 EDIT, page 36 — 10 min.

I'm from Brazil. Brazil is ~~an~~ a big country. It's a beautiful country. My family's home ~~are~~ is in Rio. We are all in different cities now. My mother and father ~~is~~ are at our home in Rio. My sister and I aren't in Rio. We ~~am~~ are students in London. My brother is in Boston. He's ~~a~~ an architect. He is married with two children. My nephews are twins. They ~~is~~ are six years old.

7 page 37 — 5 min.
Sally: This photo is interesting.
Jim: Yes, it is. He's an amazing gymnast.
Sally: He isn't a gymnast. He's an acrobat.
Jim: Oh, right.
Sally: Chinese acrobats are famous.
Jim: That's true. They're very good.

8 page 37 — 20 min.
A c. Ling School for Acrobats
B
1. Li
2. Sheng
3. Min
4. Wu
5. Jing

C Answers will vary. Possible answers:
1. Sheng is an acrobat from China.
2. Sheng's wife isn't an acrobat.
3. Sheng's grandmother owns a special school for acrobats.
4. Wu, Sheng's father, is a teacher at the school.
5. Li and Min are Sheng's children.

Connect the Grammar to Writing

1 page 38   20 min.

A *Answers will vary.*

The writer's brother's name is Jay. Hayley is the writer's sister-in-law.

B   My brother's name <u>is</u> Jay. He<u>'s</u> 29. He<u>'s</u> married. Hayley <u>is</u> his wife. She<u>'s</u> my sister-in-law. They<u>'re</u> in Scotland. Jay <u>is</u> a teacher. Hayley <u>isn't</u> a teacher. She<u>'s</u> a salesclerk. They<u>'re</u> very kind.

C *Answers may vary.*

Family Members		
Name	Jay	Hayley
Family member	Brother	Sister-in-law
Age	29	X
Married/Single	Married	Married
Job	Teacher	Salesclerk
Other information	They are in Scotland and they are very kind.	

2 BEFORE YOU WRITE, page 39   10 min.

> **WRITING FOCUS, page 39**
>
> Some students use commas (,) instead of periods (.) For additional practice, give students a paragraph with no capital letters or periods. Choose a text from the unit or type up a student sample and project it. Let students work in pairs to correct. For example:
>
> *my friend's mother is funny she is always happy her father is tall and quiet they are a nice couple their house is by the ocean their neighborhood is very quiet and peaceful I love visiting their home*

3 WRITE, page 39   20 min.

- **Alternative Writing:** Tell students to write about someone famous or known to all students in the class. Tell them not to write the name of the person. Then ask them in groups to read their paragraphs to each other. The other students must guess the person. To help, write a sample paragraph such as the following on the board.

    He lives in the United States. He's married. His wife's name is Michelle. Their daughters' names are Malia and Sasha.

UNIT 2 Celebrations

The Verb *Be*: Questions

Unit Opener

Photo: Ask students for their ideas about the photo. Point and ask questions (e.g., *Where is this? Is it a celebration? What colors do you see?*).

Location: People in India celebrate Holi, the festival of colors. Ask a student to locate India on a map.

Theme: Show students another photo of a celebration from the unit (e.g., page 59). Ask students the name of the celebration and the location. Ask the names of other celebrations.

Page	Lesson	Grammar	Examples	
42	1	Simple Present of *Be*: Yes/No Questions	**Am** I late? **Are** you from Greece?	Yes, you **are**. No, I am/I'm **not**.
50	2	Prepositions of Place; Questions with *Where* + *Be*	Our class is **in** Room 502. Their office is **on** Park Street. **Where's** the bus stop?	
58	3	Questions about Time and Weather: Prepositions of Time (Part 1)	What time is it? When's/is your class? How's/is the weather?	It's five-thirty. It's in the morning. It's warm and sunny.
66	4	*This, That, These, Those*	**This is** a great photo. **These are** our children, Anna and Jason. **Is this** your notebook?	Yes, **it is**./No, **it isn't**.
73		**Review the Grammar**		
76		**Connect the Grammar to Writing**		

Unit Grammar Terms

contraction: two words combined into a shorter form.
➤ *did not* → **didn't**   *I am* → **I'm**
➤ *Are you from New York? No, **I'm** not.*

period: a punctuation mark (.) that is used at the end of a statement. It is also called a "full stop."
➤ *This is my book.*
➤ *She lives in Moscow.*

preposition: a word that describes the relationships between nouns. Prepositions describe space, time, direction, cause, and effect.
➤ *Tomo is a student **in** my class. He's **from** Japan.*

question: a sentence that asks for an answer.
➤ *Is she a teacher?*

question mark: a punctuation mark (?) that is used at the end of a question.
➤ *What's that?*

LESSON 1   Simple Present of *Be*: Yes/No Questions

Student Learning Outcomes	• **Read** about name day celebrations. • **Ask** and **answer** *yes/no* questions with *be*. • **Listen** to information about a celebration. • **Find** and **edit** errors with *yes/no* questions and short answers with *be*. • **Speak** about a celebration. • **Read** an e-mail about a celebration. • **Write** and **role-play** a conversation with a classmate about a celebration.
Lesson Vocabulary	(n.) birthday (n.) graduation (adj.) popular (v. & n.) tango (n.) Carnival (n.) name day (n.) quinceañera (n.) wedding

EXPLORE

1 READ, page 42   10 min.

- Use the photo to elicit what students know about Greece. Students may recognize the historic site: the Acropolis. The buildings at this site are the Parthenon, the Erechtheion, the Propylaia, and the Temple of Athena. Use the globe to show Greece's location.
- In the reading, Dimitris says that five people in his family have the same name. Ask students about their families. Do people in the same family have the same name?

Be the Expert

Name days are common in parts of Europe and Latin America where people are often named after saints. Name days are not the same as birthdays. For example, someone named Patrick may celebrate his own birthday but also celebrate his name day on March 17, Saint Patrick's Day.

2 CHECK, page 43   5 min.

    1. T   2. T   3. F   4. F   5. T

- **Tip:** Have students correct the false sentences.

3 DISCOVER, page 43   5 min.

A

Yes/No Questions	Answers (Statements)
Are you from Greece?	Yes, I'm from Athens.
Is your name day your birthday?	No, it's not my birthday.
Are name days common all over Europe?	Yes, they're common in many European countries.

B   b

The word order changes. Subject + Verb changes to Verb + Subject.

- **Tip:** As you go over this answer, show students Chart 2.1 on the next page.

LEARN

Chart 2.1, page 44   5 min.

- **Notes 1 & 2:** It is helpful to show the change in word order with a nonverbal gesture illustrating the movement of the verb before the subject. Use this gesture whenever you correct mistakes in word order and question formation. This will prompt students toward the correct structure.

4 page 44   5 min.

1. Eleni is from Patras.   1. Is Eleni . . .
2. Alex is from Athens.   2. Is Alex . . .
3. Athens and Patras are . . .   3. Are Athena and Patras . . .
4. Eleni and Alex are . . .   4. Are Eleni and Alexander . . .
5. They are happy.   5. Are they . . .
6. Costas is their last name.   6. Is Costas . . .
7. Eleni and Alex are . . .   7. Are Eleni and Alex . . .
8. Eleni's name day is . . .   8. Is Eleni's name day . . .

5 page 45   10 min.

1. Are you from Mexico?
2. Is Mexico City in Mexico?
3. Are name days common in Latin America?
4. Are they from Brazil?
5. Is your birthday in November?

6. Are you a student?
7. Is she a teacher?
8. Is he Korean?

- **Tip:** Have more advanced students answer the questions with *yes* or *no*. Then, show the notes in Chart 2.2.

Chart 2.2, page 45   5 min.

- **Notes 1 & 2:** Emphasize the fact that contractions are never used in affirmative short answers while they are used in negative short answers.

6 page 46   5 min.

1. they are
2. it isn't
3. he isn't
4. it is
5. we aren't/we're not
6. she isn't/she's not
7. you are/I am
8. they aren't/they're not

- **Expansion Tip:** Show lists of cities, countries, and continents. Have students ask and answer questions to find locations:
  Student 1: *Is Tokyo in Japan?*
  Student 2: *Yes, it is. Are Seoul and Beijing in Europe?*
  Student 1: *No, they aren't.*

- **Expansion Tip:** Another way to do this activity is to have Student 1 call on Student 2 for an answer. Student 2 then asks another question, calling on Student 3 for an answer, and so on.

PRACTICE

7 page 46   10 min.

- **Tip:** Read the caption and discuss the photo before students do this exercise.

1. A: Is
   B: No, it isn't.
2. A: Is
   B: No, it isn't.
3. A: Are
   B: No, they aren't.
4. A: Is
   B: Yes, it is.
5. A: Are
   B: Yes, they are.
6. A: Are
   B: Yes, they are.
7. A: Is
   B: *Answers will vary.*
8. A: Are
   B: *Answers will vary.*

8 page 47   10 min.

1. 1. Are you
   2. I'm not
   3. I'm
   4. Is it
   5. it is
   6. It's
2. 7. Is
   8. it is
9. Are
10. we aren't
11. We're
3. 12. Are
13. I'm not
14. I'm
15. are they
16. are

9 **SPEAK,** page 47   5 min.

10 **LISTEN & SPEAK,** page 47   15 min.

- **Tip:** Before you listen, search online for *quinceañera* and show photos of *quinceañera* celebrations. Have students guess what the celebration is.

A 1. No   3. Yes   5. No
     2. No   4. Yes   6. No

11 **EDIT,** page 48   10 min.

Ken: Hi. ~~You are~~ Are you at the hotel now?
Molly: Yes, ~~I'm~~ I am. I'm in the hotel restaurant.
Ken: Is it a nice hotel?
Molly: Yes, it is. It's beautiful! It's very busy here, too.
Ken: ~~It is~~ Is it a business meeting?
Molly: No, ~~it~~ it's not. The women here are in long dresses.
Ken: ~~Is~~ Are they at the hotel for a wedding?
Molly: No, they aren't. The party is for a young girl.
Ken: ~~It is~~ Is it a *quinceañera*?
Molly: Yes, ~~it's~~ it is.

12 **READ, WRITE & SPEAK,** page 48   20 min.

A *Answers will vary. Possible answers:*
1. Is Karen in New York?
2. Is she in Rio for Carnival?
3. Are people out in the streets?
4. Is the celebration all day and night?
5. Is the celebration for four days?
6. Are the people happy?

13 **APPLY,** page 49   25 min.

- **Tip:** Have two students read the conversation. Point out the use of *really* in the last sentence. Then discuss the Real English box.

> **REAL ENGLISH, page 49**
>
> *Really* has the same meaning as *very*, but it is more informal. Ask students to replace *very* with *really* in additional sentences; e.g., *I'm very happy.* (*I'm really happy.*) *She's a very nice student.* (*She's a really nice student.*)

- If students ask, point out the use of the article *a* before the noun. Contrast with an adjective: *It's really cold. It's a really cold day.*

LESSON 2	**Prepositions of Place; Questions with** *Where* **+** *Be*
Student Learning Outcomes	• **Read** about a famous monument. • **State** location using prepositions of place. • **Ask** and **answer** questions about location using *Where* and prepositions of place. • **Read** and **speak** about a diagram showing location. • **Listen** to information about location and **label** places on a map. • **Find** and **edit** errors with prepositions of place. • **Draw** a map and **describe** locations.
Lesson Vocabulary	(adj.) amazing (n.) elevator (n.) river (n.) tour (n.) cathedral (n.) museum (n.) ticket (n.) tower

EXPLORE

1 READ, page 50   20 min.

- Use the photo. Ask students the name of the tower, the city, and the river. Point out the bridge, the river, and the park across the river. The river is the Seine.
- This reading is an advertisement for a tour of the Eiffel Tower.

Be the Expert

The Eiffel Tower was built as part of a celebration commemorating the 100th anniversary of the French Revolution. It is 1063 feet (324 meters) tall. In 1889, it was the tallest structure in the world. It took two years to complete. On the Eiffel Tower website, you can take a virtual tour of the tower and see panoramic views from the tower.

2 CHECK, page 51   5 min.

1. F   2. F   3. F   4. F   6. T

- **Tip:** Have students correct the false statements.

3 DISCOVER, page 51   5 min.

A 1. in front of   2. over   3. next to

B b

LEARN

Chart 2.3, page 52   10 min.

- Each illustration shows the meaning of the preposition in the sentence.
- Notes 2, 3 & 4: show common prepositional phrases related to locations. It may be helpful to point out that *at* is used with a specific location (the address) and with common locations we go to in our everyday life. *On* is used to show the relationship with something flat or horizontal (the street), and *in* is used with locations that you can go inside.

4 page 53   5 min.

1. above   6. on
2. between   7. behind
3. next to   8. under
4. in   9. near
5. in front of   10. across from

5 page 53   5 min.

> **REAL ENGLISH, page 53**
>
> The use of *at* is very idiomatic. We don't use "the" in front of common locations such as school, work, and home. Ask students a few questions to elicit these phrases. *Where do you do your homework? Where do you sleep? Where are most people from 8:00 to 5:00?*

1. in   5. on
2. in   6. in
3. in   7. at
4. at   8. in

Chart 2.4, page 54   5 min.

- **Note 3:** Contractions of the *Wh*-word and *is* are very common in conversations. Other examples include: *How's your class? Who's absent today? What's your name?*

REAL ENGLISH, page 53

Question words are often used alone to ask for information when both people understand the context. This happens when people need more information (as in the example). We also use a single question word with rising intonation when we didn't hear or understand something clearly and want it repeated. Give a sentence including a location that you say in nonsense syllables and ask them to clarify: *Class is in dadada.* (*Where?*) *In room 502.*

- **Tip:** In future classes, when students give an answer, use a question word to clarify or ask for repetition and point out what you are doing.
- **Expansion Tip:** Have students use their own pens and quiz each other as they move the pen into different locations.

6 page 54 — 10 min.

1. Where is our class?
2. Where is the bathroom?
3. Where's our teacher?
4. Where are our books?
5. Where is your home?
6. Where are our classmates?
7. Where's our classroom
8. Where are you?
9. Where are Chan and Meg?
10. Where's your office?

7 SPEAK, page 54 — 5 min.

PRACTICE

8 READ & SPEAK, page 55 — 20 min.

A
1. a   6. b
2. c   7. b
3. b   8. b
4. a   9. a
5. c   10. a

- **Tip:** For speaking practice, have students give the incorrect location with a preposition error about the places in the diagram. Another student will use the correct preposition and location.

- **Expansion Tip:** Use your own building for more practice. Give students a room and have them give its location in relation to other things. For example, say or write *the water fountain.* (Student: *The water fountain is near the bathrooms.*)

9 LISTEN & SPEAK, page 56 — 15 min.

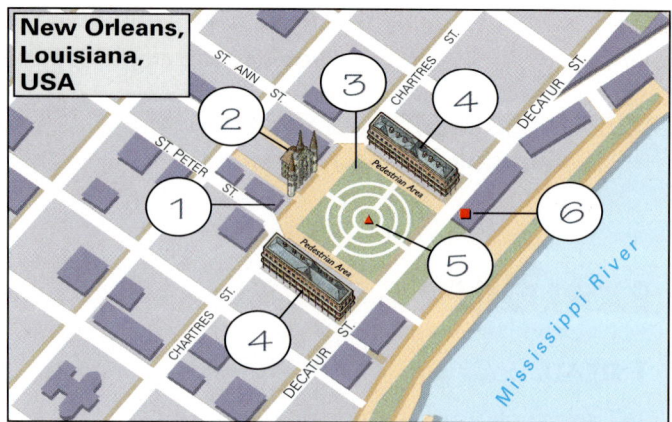

10 EDIT, page 57 — 10 min.

New Orleans is a city ~~on~~ in the United States. It is in the state of Louisiana. The French Quarter is a very old part of New Orleans. It is ~~between~~ near the Mississippi River. Jackson Square is ~~under~~ between Decatur Street and Chartres Street. The Café du Monde is ~~in~~ on Decatur Street. It is across ~~of~~ from Jackson Square. The Cathedral is on Chartres Street. It is ~~above~~ next to the Cabildo Museum. Apartments are ~~under~~ above the stores and restaurants in the Pontalba Buildings.

11 APPLY, page 57 — 20 min.

Answers will vary.

- **Alternative Activity:** Give students maps of an area near you. It could be a map of a campus, a downtown area, or a shopping center. You can use the maps for many different activities:
  - an information gap activity (white out different labels on each student's map)
  - practice asking directions (e.g., *Excuse me. Where is the bookstore?*)
  - a guessing game with prepositions (e.g., *It's next to a bookstore. What is it?*)

LESSON 3 Questions about Time and Weather

Student Learning Outcomes
- **Read** about New Year's Celebrations in different countries.
- **Use** *it* to state time and dates and describe weather.
- **Ask** questions about time and dates with *what time* and *when*.
- **Ask** and **answer** questions about the weather using *how*.
- **Find** and **edit** errors with questions about time and prepositions of time.
- **Listen** to a news report and **answer** questions about it.
- **Write** a news report about a holiday or festival.

Lesson Vocabulary

| (adj.) cold | (adj.) freezing | (n.) reporter | (adj.) sunny |
| (n.) date | (n.) midnight | (n.) summer | (adj.) warm |

EXPLORE

1 READ, page 58   15 min.

- Look at the photo. Ask students what the celebration is and what they see (fireworks, boats, water). The building with the interesting shape is the Sydney Opera House on the harbor in Sydney. It was named a UNESCO World Heritage Site in 2007.

Be the Expert

In many countries, people celebrate the New Year on December 31. They "ring in the New Year" with a countdown (10, 9, 8, 7, . . .) and fireworks at the stroke of midnight. Sydney is 14 hours ahead of London, so it's actually January 1 in Sydney in this conversation. Australia is in the Southern Hemisphere, so it's summer there.

2 CHECK, page 59   5 min.

	Time	Weather
London	midnight	cool and rainy
New York	seven o'clock in the evening	cold and snowy
Sydney	eleven o'clock in the morning	sunny and warm

3 DISCOVER, page 59   10 min.

Time	Weather
It's midnight on New Year's Eve!	It's cool and rainy…
What time is it there?	How is it in New York?
It's seven o'clock in the evening.	It's freezing here!
What time is it there?	It's cold and snowy…
It's eleven o'clock in the morning.	It's terrible!
	It's sunny and warm here!

LEARN

Chart 2.5, page 60   10 min.

It + be is the way we talk about dates, days, and time in English. In these questions and answers, the pronoun *it* does not refer to anything specific; it is a "dummy subject." The first questions in the chart use *What* + noun (*What time, What day, What month*) to ask for information.

4 page 60   10 min.

1. What month is it?
2. What time is it?
3. What day is it?
4. What's the date today?/What's today's date?
5. What day is it?
6. What month is it?
7. What year is it?
8. What time is it?

5 page 61   5 min.

1. b   5. a
2. a   6. a
3. b   7. b
4. a   8. b

6 SPEAK, page 61   5 min.

Chart 2.6, page 6   10 min.

- **Note 4:** Tell students that a *phrase* is a group of words. A prepositional phrase is a preposition + noun; e.g., *on Saturday*.
- **Notes 5 & 6:** Point out that *at* is used with specific times and *in* is used with periods of time that other units of time can fit inside.
- **Expansion Tip:** Give three students cards with the prepositions *in, on,* and *at*. Give other

UNIT 2 LESSON 3 25

students cards with the nouns that follow these prepositions: a time, day, month, year, date, season, etc. Have them arrange the cards under the correct prepositions.

- **Expansion Tip:** Have students look at a world time zone map and discuss times around the world using the time and time expressions such as *in the morning, in the afternoon, in the evening,* or *at night.*

7 page 62   10 min.

1. A: When's New Year's Eve?   B: on
2. A: When's her 21st birthday?   B: in
3. A: When's your birthday?   B: in
4. A: When's St. Patrick's Day?   B: on
5. A: When's our English class?   B: at
6. A: When's the party?   B: on
7. A: When's the exam?   B: on
8. A: When's the winter festival?   B: in

8 page 62   5 min.

1. in; on   4. in
2. in   5. on
3. on; on   6. at; in; at

- **Tip:** Use daily matching tasks or dictations that substitute a silly word for every preposition to help students memorize prepositions.
- **Expansion Tip:** Give students an information gap with holidays and dates. Have them ask and answer questions to fill in the information.

    Student 1: *When is Valentine's Day?*
    Student 2: *It's on February 14th.*
    Student 2: *When is Mother's Day?*
    Student 1: *It's in May.*

9 SPEAK, page 62   5 min.

Chart 2.7, page 63   10 min.

- **Notes 1, 2, 3 & 4:** In these questions and answers about the weather, the pronoun *it* is a dummy subject, as with questions and answers about time.
- **Tip:** Talk about the weather today.
- **Expansion Tip:** Show photos of a hurricane or blizzard and have students describe the weather. As they say adjectives, write them on the board. Then have students write sentences with the prompts, e.g., *"In a hurricane, the weather is . . . It's . . ."*

10 page 63   5 min.

1. A: How's   B: It's cold and windy.
2. A: How's   B: It's warm and sunny.
3. A: What's   B: It's rainy.
4. A: How's   B: It's cold and snowy.
5. A: How's   B: It's hot and sunny.
6. A: What's   B: It's cool and cloudy.
7. A: How's   B: It's sunny and mild.
8. A: What's   B: It's freezing.

11 SPEAK, page 63   5 min.

- **Tip:** Write names of places around the world known for a certain type of weather, e.g. *Hawaii, London, Moscow, Saudi Arabia,* etc.

PRACTICE

12 page 64   5 min.

1. 1. What time   8. date
   2. It's   9. It's
   3. at   4. 10. When's
2. 4. How's   11. on
   5. It's   12. in
   6. It's   13. in
3. 7. What's   14. at

13 EDIT, page 64   10 min.

1. Sam: Hi, Mel. What time ~~it is~~ **is it**?
2. Mika: It's ~~on~~ **in** June.
   Ben: Really? My birthday's in June, too. It's ~~in~~ **on** June 24th.
3. Chan: It's seven o'clock.
   Nora: Oh good. The movie is ~~on~~ **at** 7:30.
4. Toshi: When**'s/is** Steve's graduation party?
   Maria: No, it's ~~in~~ **at** night.

14 LISTEN & WRITE, page 65   15 min.

A b

B 1. It's 7:00 a.m.
     2. It's Wednesday.
     3. It's February.
     4. It's February 14th.
     5. It's windy and cold.

15 APPLY, page 65   20 min.

- Before doing this task, play the news report from exercise **1** again. Have students read along as they listen. Then have them compose their own news reports to perform for the class.
- **Tip:** If you have a large class, give each pair a number. To choose the pairs to perform, put the numbers in a cup, and draw several.

LESSON 4 | *This, That, These, Those*

Student Learning Outcomes	• **Read** about a popular celebration in India. • **Use** *this, that, these,* and *those* to show whether something is near or distant. • **Ask** and **answer** questions about things that are near or distant. • **Speak** about things in your classroom. • **Listen** and **respond** to questions about people, places, and things. • **Find** and **edit** errors with *this, that, these,* and *those*. • **Write** a conversation about a party or celebration.
Lesson Vocabulary	(v.) celebrate (n.) flower (v. & n.) paint (n.) seat (n.) festival (n.) laptop (n.) screen (n.) stop

EXPLORE

1 READ, page 66   15 min.

- Use the photos on this page and on pages 40–41 to ask questions about the people and the paint. *(Are the people in the photos happy or angry? Young or old? What are the colors?)*
- This reading is a conversation that takes place on the bus. Scott notices a colorful photo on Dan's computer and asks about it.

Be the Expert

The Holi Festival is a traditional Hindu festival to celebrate spring in India and in Hindu communities in other parts of the world. The night before Holi begins, people have bonfires. On the day of the festival, it is very colorful because people throw dry paint powder in the air.

2 CHECK, page 67   5 min.

1. b   2. b   3. a   4. a

3 DISCOVER, page 67   5 min.

A 1. that   2. those   3. these
    4. Those   5. this

B 1. singular   2. Plural

- **Tip:** If your students are more advanced, preview some of the notes in the next chart by asking students to look at the conversation again. Ask, *Is "this" for things that are close to the speaker or far away? Is "that" for things that are close to the speaker or far away?* Show some other examples by pointing to things close or far away from you. Then go over the notes in Chart 2.8.

LEARN

Chart 2.8, page 68   10 min.

- *This, that, these,* and *those* are called demonstratives (demonstrative adjectives and demonstrative pronouns). They show whether something or someone is near or distant from the speaker, and the same forms are used as adjectives and pronouns. The exercises that follow focus on the distinction between the singular and plural forms.
- The contraction *that's* is very common in both speaking and in informal writing. *This is* often sounds like it is contracted to *This's* in speaking, but it is never contracted in writing.

> **REAL ENGLISH,** page 68
>
> Students have probably seen or heard *this* used to introduce someone who is close to the speaker. Review introductions and have students practice introducing each other.

4 page 68   5 min.

1. These	6. These
2. That	7. These
3. This	8. Those
4. This	9. This
5. Those	10. That

5 page 69   5 min.

1. These	5. Those
2. That	6. This
3. That	7. These
4. This	8. Those

UNIT 2   LESSON 4   27

Chart 2.9, page 69   10 min.
- **Notes 1 & 2:** *This, that, these,* and *those* are used in questions, but they are not necessary in the answers.
- **Note 3:** The contraction *What's* is often used in conversation. *What are* is not contracted.
- **Expansion Tip:** Have students ask and answer questions about things that you point to in the room. Choose singular and plural things that are close to students and also far away to elicit all of the forms: *this, that, these, those.*

6 page 70   10 min.
1. A: Is that your camera?
   B: Yes, it is.
2. A: Are those Bob's sons?
   B: Yes, they are.
3. A: Are those cars expensive?
   B: No, they aren't.
4. A: Is this your jacket?
   B: Yes, it is.
5. A: Are these Cho's books?
   B: No, they aren't.
6. A: Is that our bus?
   B: No, it's not./ No, it isn't.
7. A: What is that?
   B: It's my backpack.
8. A: What are those?
   B: They're notebooks.
9. A: What are these?
   B: They're earrings.
10. A: What is this?
    B: It's a scarf.

7 LISTEN, page 70   10 min.
1. a   5. a
2. a   6. a
3. a   7. b
4. a   8. b

PRACTICE

8 page 71   10 min.
1. 1. This
   2. this

2. 3. Those
   4. that
   5. it's
   6. it's
3. 7. this
   8. it's
   9. It's
   10. that
   11. it is
4. 12. That
   13. Is
   14. it is
   15. These

9 EDIT, page 71   10 min.
Alicia: Wow! ~~These~~ This festival is amazing!
Ima: Yeah, it is. All of ~~this~~ these flowers are beautiful.
Alicia: Are ~~that~~ those roses over there?
Ima: Yes, ~~it is~~ they are.
Alicia: They're so colorful.
Ima: ~~This~~ These big yellow flowers here are beautiful, too. I think they're sunflowers.
Alicia: Are ~~that~~ those people over there farmers?
Ima: Yes, they are. They grow the flowers for ~~these~~ this festival every year.

10 SPEAK, page 72   10 min.
- **Expansion Tip:** If your class is not too large, you can have students sit in a circle and make compliments or ask questions as a chain activity. The first student begins with either a compliment or a question. The next student responds and then asks a question or compliments the next student.

11 APPLY, page 72   20 min.
- **Tip:** Another typical context for conversations with *this, that, these,* and *those* is at a farmers' market or a flea market where customers might ask, "What's this?" "How much are these oranges?" or "I'd like two of these."

UNIT 2 Review the Grammar

1 LISTEN, page 73   10 min.

1. b   5. b
2. a   6. a
3. a   7. a
4. a   8. b

2 WRITE & SPEAK, page 73   20 min.

A *Answers will vary. Possible questions:*

Is Marta's birthday on Wednesday?

When is Angela's meeting on Monday?

Where is Jack's party?

Where is the meeting on Thursday?

What time is the concert on Friday?

What day/night is the concert?

Is the Street Fair on Saturday?

Where is the Street Fair?

3 EDIT, page 74   10 min.

Delma: Hello?

Sara: Hi, Delma. Are you in Madrid now?

Delma: Yes, I am. It's beautiful here.

Sara: Where **is** your hotel ~~is~~?

Delma: It's near ~~to~~ the Prado Museum.

Sara: Is it nice?

Delma: Yes, it is. It's really nice. What time is it ~~at~~ **in** Boston now?

Sara: It's eight o'clock ~~at~~ **in** the morning. What time **is** it there?

Delma: It's ~~at~~ two o'clock ~~at~~ **in** the afternoon here. It's time for lunch. I'm hungry!

Sara: OK. Well, enjoy your vacation!

Delma: Thanks! Bye.

Sara: Bye.

4 READ, WRITE & SPEAK, page 74   25 min.

A *Answers will vary. Possible questions and answers:*

Q: Is the Harbin Festival fun?

A: Yes, it's a lot of fun.

Q: When is the festival?

A: It's in the winter./It's in January.

Q: How's the weather?

A: It's very cold.

Q: What's the weather like?

A: It's very cold.

Q: What are the ice sculptures like?

A: They're amazing.

- **Alternative Speaking:** Each year, there are many newscasts about the Harbin Ice Festival. Find a newscast online to show before or after students read about the festival. Then have students read sentences from exercise **A** as though they are doing a news report.

- **Alternative Writing:** Remind students of the first news report about New Years. Have them turn the paragraph from exercise **A** into a news report.

Connect the Grammar to Writing

1 READ & NOTICE THE GRAMMAR, page 76   25 min.

A His favorite celebration is his birthday.

B   My grandfather's favorite celebration is his birthday. It's in September. His party isn't at a restaurant. It's at our home. The weather is often warm and sunny in September, so the party is outside in our yard. My grandfather is very happy on September 3rd. It's his special day, and it's a lot of fun!

C *Answers may vary. Possible answers:*

A Favorite Celebration		
	Questions	Answers
What	What is the grandfather's favorite celebration?	His birthday.
When	When is the grandfather's birthday?	It's on September 3rd.
Yes/No question	Is his party at a restaurant?	No, it's at their house.
How	How is the weather?	It's warm and sunny.
Yes/No question	Is the party inside?	No, it's outside in their yard.

2 BEFORE YOU WRITE, page 77   10 min.

Answers will vary.

- **Alternative Writing:** Instead of interviewing and writing about someone else's favorite celebration, have students write a paragraph about their own favorite celebrations. Then have them use the interview questions in exercise **A** as a follow-up to ask other students about the celebrations they wrote about.

3 WRITE, page 77   25 min.

> **WRITING FOCUS,** page 77
>
> - A paragraph is a section of writing about one topic. The sentences in a paragraph follow each other on the same line instead of starting on a new line. The first line starts about five spaces to the right. This is called an indent.
>
> - The examples in this chart show the difference in format between a list and a paragraph. Many students are not familiar with paragraph format. They write in lists of sentences because that is what they would do in their language.
>
> - **Tip:** On the board or in a handout, write a list. Have students rewrite the information in paragraph format.

UNIT 3 Work

Simple Present: Part 1

Unit Opener

Photo: Read the photo caption to the students. Discuss the word *skyscraper* and ask the names of famous skyscrapers.

Say, *He's a worker. What's his job?* (He's an electrician.) Ask, *What's his job like?* (It's dangerous!)

Location: This building is in Chicago, Illinois in the United States. It is on the shore of Lake Michigan. When the 100-story John Hancock Tower was finished in 1969, it was one of the tallest buildings in the world.

Theme: Students will read about workers in many different jobs.

Page	Lesson	Grammar	Examples
80	1	Simple Present: Affirmative Statements; Irregular Verbs: *Do, Go,* and *Have*	We **work** every day. He **works** every day. We **go** to work at 8:00 a.m. He **goes** at 10:00 a.m.
88	2	Simple Present: Negative Statements; Prepositions of Time (part 2); *Like, Need, Want*	You **do not/don't work**. He **does not/doesn't work**. The bank opens **at nine o'clock**. He **likes to play** soccer. They **want to meet** every week.
97	3	Verbs + Objects; Object Pronouns	I teach **children**. We listen to **music** a lot. I like **her**. They know **us**.
104	4	Imperatives	**Close** the door. **Open** your books.
111	**Review the Grammar**		
114	**Connect the Grammar to Writing**		

Unit Grammar Terms

base form: the form of the verb without *to* or any endings such as *-ing, -s,* or *-ed.*
➢ *eat, sleep, go, walk*

imperative: a verb form that gives an instruction or command. Use the base form of the verb to form the imperative.
➢ **Sit** down, please.
➢ **Tell** me now!

infinitive: an infinitive is *to* + the base form of the verb.
➢ Sally wants **to talk** with you.

object: a noun or pronoun that receives the action of the verb.
➢ A supermarket sells **food**.

object pronoun: a word that takes the place of a noun as the object of the sentence: *me, you, him, her, it, us, them.*
➢ I see **her** every day in class.

31

LESSON 1   Simple Present: Affirmative Statements

Student Learning Outcomes	• **Read** about a scientist and photographer. • **Complete** simple present affirmative sentences about people and their jobs. • **Speak** about activities and jobs. • **Listen** to information about people's activities in their jobs. • **Find** and **edit** errors with the simple present form of verbs. • **Practice** the pronunciation of simple present verb endings /s/, /z/, and /əz/. • **Write** a paragraph about someone's job.
Lesson Vocabulary	(v.) carry (v.) go (v.) sleep (v.) take (v.) do (v.) help (v.) study (n.) watch

EXPLORE

1 READ, page 80   10 min.

- Use the photos to teach the meaning of *ant* and *bug*.

Be the Expert

- Mark Moffett, also known as Dr. Bugs, is a researcher at the Smithsonian Institute and a well-known author and photographer. His website has several interesting short videos, including one where he tries to get people to eat ants. (Search keyword: *Dr. Bugs*.)

- In the small photo, Mark Moffett has a *tarantula* on his hand. Tarantulas are not considered "insects." They are *arachnids* (like spiders). Interesting facts: Tarantulas are not poisonous or dangerous to humans. They eat insects and some large tarantulas eat small birds. Female tarantulas can live up to 30 years.

- **Expansion Tip:** Give students the following information about the ants in the photo. Have them underline simple present verbs.

  The ants in the photo are leaf cutter ants. They cut leaves and carry them to their nests. The ants don't eat the leaves. They use them to grow fungus for food, so they are "farmers." Ants have different roles or jobs such as queen, soldier, and worker. Soldier ants fight. Worker ants do different kinds of work such as clean or get food for the other ants. Ants live on every continent in the world except Antarctica.

2 CHECK, page 81   5 min.

Verbs	Doctor Moffett	Ants
1. studies	✓	
2. fight		✓
3. waits	✓	
4. bite		✓

3 DISCOVER, page 81   5 min.

- **Tip:** As you read the directions for exercise **A**, make sure students find additional verbs to list, not the ones already used in exercise **2**.

A Doctor Moffett: goes, watches, takes, lies, has

    Ants: eat, work, rest, sleep

B 1. end in -*s*   2. do not end in -*s*

- **Tip:** The exercises on this page will encourage students to notice the -*s* ending. Ask, *What is the rule? When do you need an* -s *on the verb?* Then, show them the answer in the top part of Chart 3.1.

LEARN

Chart 3.1, page 82   10 min.

- **Note 1:** The focus of the simple present is on general information: habits, schedules, and facts. It is also used to talk about the future (see Unit 14).

- **Note 2:** Remembering to add the -*s* ending on the third-person singular in the simple present is the most challenging aspect of this verb tense.

- **Note 3:** The addition of *be* is a common mistake.

- **Tip:** Use a nonverbal cue to remind students to add the -*s* ending.

- **Tip:** If your students add *be* to verbs in the simple present, write a sentence with the mistake on the board. Draw a huge *X* through the verb.

4 page 82   5 min.

1. loves	6. write
2. studies	7. closes
3. sells	8. takes
4. work	9. walk
5. help	10. start

5 WRITE & SPEAK, page 82 — 5 min.

6 page 83 — 5 min.
1. feeds 3. take 5. fights 7. works
2. write 4. cooks 6. play 8. dances

Chart 3.2, page 83 — 10 min.
- **Note 2:** This spelling rule makes sense to students if you point out how difficult it would be to pronounce the verb without adding the additional syllable.
- **Note 3:** Point out the difference in spelling between *play* (with a vowel before -*y*) and *try* (with a consonant before -*y*).

7 page 84 — 10 min.
1. studies 6. bites 11. fixes
2. fishes 7. buys 12. watches
3. passes 8. helps 13. likes
4. worries 9. misses 14. pays
5. explores 10. flies

Chart 3.3, page 84 — 10 min.
- The spelling of *do*, *go*, and *have* is irregular in the third-person singular.
- **Tip:** This is a good time to point out how English spelling does not correlate to pronunciation. For example, *does* and *goes* look similar in spelling but sound completely different.

8 page 84 — 10 min.
1. have 6. go 11. has
2. goes 7. goes 12. has
3. goes 8. does 13. goes
4. have 9. goes 14. have
5. have 10. does

PRACTICE

9 page 85 — 10 min.
1. have 4. help 7. flies
2. fly 5. has 8. takes
3. carry 6. owns 9. goes

10 EDIT, page 85 — 5 min.
Bill is a mechanic. He ~~know~~ **knows** a lot about cars. He ~~work~~ **works** at a garage. He ~~fix~~ **fixes** cars and talks to customers. They ~~asks~~ **ask** questions about their cars. Bill works from 8:00 a.m. to 6:00 p.m. every day. He ~~have~~ **has** a busy schedule, but he ~~like~~ **likes** his job very much.

11 PRONUNCIATION, page 86 — 15 min.
- **Tip:** Focus on Note 3 in this chart for lower-level students. Point out that it would be very difficult to hear the -*s* ending on verbs that end in the sounds listed. If your students are more advanced, point out the ending sounds: /s/ after final consonants that are voiceless; /z/ after final consonants that are voiced. Have them put their hands on their throats as they repeat the words with voiced final consonants in the second list.

A
1. /s/ 4. /əz/ 7. /əz/ 10. /z/
2. /z/ 5. /s/ 8. /z/ 11. /əz/
3. /s/ 6. /z/ 9. /s/ 12. /z/

12 LISTEN & SPEAK, page 86 — 25 min.

	Alvaro	Galina
1. lives in Ecuador	✓	
2. lives in Russia		✓
3. teaches at a university	✓	
4. teaches at a high school		✓
5. teaches biology	✓	✓
6. gets up early		✓
7. goes home at 3:00 p.m.		✓
8. goes home at 6:00 p.m.	✓	
9. meets with students after class	✓	
10. relaxes on Saturday	✓	✓

- **Tip:** As students discuss their charts, listen for the correct pronunciation of the verb endings.
- **Expansion Tip:** Ask students to talk about a favorite teacher. Model or give students cues to get them started, e.g., *My favorite teacher is... She/He lives in...*

13 READ, SPEAK & WRITE, page 87 — 10 min.
- **Tip:** Do exercise **A** in class. Assign the writing in exercise **B** for homework and have students exchange papers the next day.

A Rosa is a sales representative.

- **Expansion Tip:** Throughout PRACTICE, there is a lot of job-related vocabulary. Put students in teams. Give them six minutes to list as many tasks as possible for each of these jobs: a pilot, a bush pilot, a mechanic, a teacher, a dancer, and a salesperson. Give a point for each correctly spelled verb.

14 APPLY, page 87 — 20 min.
- **Alternative Writing:** Instead of writing about a friend or family member's job, students can write about any job.

LESSON 2	Simple Present: Negative Statements and Contractions
Student Learning Outcomes	• **Read** about a typical schedule for astronauts on the International Space Station. • **Make** negative statements in the simple present. • **Describe** schedules using prepositions of time. • **Use** verbs with infinitives to state likes, wants, and needs. • **Read, speak** and **listen** about people's work schedules. • **Find** and **edit** errors with negatives and prepositions of time. • **Write** about people's schedules.
Lesson Vocabulary	(n.) astronaut (v.) exercise (v.) like (n.) schedule (adj.) different (v.) go (n.) pilot (n.) space station

EXPLORE

1 READ, page 88   15 min.

- Use the photo and ask questions about the Space Station. Ask, *What is this? Where is it? Who is on it? What nationalities are they?* Teach the word *astronaut*.

- After students listen, ask them, *Is this a difficult job? Why?*

- Have them fill in a schedule of a typical day on the space station with breakfast, lunch, and dinner already written in.

Be the Expert

- The living module of the International Space Station is 167 feet (51 meters) in length. It has more living space than a typical six-bedroom house. Fifteen countries worked together for over ten years to build the International Space Station. The first astronauts stayed there in 2000. Since then, over 200 astronauts have stayed there.

- For their daily exercise, astronauts ride a stationary bicycle, lift weights, or run or walk on a treadmill. Astronauts also have some time for hobbies. For example, some play a musical instrument, play basketball, or read. Students can search online for *astronaut Chris Hadfield* to find some famous videos of him singing and playing guitar.

2 CHECK, page 89   5 min.

    1. d   2. a   3. e   4. b   5. c

3 DISCOVER, page 89   5 min.

A   1. do   2. work   3. end

- **Tip:** If your students are advanced, after doing exercise **A**, have them look at the reading and list all the negative verbs. They will find one negative with *be* and three other negatives. Ask them to create a chart for forming the negative of the simple present.

B   1. T   2. F

LEARN

Chart 3.4, page 90   5 min.

- **Note:** We usually use the contraction forms *don't* or *doesn't* + the base verb to form the negative in the simple present.

4 page 90   10 min.

    1. doesn't   5. don't
    2. don't   6. doesn't
    3. doesn't   7. doesn't
    4. don't   8. don't

5 page 90   10 min.

    1. My brother doesn't have a job.
    2. I don't drive to work.
    3. Pilots don't fix planes.
    4. Our teacher doesn't do homework.
    5. I don't go to the gym in the morning.
    6. We don't have class on Sunday.
    7. You don't teach biology.
    8. We don't have an exam on Saturday night.

6 SPEAK, page 91   10 min.

Chart 3.5, page 91   10 min.

- Students have studied prepositions used with addresses (Chart 2.3, page 52) and time (Chart 2.6, page 61). Now the concept of prepositional phrases is introduced as they learn about prepositions necessary to discuss schedules.

> **REAL ENGLISH,** page 91
>
> For additional practice, write these sentences on the board for students to complete: *I get home each day . . . , I eat dinner . . . , I usually go to sleep . . . , On weekends, I wake up . . . , My bus comes . . .* They can use *around* or *about* for the imprecise times, but not for exact times (e.g., the TV news or the alarm).

7 page 91   5 min.

1. We have class <u>from 9:40 to 10:50</u>.
2. <u>On Wednesday</u>, I have class <u>until 3:30</u>.
3. The party is <u>on Saturday night</u>.
4. The meeting doesn't end <u>until 3:00</u>.
5. My workweek is <u>from Monday to Friday</u>.
6. I work <u>from 9:00 to 7:00</u> <u>on Tuesday and Wednesday</u>.
7. I don't work <u>on weekends</u>.
8. She doesn't get home <u>until 4:00 in the afternoon</u>.

8 page 92   5 min.

1. at
2. on
3. until; in; on
4. from; to
5. at; in
6. at
7. until; at
8. from; to
9. at; on
10. from; to; in

9 WRITE & SPEAK, page 92   5 min.

- **Tip:** Remind students that they can use *about* or *around* when the time is not exact.
- **Expansion Tip:** Have students compare their schedules on weekdays and weekends or vacations.

Chart 3.6, page 92   5 min.

- The verbs *like, need,* and *want* can be followed by a noun *(I like ice cream.)* or by another verb. We call *to* + verb an infinitive. If students ask about the use of a gerund after *like* (e.g., *I like shopping.*), tell them that some verbs, including *like,* can take either an infinitive or a gerund.

10 page 93   10 min.

1. They need to work on Saturday.
2. He wants to have lunch at 1:00.
3. You need to work until 7:00 tonight.
4. I need to buy a new computer.
5. She likes to play tennis.
6. We want to watch the game.
7. He likes to study in the library.
8. I need to do my homework.
9. I need to call my mother.
10. She wants to ask a question.

PRACTICE

11 SPEAK, page 93   15 min.

> **REAL ENGLISH,** page 93
>
> Point out the plural ending in *on weekends* in the choices for exercise **A**. Tell students that *on the weekend* (the singular) is also possible when talking about regular occurrences. The plural emphasizes the idea that it happens again and again. *I have class on Tuesdays. We get together on weekends.* Call on students to give sentences about what they do and don't do on weekends.

12 READ, SPEAK & WRITE, page 94   15 min.

A
1. cooks
2. has; from; to
3. goes; on
4. doesn't cook
5. has; at; in
6. doesn't have; in
7. works; from; to/until; from; to
8. studies; wants to
9. has; from; to; at; on
10. doesn't have
11. doesn't go; on
12. is
13. misses

B

- **Tip:** If your students are living at home, their lives may be more similar to Lia's life in Indonesia than in Toronto. They can specify that in item 1.

UNIT 3 LESSON 2

13 EDIT, page 95   10 min.

Iris is a reporter. She works for a newspaper. She asks questions and writes articles. She ~~don't~~ doesn't drive to work. She walks. She ~~don't~~ doesn't work in the morning. She works from 2:00 p.m. ~~in~~ to 11:00 p.m. She doesn't ~~goes~~ go to bed early. She goes to bed ~~on~~ at 1:00 a.m. She doesn't work ~~at~~ on Saturday and Sunday. She relaxes ~~in~~ on weekends.

> **REAL ENGLISH, page 95**
>
> Students many already know the use of *How about you?* to reciprocate in a question. This introduces *how about* for making suggestions. It means, *What do you think about this idea?* Have two students role-play the conversation in exercise **14**. Point out the use of *how about*. Then, in pairs, have students practice using *how about* in suggestions. Tell them to discuss possible things to do after class.

14 page 95   15 min.

1. in; on
2. have
3. at
4. have; from; to
5. work; from; to
6. at

15 SPEAK, page 95   15 min.

16 LISTEN & SPEAK, page 96   20 min.

	M	T	W	Th	F	Sa	Su
Canada	✓	✓	✓	✓	✓		
United States	✓	✓	✓	✓	✓		
Thailand	✓	✓	✓	✓	✓		
Austria	✓	✓		✓	✓ (1/2)		
Saudi Arabia	✓	✓	✓			✓	✓
UAE	✓	✓	✓	✓			✓
Japan	✓	✓	✓	✓	✓	✓ sometimes	
India	✓	✓	✓	✓	✓	✓	

17 APPLY, page 96   15 min.

- **Alternative Writing:** Have students write about school schedules in different countries or for different levels (grade school, high school, college).

LESSON 3	**Verbs and Objects**
Student Learning Outcomes	• **Read** about orphan elephants and their keepers. • **Identify** the object of a verb. • **Use** object pronouns in place of nouns. • **Listen** to information about people's jobs. • **Read** and **report** on a person's job. • **Write** a description of a person's job.
Lesson Vocabulary	(n.) crocodile (v., n.) golf (n.) keeper (v.) taste (n.) gear (n.) hunter (n.) orphan (n.) trunk

EXPLORE

1 READ, page 97   15 min.

- Have students look at the photo. Point out the *elephant(s), trunk(s), bottle,* and *blanket.*
- After they listen, ask, Is this an easy or a difficult job? Why?

Be the Expert

- Hunters kill adult elephants for their ivory tusks. The baby elephants in the photo are cared for at the David Sheldrick Wildlife Trust in Nairobi. When they no longer need milk, they will go to Tsavo National Park, where they will transition back into the wild. Sometimes it takes eight to ten years there before this happens. To find out more, search the Internet for keywords: *orphan elephants* or *David Sheldrick.*

- Some reports have shown that grown elephants still recognize their keepers years later. Sometimes they come back as adults and show off their babies to their keepers.

2 CHECK, page 98   5 min.

1. The keepers feed the ~~baby~~ elephants.
2. Ivory hunters killed the ~~baby elephants~~ elephants' mothers.
3. The keepers work in ~~Botswana~~ Kenya.
4. The keepers sleep in ~~houses with their families~~ a building with the elephants.

3 DISCOVER, page 98   5 min.
B b

LEARN

Chart 3.7, page 99   5 min.

- **Note 1:** The object of a sentence is a noun, pronoun (Chart 3.8), or noun phrase.

- **Note 2:** A verb + preposition combination is always followed by an object (a noun or pronoun). Students need to memorize the prepositions that go with the verbs. Additional examples are *ask for, apply for, belong to, consist of, laugh at, look at, look for, work for.*

4 page 99   5 min.

1. He (helps) baby elephants.
2. They (play) soccer.
3. He (likes) his job.
4. She (writes) articles.
5. We (visit) customers every day.
6. You (need) a new computer.
7. I (ride) my bike to work.
8. Makiko (loves) weekends.

5 page 99   10 min.

1. He has a new job.
2. A mechanic fixes cars.
3. Jasmin has a huge office.
4. Zookeepers feed animals.
5. Deanna talks to her boss every day.
6. Jay takes beautiful photographs.
7. I listen to music at night.
8. Katrina misses her friends.

6 WRITE & SPEAK, page 100   15 min.

- **Alternative Activity:** Play a circle memory game to practice third-person singular verbs. Student 1 says his/her name and chooses one of the sentences to complete. Student 2 repeats the information about Student 1, says his/her name and says another sentence. This continues with each student having to remember and report more information.

Chart 3.8, page 100　　　　　　　　　　　10 min.

- **Note 1:** Object pronouns follow verbs and prepositions.
- **Note 2:** Students may not know what *refer back to* means. It is easy to show with the arrow in the example.
- **Tip:** On the board, write *I live with him.* Put a *?* above *him*. Show that you need an earlier sentence, for example, *This is my brother. My brother is a student here.*

7 page 100　　　　　　　　　　　　　　　　5 min.

A & B

1. Angel has a new job. He likes *it* a lot.
2. I'm Cory's boss. He works for *me*.
3. Sally is Joe's employee. She works for *him*.
4. My sister lives in Australia. I miss *her* a lot.
5. It's an excellent newspaper. I read *it* every day.
6. You are in my class. I sit behind *you*.
7. We go to the park on Saturday. Henri sometimes comes with *us*.
8. Paulina has two dogs. She walks *them* in the park every morning.

- **Tip:** As students begin exercise 8, ask, *In number 1, who is "her?" What about number 2? I need to call who? My father.* Think about the meaning of each sentence.

8 page 101　　　　　　　　　　　　　　　10 min.

1. her	6. you
2. him	7. them
3. them	8. me
4. it	9. us
5. them	10. it

PRACTICE

9 page 101　　　　　　　　　　　　　　　15 min.

A 1. He thinks about Linda every day.
2. We sometimes visit Mr. and Mrs. Lee.
3. I don't call my parents every day.
4. Kate loves her sister.
5. He sees Fiona and Ken at work.
6. He doesn't listen to music every night.
7. I ride my bike on weekends.
8. He doesn't like his job.

B 1. He thinks about *her* every day.
2. We sometimes visit *them*.
3. I don't call *them* every day.
4. Kate loves *her*.
5. He sees *them* at work.
6. He doesn't listen to *it* every night.
7. I ride *it* on weekends.
8. He doesn't like *it*.

10 LISTEN, WRITE & SPEAK, page 102　　25 min.

A 1. a　　2. c　　3. b

B 1. F　　3. F　　5. T　　7. F
　　2. T　　4. F　　6. F　　8. T

C 1. Tim doesn't look for them in the ocean. He looks for them in the lake.
2. Tim doesn't sell them. The store sells them.
3. Tim likes it.
4. Tim watches for it.
5. Kelly doesn't like it.
6. People don't want it.
7. Kelly doesn't eat it. She tastes it.
8. The pet food company does pay her. / The company pays her.
9. An animal park doesn't pay them. The government pays them.
10. Most people worry about them.

11 READ & SPEAK, page 103　　　　　　10 min.

- **Tip:** Give students five minutes to read and try to remember the information. To build fluency, have students get together with others who have the same story to practice. Then have them tell the story to two people who had the other story.

12 APPLY, page 103　　　　　　　　　　　10 min.

- **Alternative Activity:** In class or for homework, have students think about a great job. Ask them to list the typical tasks in that job. (*A doctor talks to patients. He or she gives medicine to them.*) Then ask them to list the benefits (*A doctor makes a lot of money.*) or difficulties of the job (*A doctor is very busy.*).

LESSON 4 — Imperatives

Student Learning Outcomes	
	• **Read** advice about how to get a job in game design.
	• **Identify** common signs and **state** their meanings using imperatives.
	• **Find** and **edit** errors with imperatives.
	• **Listen** to advice about a job and **restate** the advice using imperatives.
	• **Write** advice using imperatives.
	• **Give** advice about ways to improve English skills.

Lesson Vocabulary			
(n.) advice	(n.) experience	(n.) skill	(v.) volunteer
(n.) employee	(v.) improve	(v.) use	(v.) worry

EXPLORE

1 READ, page 104 — 15 min.

- Look at the photos. Before reading the caption, ask, *Do you like to play computer games? Children like to play games, too, and even animals at the zoo play games.* In the second photo, you may need to explain the meaning of a Buddhist monk.

Be the Expert

- Many people love to play online games and would like to work in the industry. Write *jobs in game design* on the board and have students brainstorm a list. (game designer, programmer, animator, writer, audio engineer, tester, and technical support)

2 CHECK, page 105 — 5 min.

Ideas	Good Idea	Bad Idea
1. make games	✓	
2. play games all the time		✓
3. worry about a college degree		✓
4. get experience	✓	
5. ask for a lot of money		✓

3 DISCOVER, page 105 — 5 min.

A 1. Don't play   4. Keep
   2. Don't worry   5. Work
   3. Show

B 1. F   2. T   3. T

LEARN

Chart 3.9, page 106 — 10 min.

- **Note 1:** The list shows when people use imperatives.
  a. Commands are used by people in authority, e.g., a police officer or a parent.
  b. Instructions are often given by teachers, or by someone in charge of a process.
  c. Directions are simple ways to tell people how to get somewhere.
  d. Warnings are given as imperatives because it's important to communicate them quickly.
  e. Advice can be given using imperatives if the speakers are friends or the context is informal.

- **Tip:** Write *Teacher* on the board. Ask students what imperatives teachers often give, e.g., *Open your books; Turn to page. . . ; Get into a group.* You can also point out the direction lines on this Student Book page for more examples of the imperative.

- **Note 3:** It is not common to use *you* in imperatives; however, one exception is when a parent says to a child (in an angry voice), *You come here right now!*

- **Note 4:** The use of *please* changes a direct command into a request.

- **Tip:** Demonstrate how a person's tone of voice can make an imperative harsh or kind. Say, *Sit down, please* with an angry tone, a routine tone, and a kind tone.

4 page 106 — 5 min.

1. <u>Try</u> to meet people at game companies.
2. <u>Ask</u> people at game companies about their jobs.
3. Please <u>tell</u> me the truth. Do you really like your job?
4. Bob, please <u>call</u> me when you get this message.
5. <u>Read</u> the directions.

UNIT 3   LESSON 4   39

6. It's hot in here. Please <u>open</u> the window.
7. <u>Turn</u> right on Elm Street.
8. Please <u>pass</u> your papers to the center of the room.

5 page 107 — 10 min.

| 1. Study | 3. Be | 5. Stay | 7. Wear |
| 2. Go | 4. Eat | 6. give | 8. Ask |

6 SPEAK, page 107 — 10 min.

- **Expansion Tip:** Teach common expressions used in directions (*go straight, go two blocks, turn left/right, at the corner,* etc.). You can also teach students how to clarify when they don't understand: *Sorry? Two blocks?* Use a map of nearby streets to have them give each other directions and mark the route.

Chart 3.10, page 107 — 15 min.

- **Tip:** Write *Parents* on the board. Ask students what imperatives parents often give. Make two columns and write *Affirmative* and *Negative* across the top. Then write the imperatives students suggest, e.g., *Go to sleep; Do your homework; Don't stay out late; Don't spend so much time on the computer.*

> **REAL ENGLISH,** page 107
>
> In these imperatives with the full form of *do not. . . ,* the *not* is emphasized: *Do NOT tell your parents!* Give additional examples of times when someone might emphasize an imperative by not using the contraction (e.g., *Do NOT forget to give me your homework. Do NOT forget to put the -s on the verb after he, she, or it!*) Elicit additional examples from students, making sure they use the appropriate stress for emphasis.

7 page 107 — 5 min.

1. It's cold. <u>Don't open</u> the window.
2. <u>Don't worry</u>. Everything is OK now.
3. Please <u>don't sit</u> there.
4. <u>Don't stay</u> up late tonight. You have a meeting at 8:00 a.m. tomorrow.
5. I want to read that book. Please <u>don't tell</u> me the ending.
6. <u>Don't forget</u> Eva's birthday. It's tomorrow.
7. <u>Don't be</u> late tomorrow. We have a test.
8. <u>Don't go</u> to that restaurant. The food there is terrible!

8 SPEAK, page 108 — 5 min.

1. Don't eat	6. Don't open
2. Don't be late	7. Don't park
3. Don't sit	8. Don't feed

4. Don't use   9. Don't close
5. Don't call   10. Don't use

- **Expansion Tip:** If all students are able, have them stand up. Give affirmative and negative commands for different movements, e.g., *Clap your hands. Smile. Don't smile. Put your hands on your knees. Don't touch your knees. Run in place. Stop.*

PRACTICE

9 SPEAK & WRITE, page 108 — 10 min.

| 1. a | 3. g | 5. e | 7. d |
| 2. f | 4. c | 6. h | 8. b |

10 EDIT, page 109 — 10 min.

1. Be on time. ~~Doesn't~~ Don't be late.
2. Be friendly and polite to customers. ~~You~~ Say "thank you."
3. Don't be rude to coworkers.
4. Don't ~~leaves~~ leave work early. Stay until five o'clock.
5. Do not ~~you~~ use your cell phone in meetings.
6. ~~Doesn't~~ Don't play computer games at work.

11 page 109 — 10 min.

1. Don't take; Take
2. Don't quit; Get
3. Don't go; call; stay; drink
4. go; don't drink
5. Don't go; Stay; save

12 LISTEN, SPEAK & WRITE, page 110 — 20 min.

A

	Good Idea	Bad Idea
1. Swim a lot.	✓	
2. Learn about the ocean.	✓	
3. Try to catch fish.		✓
4. Choose the right camera.	✓	
5. Practice in a swimming pool.	✓	
6. Jump into the water with your camera.		✓
7. Leave your camera in the sun.		✓
8. Have fun.	✓	

13 APPLY, page 110 — 15 min.

- **Alternative Writing:** Ask students to make a list of advice for visitors to your city or new students in your program. Have them make a poster or slide show to display their advice.

UNIT 3 Review the Grammar

1 page 111   15 min.
1. She doesn't read it every morning.
2. She doesn't work with them.
3. My brother doesn't have it.
4. She doesn't teach us.
5. We don't talk to them every day.
6. She doesn't study it.
7. He doesn't know her.
8. He doesn't fix them.

2 page 111   15 min.
1. works; to/until
2. doesn't work; on
3. works; until
4. has; at
5. doesn't work; in
6. work; at
7. has; at
8. works; from; to/until
9. doesn't work; on
10. have; in

- **Expansion Tip:** Use a page from a college schedule. White out some of the times on two sets of the schedule for students to complete an information gap activity.

3 EDIT, page 112   10 min.

Max Kraushaar ~~studys~~ studies in Seattle. He likes to bake. ~~At~~ On Friday and Saturday morning, he ~~bake~~ bakes pies. ~~In~~ At night, people call or text Max. They order pies, and Max delivers them. He doesn't ~~drives~~ drive a car. He rides a bicycle and ~~carrys~~ carries the pies in a basket. He takes orders until 3:00 a.m. Max's company ~~have~~ has a funny name. He calls it "Piecycle."

4 page 112   15 min.
1. works
2. in
3. has
4. fishes
5. from
6. to
7. drop
8. pull
9. doesn't like
10. is
11. doesn't stop
12. are
13. doesn't rise
14. until
15. goes
16. at
17. worries
18. says
19. Be
20. Don't fall
21. says
22. Don't worry

- **Expansion Tip:** Have students change *Chris* to *Chris and Tom* in exercise **4** and rewrite the paragraph using the correct verb forms.
- **Expansion Tip:** Give pairs of students a card with a job on it (e.g., *nurse, firefighter, police officer, soldier, pilot*) and a T-chart with (+) and (–) at the top. Have the class compete to write as many sentences as possible about the good and bad aspects of those jobs.

5 SPEAK & WRITE, page 113   20 min.
Answers will vary.

6 LISTEN, SPEAK & WRITE, page 113   20 min.
A 3   2
       1   4

B *Answers may vary. Possible answers:*
1. Tom has a new job. He doesn't have a car
2. Sue has an important meeting. She has a bad headache.
3. Jay and Bill have a test tomorrow. The party starts at ten o'clock.
4. Ann and Jim's new baby has a bad cold. Ann wants to take him to the emergency room, but Jim doesn't want to go.

C *Answers may vary. Possible answers:*
1. Don't miss work! Ask a friend for help.
2. Take some medicine. Don't miss the meeting.
3. Study for the test. Don't go to the party. Don't stay up late.
4. Call your doctor. Ask him or her for advice.

- **Expansion Tip:** Give students cards with problems on them, e.g., *I'm tired all the time. I don't have many friends here. My roommate snores. I have too much homework. I'm hungry. I'm bored on weekends.* Have them tell another student the problem. The other student gives advice using affirmative or negative imperatives. After that, students exchange cards and talk to a different student.

Connect the Grammar to Writing

1 page 114   15 min.

A Learn your students' names on the first day.

B   I <u>am</u> a teacher. I <u>work</u> from 8:00 a.m. to 1:30 p.m. I <u>teach</u> four English classes. In class, I <u>write</u> on the board. I <u>ask</u> a lot of questions. I <u>use</u> pictures when I teach vocabulary. I <u>don't arrive</u> late. At home, I <u>plan</u> my lessons. I <u>correct</u> homework and tests. My advice for new teachers— (learn) your students' names on the first day.

C

The Job of a Teacher	
In Class	**At Home**
A teacher asks a lot of questions. A teacher writes on the board. A teacher uses pictures to teach vocabulary. A teacher doesn't arrive late.	A teacher plans lessons. A teacher corrects homework and tests.
Advice: Learn your students' names.	

2 BEFORE YOU WRITE, page 115   15 min.

3 WRITE, page 115   15 min.

> **WRITING FOCUS,** page 115
>
> Show a paragraph with no indentation. Show the same paragraph with the first line indented. If possible, show students the tab key on a keyboard. After students have written their paragraphs, ask them to double-check that they have indented the paragraphs before handing in their work.

- **Alternative Writing:** If your students have jobs, have them write about their job. First, have them fill out the graphic organizer chart in exercise **2** for their jobs. Then, have them write their paragraphs.

UNIT 4 Lifestyles
Simple Present: Part 2

Unit Opener

Photo: Have students look at the photo. Ask, *What do you see in this photo?* Elicit: *boats, food, fruit, vegetables, bananas, workers, hats,* etc. Say, *They have fruit and vegetables in their boats. Why?* (They sell the food from their boats.) Have students read the caption with you. Find Thailand on the map.

Location: Damnoen Saduak in Thailand has a special market. It is a floating market. Vendors sell food from their boats to people along the river.

Theme: Lifestyles include the way people live and choices they make about how they spend their time. This unit includes information about people with different lifestyles from around the world.

Page	Lesson	Grammar	Examples
118	1	Simple Present: *Yes/No* Questions and Short Answers	**Does** she **work** a lot? Yes, she **does**./No, she **doesn't**.
125	2	Frequency Adverbs and Expressions	I **sometimes** drink coffee at night. We go to the movies **once a week**.
131	3	Simple Present: *Wh-* Questions	**What do** they **do** for fun? **When do** you **get up**?
139	**Review the Grammar**		
142	**Connect the Grammar to Writing**		

Unit Grammar Terms

frequency adverb: an adverb that indicates how often something happens. Some common frequency adverbs are *never, seldom, sometimes, frequently, usually,* and *always*.
➢ We **rarely** see my cousins.
➢ She is **always** late to class.

frequency expression: a group of words that tells how often something happens.
➢ They go to a movie **once a week**.
➢ I visit my grandparents **every Sunday**.

Wh- question: a question that asks for specific information, not *"Yes"* or *"No."*
➢ **Where** does your brother work?
➢ **What** do you usually do on weekends?

Yes/No question: a question that can be answered only by *yes* or *no*.
➢ A: **Do you work on Saturdays?**
   B: Yes, I do./No, I don't.
➢ A: **Does she live in Dublin?**
   B: Yes, she does./No, she doesn't.

43

LESSON 1   Simple Present: Yes/No Questions and Short Answers

Student Learning Outcomes
- **Read** about the lifestyle of long-lived people from the Nicoya Peninsula.
- **Ask** and **answer** yes/no questions in the simple present.
- **Find** and **edit** errors with yes/no questions and short answers.
- **Listen** and **ask** questions about people's lifestyles.
- **Write** yes/no interview questions.
- **Interview** a classmate to find out about his or her lifestyle.

Lesson Vocabulary

| (n.) diet | (adj.) healthy | (n.) lifestyle | (n.) vegetable |
| (n. & v.) exercise | (v.) hike | (n.) meat | (n.) water |

EXPLORE

1 READ, page 118   15 min.

- Have students read the title and the caption. Ask, *Where is the Nicoya Peninsula? How old is the man on the horse? What is his job? Isn't he old for a cowboy?*

Be the Expert

In 2005, a demographer named Dr. Luis Rosero-Bixby found that people on the Nicoya Peninsula in Costa Rica lived longer than people in the rest of the country. The people who live inland on this peninsula are small farmers, laborers, and cowboys (on large ranches). It is thought that these aspects of their lifestyle lead to their longevity: healthy food, active lives with hard work, and close relationships with family. A *National Geographic* writer, Dan Buettner, called this and other areas where people live longer *Blue Zones*.

2 CHECK, page 119   5 min.

1. T   2. F   3. F   4. T

3 DISCOVER, page 119   10 min.

A

Questions	Answers
Do they have a healthy diet?	Yes, they do.
Do they eat a lot of meat?	No, they don't.
Does the article talk about exercise?	Yes, it does.

B *Do* is used with all subjects except for the third-person subjects, *he, she,* and *it*. Use *does* with these pronouns or with a singular noun as subject.

- **Tip:** Show the answer to exercise **B** by having students turn to Chart 4.1 on page 120.

LEARN

Chart 4.1, page 120   5 min.

- **Notes 1 & 2:** To make questions in English, a verb or auxiliary (sometimes called an *operator*) is used before the subject. With the simple present, the operator is *do* or *does*.

- **Tip:** To show how to make questions, write these sentences on the board: *I work here. They study. She likes pizza. Class starts at 9:00.* Then show the question forms. Draw an arrow from the *-s* in *likes* and *starts* to the *-s* in *Does*.

- **Tip:** Use a gesture to show the change in word order in questions. Then use this same gesture to correct student mistakes.

REAL ENGLISH, page 120

It sounds strange to say *do you do*, but it's a good illustration of the use of *do* and *does* as the operator in simple present questions. *Do* is used in fixed expressions such as *do homework, do the dishes, do business, do errands,* and *do a (good) job*. Write *do homework every night* and *do the dishes* on the board. Have students ask a partner these questions.

4 page 120   10 min.

1. Do   5. Do
2. Do   6. Do
3. Does   7. Does
4. Does   8. Does

5 page 120   10 min.

1. Does Abuela Panchita walk every day?
2. Do people from the Nicoya Peninsula eat beans and rice?
3. Do they live in Costa Rica?
4. Does he have a big family?
5. Do we/you have a healthy lifestyle?
6. Do you live with your grandparents?
7. Does she hike six miles every day?
8. Is he healthy and happy?

- **Tip:** Item number 8 reminds students of Note 2 in Chart 4.1. To make questions with *be*, we change the order of the subject and verb. We don't use *do* or *does*.

Chart 4.2, page 121

- **Tip:** Short answers use the auxiliary *do* or *does* rather than the base verb. Students sometimes want to use just the base verb. For example, to answer *Do you walk to school?* they might say, *I walk*. Since this is a *yes/no* question, these are the correct short answers: *Yes./Yes, I do. No./No, I don't*.

6 page 121   10 min.

1. they do
2. she does
3. they don't
4. she doesn't
5. he doesn't
6. I don't
7. we do
8. you do

7 page 121   10 min.

- **Tip:** Show students that they must change the subject of the items in exercise **6** to ask each other the questions.

PRACTICE

8 page 122   15 min.

A
1. Do you like
2. Yes, I do
3. Do you miss
4. Yes, I do
5. Do you like
6. No, I don't
7. Do you eat
8. Yes, I do
9. Do you help
10. Yes, I do
11. Do your parents
12. No, they don't
13. Do you have
14. Yes, I do
15. Do you all
16. Yes, we do

- **Tip:** After checking the answers for **A**, discuss more informal ways of answering *yes/no* questions with only *uh huh, yeah, yep* for affirmatives and *uh uh* or *nope* for negatives. Then have students do exercise **B** using the informal short answers.

9 EDIT, page 123   10 min.

1. B: No, he ~~hasn't~~ doesn't.
2. A: ~~You~~ Do you live in Toronto?
3. A: Does Richard ~~likes~~ like his job?
4. B: No, it ~~don't~~ doesn't.
5. A: ~~Do~~ Are you from Italy?
6. B: Yes, I ~~eat~~ do.

- **Tip:** An alternative correction for item 5 is *Do you come from Italy?* However, *Are you from . . .* is more common.

- **Tip:** Students sometimes make a mistake and use the base form instead of *do* and *does* with transitive verbs. For example, in item 3, they might say *Yes, he likes* instead of *Yes, he likes it*.

10 LISTEN & SPEAK, page 124   10 min.

Kate: 1, 4, 5, 7, 8, 10
Rena: 1, 2, 3, 6, 9

11 APPLY, page 124   10 min.

- **Expansion Tip:** Have students ask each other about the classmates they interviewed. *Does Saleh have a healthy lifestyle?* They use the information in their charts to answer.

- **Expansion Tip:** Have students think of a famous person. The other students take turns asking *yes/no* questions to guess who it is. After ten questions, the first student says who it is. For example:

  A: Is it a man?   *B: No, it isn't.*
  A: Is she from our city?   *B: Yes, she is.*

- **Expansion Tip:** Do a "Find someone who . . ." activity. Write interesting information about students in a list with a blank in front of each and the base form of each verb. Have students turn each item into a *Yes/No* question and find someone who answers *yes* to the question. A student's name can only be written once.
  Example: _____ *has a brother.*
  Student 1: *Do you have a brother?*
  Student 2: *Yes, I do.* (Student 1 writes Student 2's name in the blank.)

LESSON 2 | Frequency Adverbs and Expressions

Student Learning Outcomes
- **Read** about night markets in Asia.
- **Use** frequency adverbs and frequency expressions in affirmative statements.
- **Complete** sentences and paragraphs that express how often something happens.
- **Listen** and **write** the missing words in a blog about floating markets.
- **Listen** to information about differences in someone's lifestyle.
- **Discuss** your lifestyle and how often you do certain things.

Lesson Vocabulary
(adj.) crowded	(n.) groceries	(n.) market	(n.) shopping
(n.) entertainment	(n.) mall	(adj.) open	(n.) snack

EXPLORE

1 READ, page 125 — 10 min.
- Use the photos to discuss *night market, snack, buy,* and *sell*. Ask students if they ever go to markets. Discuss the difference between a supermarket and a market.
- The word *vendor* is in the caption on page 126. Ask, *What do vendors sell at these markets? What is on the woman's table?*

Be the Expert

Night markets are more than just a place to shop; they are also a form of entertainment and a place to socialize. Night markets are common in many cities in Asia, but they also exist in other parts of the world such as Morocco, Canada, Peru, and France. To find out more information, do a web search for the world's top night markets.

2 CHECK, page 126 — 10 min.
1. T   2. T   3. F   4. F   5. T

3 DISCOVER, page 126 — 10 min.
A 1. usually
   2. often
   3. always
B c

LEARN

Chart 4.3, page 127 — 5 min.
- **Notes 1 & 4:** Students are often unfamiliar with the negative words *hardly ever* and *rarely*. You could explain that these words are probably about 5 percent on the continuum, and *almost always* is about 95 percent of the time.
- **Notes 2, 3, & 5:** The most difficult part of frequency adverbs is where they go in the sentence. Exercises through the lesson help students learn this.
- **Tip:** Explain the examples with days of the week. (e.g., *She always eats eggs for breakfast. That's Monday, Tuesday, Wednesday, etc.*)

4 page 127 — 10 min.
1. The night market is **usually** open on weekends.
2. We **always** go to the market with friends.
3. I **usually** buy a snack at the night market.
4. The market is **rarely** open in the morning.
5. She **almost always** goes shopping on Saturday afternoon.
6. He **never** buys groceries.
7. **Sometimes** I eat dinner at ten o'clock. / I **sometimes** eat dinner at ten o'clock. / I eat dinner at ten o'clock **sometimes**.
8. Marta **almost never** eats dessert.

5 page 127 — 10 min.
1. usually shop
2. is always busy
3. rarely shops
4. am never hungry
5. always buy
6. are often open
7. almost never walks
8. is never open

6 SPEAK, page 128 — 5 min.
Answers will vary.

Chart 4.4, page 129
- **Notes 1 & 2:** Frequency expressions give more specific information than adverbs of frequency. They are placed at the beginning or at the end of sentences.

46 SIMPLE PRESENT: PART 2

7 page 128 — 10 min.

1. Saturday
2. once
3. night
4. two
5. a week
6. times
7. day
8. a month
9. day
10. days

8 SPEAK, page 129 — 10 min.

Answers will vary.

- **Expansion Tip:** Give short verb phrases and a frequency expression. Have students make sentences. For example:

  Teacher: be late to class—sometimes
  Student: Sometimes Marco is late to class.
  Teacher: never
  Student: You are never late to class.
  Teacher: come to class on time—always
  Student: The teacher always comes to class on time.
  Teacher: have homework—every night

PRACTICE

9 LISTEN & WRITE, page 129 — 25 min.

A

1. often travel
2. twice a year
3. almost always go
4. usually have
5. often go
6. every time
7. almost never go
8. it's usually

B

1. b
2. a
3. b
4. a
5. a
6. b
7. a
8. a

C page 130

Answers may vary. Possible answers:

1. People always sell things from their boats at the floating markets.
2. They almost always have colorful umbrellas and wear large hats.
3. The Amphawa market is open every weekend.
4. The Damnoen Suduak market is always open.
5. It is almost always crowded.

- **Expansion Tip:** *Wh-* questions are taught in Lesson 3, but you could model a *how often* question. Then have students ask *how often* questions about the statements in exercise **9B**. Note: Most people do not pronounce the *t* in *often*.

10 LISTEN, page 130 — 10 min.

In Canada	In France
Sophie almost never cooks. She rarely goes to the grocery store.	Sophie walks to the market every morning. She buys bread or pastries twice a day. She cooks dinner every night.

11 APPLY, page 130 — 15 min.

Answers will vary.

> **REAL ENGLISH, page 130**
>
> *Me, too* and *Me neither* are very common rejoinders in conversation. They show that people share affirmative or negative statements. Have students respond to some true statements that they share with you: *I live in [your city]. Me, too. I don't live in Australia. Me neither.* Explain that if they don't share, they can say various responses such as *Oh really? Oh, that's interesting.*

- **Expansion Tip:** Have students discuss or write about lifestyles or customs in different cultures. For example, *Life in [Spain] is different from life in the United States. In the U.S., people usually eat dinner at about 6:30. In Spain, we never eat dinner at this time. We always eat dinner after 9:00.* They could also discuss or write about differences in generations (their grandparents' lifestyles and their lifestyles).

LESSON 3 Simple Present: *Wh-* Questions

Student Learning Outcomes	• **Read** about the Amish lifestyle. • **Write** and **ask** information questions in the simple present. • **Ask** questions with *Who* as the subject. • **Listen** to an interview. • **Write, ask,** and **answer** questions about lifestyle. • **Find** and **edit** errors with *Wh-* questions in the simple present.
Lesson Vocabulary	(n.) buggy (n.) farm (v.) ski (adj.) traditional (n.) cap (adj.) plain (n.) snowshoes (n.) vacation (n.) electricity (adj.) retired

EXPLORE

1 READ, page 131   10 min.

- Look at the photos. Ask, *What's in this photo? What do you see?* Elicit the words *horse, buggy, cap, hat, clothes,* and possibly *old-fashioned.*

Be the Expert

The Amish live apart from non-Amish. They make their own clothes, which are very simple. The men's pants have no creases or cuffs. Amish women use solid colors for their dresses. Men have beards, but no mustaches, and women don't cut their hair. However, each group follows its own set of rules, called *Ordnung.*

- After students listen, ask, *How is their life different from yours?* List similarities and differences on the board.

2 CHECK, page 132   5 min.

1. a   2. b   3. b   4. b   5. a

3 DISCOVER, page 132

A 1. Where   2. Why   3. What   4. What

B These questions ask for other information.

- **Tip:** When you discuss the answer to exercise **B**, show students the *Wh-* words in Chart 4.5. Read Note 1.

LEARN

Chart 4.5, page 133   5 min.

- **Note:** Questions with *how* can ask for many different types of information; e.g., *How do you get to school? How do you like your new phone? How do you know her?*

- **Note:** A question with *why* sometimes has a negative verb, e.g., *Why don't you eat meat?* Sometimes a *Why* question with a negative verb is a suggestion, e.g., *Why don't you come with us?*
- **Note 2:** Remind students that verbs in the simple present use *do* and *does* to form questions.

> **REAL ENGLISH,** page 133
>
> In conversation, we ask for additional information by using a single *Wh-* word. *Why* by itself is a common question. Say another statement, e.g., *I get up early.* Students can ask *Why?* to find out more information.

4 page 133   5 min.

1. Where **do** many Amish people live?
2. How often **do** they visit other families?
3. What **does** an Amish woman wear?
4. Why **do** they live on farms?
5. What **does** an Amish child do for fun?
6. How often **do** they go to big cities?
7. What **does** *cap* mean?
8. When **do** they go to restaurants?

5 page 133   5 min.

1. Where do you live?
2. Who does she visit?
3. Where do you exercise?
4. Why does he play baseball?
5. What does she teach?
6. What do they do in their free time?
7. How often do you visit your parents?
8. When do they eat dinner?

Chart 4.6, page 134 — 5 min.

- **Notes 1 & 2:** When *who* is the subject of the question, the word order is the same as a statement. It's not necessary to use *do* or *does* to form the question.
- **Note 3:** Students may ask about questions with *who* and the verb *be*. In many questions with *Who is* or *Who are*, the question is about a complement, not a subject. If students ask, explain that when the verb is *be*, the verb can be singular or plural, depending on the complement, e.g., *Who are they? What are those?*

6 page 134 — 10 min.

1. Who lives on that farm?
2. Who has a traditional lifestyle?
3. Who plays baseball?
4. Who wants coffee?
5. Who is absent today?
6. Who does your laundry?
7. Who speaks Japanese?
8. Who drives to class?

7 SPEAK, page 134 — 5 min.

- **Tip:** Teach the answers: *No one./No one does.* and *Everyone./Everyone does.* Students may use these in exercise **6**.

PRACTICE

8 WRITE, LISTEN & SPEAK, page 135 — 15 min.

1. Where
2. Who
3. Where
4. How
5. When
6. What
7. Who
8. How often
9. Where
10. Why

> **REAL ENGLISH,** page 135
>
> We use *well . . .* to give us time to think about what we want to say. Students will also hear people use *let's see, uh, so,* and *um* in this way. Sometimes they use several of these together, e.g., *What do you think? Well, uh, let's see. I'm not sure.* Ask students questions and have them use *well* in their answers.

9 LISTEN, page 136 — 5 min.

1. a
2. b
3. b
4. b
5. b
6. a
7. b
8. a

10 READ, WRITE & SPEAK, page 136 — 25 min.

A   Jeremy Stubbs <u>lives</u> in Tacoma, Washington. He <u>teaches</u> math at a high school. On weekends, he <u>likes</u> to go on hikes. In fact, he <u>goes</u> on a hike every weekend, 52 times a year!

In the winter, Jeremy sometimes <u>climbs</u> a mountain trail in snowshoes and <u>carries</u> his skis. Then he <u>has</u> a fast trip back down the mountain on the skis!

Jeremy sometimes <u>goes</u> on hikes alone, but other teachers and students usually <u>go</u> with him. Sometimes he <u>writes</u> and <u>posts</u> photos on his blog, "52 Hikes 52 Weekends."

B
1. does Jeremy
2. does he teach
3. does he like
4. does he go
5. does he; do
6. does he carry
7. goes
8. does he; do

> **REAL ENGLISH,** page 137
>
> In exercise **C**, model the conversation and have students answer the questions in exercise **B** with incomplete sentences. Point out that although abbreviated answers are used in spoken English, *Because I like it* is not a complete sentence. In writing we do write the complete sentence: *He hikes all the time because he likes it.*

11 EDIT, page 137 — 5 min.

1. A: Where ~~he does~~ does he live?
2. A: When ~~he goes~~ does he go on hikes?
3. A: When **does he** have a vacation?
4. Correct
5. A: Who ~~does~~ goes on hikes with him?
6. A: Where ~~he teaches~~ does he teach?

12 LISTEN, WRITE & SPEAK, page 138 — 25 min.

- **Tip:** For exercise **B**, put students in teams and make this a competition to see which team can write the most correct questions in a limited time.

13 APPLY, page 138 — 15 min.

- **Tip:** Have students write the information they learned about their partners after they ask their questions.
- **Expansion Tip:** Write answers on the board or on cards. In pairs or teams, students must say the questions. Give a point for every correct question. For example, write *fixes cars.* (Question: *What does a mechanic do?*)

Review the Grammar — UNIT 4

1 page 139 10 min.

1. What
2. Does
3. Where
4. How often
5. When
6. Do
7. What
8. Who
9. How
10. Why

- **Tip:** Students may want to use or *At what time* for item 5. These are also acceptable.

2 LISTEN, page 139 5 min.

1. b
2. b
3. b
4. a
5. b
6. a
7. a
8. a
9. b
10. a

- **Tip:** Remind students that in item **4a**, *Because it's good exercise,* is not a complete sentence and is only used in speaking.
- **Expansion Tip:** Have students think of a job. The other students take turns asking *Yes/No* and *Wh-* questions to try to guess what job they do. After ten questions, the first student says what job it is.

3 EDIT & SPEAK, page 140 10 min.

A 1. A: Who's that?
   B: That's my sister Katie.
   A: Does she ~~visits~~ visit you often?
   B: No, she doesn't. She ~~comes rarely~~ rarely comes to California.

2. A: How often do you travel for your job?
   B: Once a month.
   A: Wow, that's a lot. ~~You do~~ Do you like it?
   B: Yes, I do/Yes, I like it, but sometimes it's difficult. I miss my family.

3. A: Where ~~you do~~ do you live?
   B: I live on River Road.
   A: How do you get to class?
   B: I usually take the subway.

4. A: Do you exercise every day?
   B: Yes, I go to the gym every ~~days~~ day.

- **Tip:** Remind students that *like* is a transitive verb. It always has an object, so for item 2 a short answer of *"Yes, I like."* is not correct.

4 LISTEN & SPEAK, page 141 25 min.

A (Column 1)   **B** (Column 2)

Internet Activity	How Often
✓ Sends or reads e-mail	Three times a week.
✓ Watches videos online	----------
✓ Uses a social networking site	Once a week
✓ Banks online	Never
✓ Plays online games	Never
✓ Shops online	Sometimes
Reads the news	----------

C Answers will vary.

- **Expansion Tip:** Have students report on interesting information they learn about their classmates.

5 WRITE & SPEAK, page 141 25 min.

Answers will vary.

- **Alternative Activity:** For homework, have students interview two people and write about the differences between the two people in their Internet activities.

Connect the Grammar to Writing

1 READ & NOTICE THE GRAMMAR,
page 142   25 min.

B   Pradit lives in Bangkok, Thailand. He works in a trading company. He <u>often</u> travels because of his job. <u>Every night</u> he goes out with his friends. They <u>usually</u> go to a restaurant. <u>Sometimes</u> they go to the movies. On weekends, he <u>usually</u> visits his parents or goes to the beach. He enjoys his life in Bangkok.

C *Answers may vary. Possible answers:*

Information about Pradit		
	Questions	Answers
Where	Where does Pradit live?	In Bangkok.
What	What does he do for work?	He works for a trading company.
Why	Why does he travel?	He travels because of his job.
How often	How often does he go out with friends?	Every night.
Who	Who does he visit on the weekends?	His parents.
Yes/No	Does he enjoy his life in Bangkok?	Yes, he does.

2 BEFORE YOU WRITE, page 143   25 min.

3 WRITE, page 143   25 min.

> **WRITING FOCUS, page 143**
>
> Subject-verb agreement is one of the most common mistakes in student writing at all levels. Tell students to make a habit of checking every subject and verb in their writing to avoid this mistake.
>
> It is a good idea to use a special editing mark on student papers to indicate this mistake. Students will become familiar with the mark and know immediately what to do when they see it.
>
> For additional editing practice, rewrite a paragraph from exercise **10A** (the story about Jeremy Stubbs) with mistakes in subject-verb agreement. Show the paragraph to the class to edit together or distribute it to pairs of students.

• **Alternative Writing:** Students sometimes don't have an opportunity to interview anyone in English outside of class. If this is an issue, suggest that they write about an imaginary person in a job or even an animal (A Dog's Life). However, encourage them to complete exercise **2A** first to practice writing questions.

UNIT 4 CONNECT THE GRAMMAR TO WRITING **51**

UNIT 5 Food and Hospitality

Count and Non-Count Nouns

Unit Opener

Photo: Have students look at the photo. Ask, *What do you see in this photo?* Elicit: *birds, bread, bottle, water, plate, glass, salt, and pepper.* Ask, *Why are these things on the table?* Have students read the caption with you. Find Uganda on the map.

Location: Queen Elizabeth National Park is the most visited park in Uganda. There are many animals there, including tree-climbing lions.

Theme: Food and hospitality are linked topics. Hospitality refers to receiving and entertaining guests, visitors, and strangers. It includes providing food, housing, and entertainment.

Page	Lesson	Grammar	Examples
146	1	Count and Non-Count Nouns; Articles	I eat an **apple** every morning. Andrea eats two **apples** every day. **Sugar** is sweet. **a** suitcase/**an** old suitcase/**the** Earth
154	2	Measurement Words; *Some, Any*	We need a **bag of** rice. Would you like a **cup of** coffee? I have **some** onions. We don't need **any** onions.
163	3	*Much, Many, A Lot Of; A Few, A Little*	They don't eat **much** meat. Do you eat **many** snacks? I eat **a lot of** honey. I drink **a few** cups of tea every day. We have **a little** time before class.
171		Review the Grammar	
174		**Connect the Grammar to Writing**	

Unit Grammar Terms

count noun: a noun that names something you can count. They are singular or plural.
➤ I eat an **apple** every morning.
➤ Andrea eats two **apples** every day.

definite article: *the*; it is used before a specific person, place, or thing.
➤ **The** earth is round. (only one)
➤ Do you have **the** suitcases? (specific suitcases)
➤ I always stay at a hotel downtown. **The** hotel is very nice. (second reference)

indefinite article: *a* and *an*; they are used before singular count nouns that are not specific.
➤ I have **a** sandwich and **an** apple for lunch.

non-count noun: a noun that names something that cannot be counted.
➤ **Sugar** is sweet.
➤ Carlos drinks a lot of **coffee**.

LESSON 1	**Count and Non-Count Nouns; Articles**			
Student Learning Outcomes	• **Read** a conversation between a hotel guest and a front desk clerk. • **Identify** count and non-count nouns. • **Speak** and **write** sentences using correct articles. • **Find** and **edit** errors with articles. • **Listen** and **complete** conversations with articles. • **Role-play** conversations using count and non-count nouns.			
Lesson Vocabulary	(n.) coin (n.) double room	(n.) elevator (n.) fitness center	(n.) luggage (n.) reservation	(n.) traffic (n.) vending machine

EXPLORE

1 READ, page 146   15 min.

- Have students read the title and the caption. Ask, *Where is Negril Beach? What is this hotel like?* Ask students about Jamaica: *What is the climate?* (tropical) *What is it known for?* (tourism, Reggae music)

Be the Expert

Negril Beach is on the west side of Jamaica and is more than four miles long. Along the beach there are many resorts, hotels, and tourist attractions.

2 CHECK, page 147   5 min.

1. Front Desk Clerk   4. Mike Martin
2. Front Desk Clerk   5. Mike Martin
3. Front Desk Clerk

3 DISCOVER, page 147   5 min.

Luggage is a non-count noun; *bag* is a count noun. We use *a* with a singular count noun.

- **Tip:** Show the answer by having students turn to Chart 5.1 on page 148.

LEARN

Chart 5.1, page 148   10 min.

- **Note 1:** Singular count nouns require an article. It is the way we indicate there is only one of something.
- **Note 2:** Non-count nouns include liquids, abstractions, and activities. Things that are too small or too many to count (sand, salt grains, rice) or too big to count (dirt, space) are usually non-count.

- **Tip:** To illustrate the meaning of *count nouns*, point to things in the room (e.g., two students, five books) and elicit the number. Contrast these nouns with non-count nouns (e.g., *Do we count weather? Fun?*).
- **Tip:** Emphasize the meanings of singular and plural. Hold up one item and say the singular form (e.g., *a pen*). Hold up two items and say the plural form (e.g., *two pens*). Write the singular and plural forms on the board.

REAL ENGLISH, page 148

Some nouns such as *pizza, chicken,* and *cake* are usually used as non-count nouns because they are too large to eat all at once. However, when we talk about food for a group or animals, we talk about them as whole units, so they are count nouns. Write *pizza, chicken,* and *cake* on the board and elicit examples. (E.g., *There are three chickens in the yard. We need enough chicken to feed eight people. We need two cakes for the party. I ate too much cake.*)

4 page 148   10 min.

Count Noun: 2, 3, 4, 8, 9

Non-Count Noun: 1, 5, 6, 7, 10

5 page 149   10 min.

1. traffic   6. furniture
2. homework   7. money
3. time   8. weather
4. luggage   9. fruit
5. jewelry   10. clothing

- **Tip:** With books closed, call on students and name a category (e.g., *clothing*). Elicit examples.

UNIT 5 LESSON 1 53

- **Expansion Tip:** Create a memory game. Collect photos of examples of each category. Write each category on a piece of paper. Tape the photos and categories, face down on the board. Divide the class into teams. Call a member from a team to the board to turn over two pieces of paper to find a match. Each correct match earns a point.

Chart 5.2, page 149   5 min.

- **Note:** Point out that *an* is used before singular nouns that begin with a vowel sound, not necessarily a vowel. For example, we say *a university* because it begins with a *y* sound, but *an hour* because the *h* is silent.

6 page 149   10 min.

1. a
2. an
3. a
4. Ø
5. Ø
6. an
7. Ø
8. Ø

7 page 150   10 min.

1. Ø
2. a
3. a
4. Ø
5. a
6. Ø
7. an
8. Ø
9. an
10. a
11. Ø
12. an
13. Ø
14. an
15. Ø

8 SPEAK, page 150   10 min.

Chart 5.3, page 150   5 min.

- **Note 2:** Students often overuse *the*. Provide more examples of each case, e.g., a: *the sun, the president;* b: *the board, the classroom;* c: *I have a new car. The car is red.*

9 page 150   10 min.

1. the
2. the
3. Ø
4. the
5. a
6. the
7. The
8. Ø; The
9. the
10. The
11. a; the
12. the

PRACTICE

10 page 151   15 min.

1. A: the   B: a
2. A: a   B: the; the
3. A: a   B: the
4. A: a   B: the
5. A: Ø   B: Ø
6. A: the; Ø   B: The
7. A: The   B: The
8. A: a; the   B: the

- **Tip:** When you go over the answers, ask students to identify the reason why *the* is required in each case. Refer them to Chart 5.3 for the reasons.

REAL ENGLISH, page 151

Point out that *Let's* is followed by the base form of the verb (Unit 4) in affirmative suggestions and by *not* + base verb in negative suggestions. Say a few prompts and have students respond with suggestions. e.g., *I'm hungry.* (Let's eat!) *It's hot.* (Let's go to the pool.) *I'm tired.* (Let's not go out tonight.)

11 EDIT, page 152

We have **a** big hotel in our city. **The** name of **the** hotel is Barney's. It's expensive, but many people like to stay there. It has **a** pool. It also has **a** restaurant with very good food. **The** restaurant's name is Martindale by the Sea. Sometimes my family goes there for special celebrations.

12 SPEAK, page 152   5 min.

- **Tip:** Direct attention to the photo and caption. Ask, *Do you want to go there? Why, or why not?*

13 LISTEN, page 152   15 min.

A a. 3   b. 1   c. 4   d. 2
B 1. b   2. b   3. a   4. b
C page 153

Conversation 1: help; a; the TV

Conversation 2: a map; the city; information; trains; a train

Conversation 3: work; traffic; traffic; roads

Conversation 4: the office; an hour; work; a new job

REAL ENGLISH, page 153

Ask two students to role-play Conversation 2. Point out *would like* in the woman's question and *would* in the traveler's answer. For contrast, write on the board: *A: Do you want a map of the city? B: Yes, I do.* Explain that this exchange has the same meaning, but it sounds more abrupt and informal.

14 APPLY, page 153   15 min.

- **Expansion Tip:** Have each pair write a scenario (e.g., a parent and a teenager arguing over schoolwork) on a piece of paper. Collect and redistribute them so that each pair gets a new scenario. Have pairs create conversations for the scenario, using words from the box.

- **Expansion Tip:** Have students compete to use as many words from the box as they logically can in their conversations.

LESSON 2 Measurement Words; Some, Any Some/Any

Student Learning Outcomes	• **Read** a blog about food in Budapest. • **Use** measurement words to talk about food. • **Complete** sentences and paragraphs that express amounts of food items. • **Listen** and **complete** a chart to show the quantities of ingredients in a recipe. • **Ask** and **answer** questions to make a shopping list. • **Write** and **discuss** recipes.			
Lesson Vocabulary	(v.) boil (v.) chop	(v.) heat (n.) ingredient	(v.) mix (n.) recipe	(v.) serve (v.) stir

EXPLORE

1 READ, page 154 — 10 min.

- Use the large photo to introduce the city of Budapest in Hungary. Ask students what they know about Hungary. (e.g., It's in Eastern Europe.)
- Direct students' attention to the small photos of food and elicit the vocabulary. *Ask, Do you make any dishes out of these ingredients? What are they?* Note that the format of the blog itself looks like a recipe card.

Be the Expert

Goulash is a traditional Hungarian dish, but it is also popular in many other European countries. Students can find many variations of goulash recipes on the Internet.

2 CHECK, page 155 — 10 min.

1. c   2. f   3. b   4. d   5. a   6. e

- **Tip:** Recycle the grammar from Lesson 1 by having students identify the count and non-count nouns in the photos. Have students work in pairs to take turns saying sentences with each of the words. (e.g., I often have meat for dinner. I put an onion in my soup.)

3 DISCOVER, page 155 — 10 min.

A   1. some   2. any   3. any   4. some

B Any is used in negative statements. Some is used in affirmative statements.

LEARN

Chart 5.4, page 156 — 5 min.

- **Note 1:** Measurement words are especially helpful in giving information about non-count nouns.

- **Note 2:** Almost all measurement words will make a count noun plural. Exceptions would be when the measurement refers to only part of the noun (e.g., a tablespoon of chopped onion).
- **Tip:** After going over the chart, call on students and say a measurement word (e.g., *a bunch of . . .*). Elicit a correct completion (*bananas*). Then call on students and say a noun to elicit a correct measurement word.

4 page 156 — 10 min.

1. carton   5. bowl
2. stick   6. cup
3. glass   7. jar
4. piece   8. loaf

5 page 156 — 10 min.

1. b   3. c   5. a   7. b
2. b   4. b   6. a   8. c

- **Expansion Tip:** Have students work in pairs to take turns saying the sentences with another correct word in the blank, e.g., *I'd like a glass of juice, please*.

6 WRITE & SPEAK, page 157 — 5 min.

Answers will vary.

Chart 5.5, page 157 — 5 min.

- **Notes 1, 2 & 3:** Students may get *some* and *any* confused. Noting the *n* in *any* may help them remember that it is used in negative statements.

7 page 158 — 10 min.

1. any   6. some
2. some   7. any
3. any   8. any
4. some   9. some
5. any   10. any

- **Expansion Tip:** To recycle simple present and the use of *some* and *any*, have students make negative statements affirmative and affirmative statements negative.

8 WRITE & SPEAK, page 158 5 min.

Answers will vary.

PRACTICE

9 page 158–159 15 min.

A
1. a glass
2. any
3. some
4. glass
5. bowl
6. any
7. pieces
8. any
9. slice
10. some
11. any
12. box
13. jar
14. some

> **REAL ENGLISH,** page 159
>
> These words are often used when ordering in restaurants. Have students role-play in pairs to practice. One student is the server, and the other is the customer. Elicit and write menu items on the board as prompts (*soup/salad, coffee/tea, vanilla ice cream/chocolate ice cream, etc.*).

- **Expansion Tip:** Have students practice Conversation 1 using their own ideas for food and drinks. Suggest they use *or* to offer choices and *also* to add to their orders.

10 EDIT, page 159 5 min.

This is an easy recipe for fried rice. You need two or three eggs, four ~~cup~~ cups of rice, ~~any~~ some green onions, and some oil. ~~Any~~ Some people also use some small ~~piece~~ pieces of chicken or shrimp. First, chop the onions and mix the eggs. Then, cook the eggs in two ~~tablespoon~~ tablespoons of oil, and add some salt. Next, fry the rice in some oil. Add the eggs and onions. This is also delicious with a cup of ~~vegetable~~ vegetables such as peas.

- **Tip:** Direct students' attention to the photo. Ask, *What do you see? Where is she? What is in the pan?*

11 LISTEN, SPEAK & WRITE, page 160 25 min.

- **Tip:** Ask students to describe what they see in the photo. This will elicit the food vocabulary that they know.

Potatoes: a large bag
Eggs: a carton
Onions: 1
Flour: 2 tablespoons
Oil: 2 cups
Salt: some

- **Tip:** For added scaffolding in exercise **C**, have students write their questions first, or model the activity by calling on students and asking *Yes/No* questions.

D WRITE, page 160 10 min.

Answers will vary. Possible answers:
1. They have a large bag of potatoes.
2. They have a carton of eggs.
3. They don't have any onions.
4. They have a lot of flour.
5. They don't have any oil.
6. They have a lot of salt.

12 READ, SPEAK & WRITE, page 161 25 min.

- **Expansion Tip:** Write the verbs from the recipe on slips of paper. Call on students to choose a slip and mime the action for the class.

13 APPLY, page 162 15 min.

- **Expansion Tip:** Have students stand and walk around the room to share recipes with at least five classmates. When they are finished, ask students which recipes they want to try.

56 COUNT AND NON-COUNT NOUNS

LESSON 3	**Much, Many, A Lot Of; A Few, A Little**
Student Learning Outcomes	• **Read** about the Hadza people in Tanzania. • **Use** *much, many, a lot of, a few,* and *a little* in sentences. • **Ask** and **answer** questions with *How much* and *How many*. • **Listen** to a conversation about diets. • **Ask** and **answer** questions about someone's diet. • **Find** and **edit** errors with *much, many, a lot of, a few,* and *a little*. • **Report** about your own and a partner's diet.
Lesson Vocabulary	(n.) berry (n.) diet (n.) lifestyle (n.) shelter (n.) calorie (v.) gather (adj.) permanent (n.) vitamin

EXPLORE

1 READ, page 163   10 min.

• Look at the photos. Ask students, *Where is Tanzania? What do you see in the photo? What do you think their lives are like?* Then, listen to or read the passage.

Be the Expert

The Hadza have one of the last hunter/gatherer cultures in Africa. They have followed this way of life in Tanzania for thousands of years. Today, their culture numbers less than a thousand people. Their language is very unique, unrelated to other languages.

• After reading, ask, *How is their life different from yours? How is it the same?* List similarities and differences on the board.

2 CHECK, page 164   5 min.

1. F   2. T   3. F   4. T   5. F

3 DISCOVER, page 164   5 min.

A
1. Many   2. a lot of   3. a lot of   4. much

B
1. F   2. T   3. T   4. T

• **Tip:** When you discuss the answers to exercise **B**, read the notes for Chart 5.6.

LEARN

Chart 5.6, page 165   5 min.

• **Note:** *A lot of* can be used in every situation; *many* can be used in all situations with count nouns. *Much* is the most limited in its use as it is only used with non-count nouns in questions and negative statements.

• **Note 2:** Remind students that they cannot use *much* in affirmative statements.

REAL ENGLISH, page 165

Point out that we are much more likely to use *lots of* in conversation than in writing because it is informal. Ask a few questions to elicit the structure from students; e.g., *What do you eat a lot of?* (I eat lots of fruit.) *Do you have many books?* (Yes, I have lots.)

4 page 165   10 min.

1. a lot of   7. a lot of
2. much   8. Many
3. a lot of   9. much
4. many   10. many
5. a lot of   11. many
6. a lot of   12. much

5 SPEAK, page 165   5 min.

Chart 5.7, page 166   5 min.

• **Notes 1, 2 & 3:** Unlike with large quantities, there isn't one expression like *a lot of* that can be used in all situations. Students need to focus on whether the noun is count or non-count to express themselves correctly.

• **Tip:** In pairs, have students make two sentences for each expression about things in the classroom. (E.g., *Ana has a few books on her desk. I have a little water in my bottle.*)

6 page 166   10 min.

1. a few   6. a little
2. a little   7. A few
3. a few   8. a few

LESSON 2 | Adverbs of Manner and Adjectives

Student Learning Outcomes
- **Read** a news article about an encounter with a gorilla.
- **Use** adverbs to talk about yourself.
- **Complete** sentences with linking verbs.
- **Identify** adjectives and adverbs.
- **Listen** to a true story and **answer** questions.
- **Find** and **edit** errors with adverbs or adjectives and linking verbs.
- **Share** personal stories in a group.

Lesson Vocabulary
(adj.) calm	(n.) encounter	(n.) guide	(adv.) patiently
(v.) control	(adv.) gently	(v.) knock	(v.) sniff

EXPLORE

1 READ, page 320 — 15 min.

- Use the photo to teach the meaning of *impenetrable* and *gorilla*. Elicit ideas about what the park might be like.
- **Tip:** After students read and listen, have them work in pairs to discuss what each *-ly* adverb means, and use it in an original sentence.

Be the Expert

- Bwindi Impenetrable National Park is a UNESCO World Heritage Site. It is in southwestern Uganda along the border with the Republic of Congo. The forest is very diverse with hundreds of plant and animal species. It is best known for the mountain gorillas—it has half of the members of this endangered species. Tourists can visit the gorillas, which are used to people.
- Mountain gorillas live in troops, or bands, that can include up to 30 animals. Each group is led by a dominant male called a silverback, because of the male's identifying streak of silvery fur. The animals are typically calm and nonaggressive, but they do pack incredible physical power, which makes any close encounter potentially dangerous. Elicit what students know about gorillas.

2 CHECK, page 321 — 5 min.

1. F
2. T
3. F
4. T
5. F

- **Tip:** Have students correct the false statements.
- **Expansion Tip:** Have students work in pairs to ask and answer questions formed by the statements in exercise **2**. (e.g., *Are the gorillas in cages in the park?*)

3 DISCOVER, page 321 — 5 min.

A
1. carefully
2. patiently
3. slowly
4. suddenly
5. lightly

B b

- **Tip:** Have students circle the verbs that the words in exercise **3** describe. Point out that these are action verbs, leading into the first note on page 322.

LEARN

Chart 10.4, page 322 — 10 min.

- **Notes 1 & 2:** If students ask, explain that adverbs can modify anything except nouns, including verbs, adjectives, and clauses. An adverb of manner tells how an action is performed.
- **Note 3:** Adverbs do not come between a verb and its object. Write example sentences on the board. Call on students to add adverbs of manner to the sentences (e.g., *I (gently) picked up the tiny mouse*).

4 page 322 — 5 min.

- **Tip:** Have students work in pairs to take turn asking and answering questions about how the subject of each sentence does things. (e.g., *How does the park control the number of visitors? Carefully.*)

1. The park <u>carefully</u> controls the number of visitors.
2. The gorillas move <u>freely</u> in the park.
3. John King sat beside the path and waited <u>patiently</u>.
4. The gorillas walked <u>slowly</u> past King.

104 ADJECTIVES AND ADVERBS

4. a little   9. a little
5. a few   10. a few

Chart 5.8, page 166 — 10 min.

- **Notes 1, 2 & 3:** Point out that the *-s* ending on a noun is a good clue to indicate whether the noun is singular or plural and if *How much* or *How many* should be used.
- **Tip:** Review the type of nouns that are often non-count (categories, liquids, activities, abstract nouns, things that are too small or too big to count).

> **REAL ENGLISH,** page 166
> Remind students that speakers often drop words that are repeated. For example, in answers to *Wh-* questions, we often give short answers. (e.g., *What do you usually eat for lunch?* ~~I usually eat~~ *a sandwich.*)
> Have students practice this structure in a chain, asking about items in the classroom. One student asks another a *How much/How many* question. The other student responds with a short answer and asks another student a question.

7 page 167 — 15 min.

Answers will vary. Possible answers:
1. How many cups of coffee do you drink every day?
2. How much meat do you eat every day?
3. How many meals do you have every day?
4. How much junk food do you eat?
5. How much money do you spend on food every week?
6. How much free time do you have every day?
7. How many hours do you sleep every night?
8. How many brothers do you have?
9. How much homework does our teacher give?
10. How many hours do you spend on homework every day?
11. How much English do you know?
12. How many languages do you speak?

8 SPEAK, page 167 — 10 min.

PRACTICE

9 page 168 — 15 min.
1. a lot of; How much honey does she put in her tea?
2. many; How many calories does yogurt have?
3. a few; How many pieces of fruit does she eat every day?
4. much; How much sugar do you put in your coffee?
5. much; How much salt does Samir use?
6. much; How much flour do we need for the recipe?
7. a lot of; How much milk does your daughter drink?
8. a lot of; How much homework does Hilda have?
9. A few; How many students are absent today?
10. a few; How many languages does Marco speak?
11. a lot of; How much English does Pedro know?
12. many; How many people do you know in this city?
13. a lot of; How much free time do you have these days?
14. a lot of; How much (money) do these flowers cost?

10 EDIT, page 169 — 10 min.

- **Tip:** Direct students to the graphic. Ask, *What is at the bottom? Does this diet have a little bread and rice or a lot? Does this diet have much red meat?*

   This food pyramid shows the Mediterranean diet. In general, Mediterranean people eat ~~much~~ a lot of brown rice and pasta. They eat ~~much~~ a lot of vegetables. They eat a lot of fruit and nuts. They eat a ~~few~~ a little cheese and yogurt. They also eat fish ~~a little~~ a few times every week, but they don't eat ~~many~~ much meat. They also don't eat ~~much~~ many sweets. They usually have fresh fruit for dessert. They drink a lot of water—six to eight glasses a day.
   The Mediterranean lifestyle is also very healthy. Mediterranean people get a lot of exercise, and they spend ~~much~~ a lot of time with their families. This is the Mediterranean secret to a long and happy life!

11 LISTEN & SPEAK, page 170 — 20 min.

A True for Sunil: 1, 2, 4, 5, 7, 10, 11, 12
True for Henry: 3, 6, 8, 9, 12

12 APPLY, page 170 — 15 min.

- **Expansion Tip:** After students ask their questions, have them write the information they learned about their partner into a report.

58 COUNT AND NON-COUNT NOUNS

UNIT 5 Review the Grammar

1 page 171   5 min.
1. Ø
2. Many
3. some
4. Ø
5. a
6. Some
7. a lot of
8. much
9. Ø
10. a lot of

- **Expansion Tip:** Have students write three *How much/How many* questions about the paragraph and then ask and answer the questions in pairs.

2 LISTEN, WRITE & SPEAK, page 171   25 min.

A
1. coffee; Ethiopia
2. hours
3. A few
4. a few
5. a lot of

B
1. How much time do people usually spend
2. How much time does the coffee ceremony take
3. How many neighbors come
4. How many minutes does she boil the coffee
5. How many cups of coffee do they usually have

D

- **Expansion Tip:** Have students work in pairs to plan one-minute presentations on a food or drink custom in their cultures. Then have students present in small groups.

3 EDIT, page 172   5 min.

The definition of *barbecue* is "to cook meat or other food over **an** open fire, usually outside." It's common all over **the** world. In many countries, people barbecue on **a** grill. Other people use a spit. **The** spit turns to cook the meat. It's **a** great idea for **a** party!

4 LISTEN & SPEAK, pages 172–173   25 min.

A
1. hamburgers
2. corn
3. apple pie and vanilla ice cream

B **Check (√):** hamburger, tomatoes, onions, corn, ice cream, apple pie, rolls

C *Answers will vary.*

- **Expansion Tip:** Have students work in pairs to figure out the amount of food they need for 30 people.

5 SPEAK & WRITE, page 173   25 min.

Answers will vary.

- **Alternative Activity:** Have students plan a nice dinner party. Students may need to brainstorm additional or different menu items other than what's included in the Student Book that are appropriate for a formal meal.

Connect the Grammar to Writing

1 READ & NOTICE THE GRAMMAR,
page 174   25 min.

A A potluck dinner

- **Expansion Tip:** Dictate the sentences from the paragraph in random order. Have students work in pairs to put the sentences in the correct order to make a paragraph, then check their answers in the book.

- **Expansion Tip:** Have students look through their books to choose a reading. Have them underline the indefinite articles and circle the definite articles and then share their ideas in pairs.

B   5 min.

It's very easy to plan (a) potluck dinner. Here are some things you need to do. First, choose (the) date and (the) time. Next, invite some friends. Prepare or buy some food. Put some plates and glasses on (a) table. Leave some space on (the) table for a lot of other dishes. Last, put on some music. Have (a) great party!

C *Answers may vary. Possible answers:*

How to Plan a Potluck
1. Choose the date and the time.
2. Invite some friends.
3. Prepare or buy some food.
4. Put some plates and glasses on the table.
5. Leave some space for a lot of other dishes.
6. Put on some music.
7. Have a great party!

2 BEFORE YOU WRITE, page 175   10 min.

- **Tip:** After students complete the chart, have them share and discuss their ideas with a partner. This will help them clarify their ideas before writing.

3 WRITE, page 175   25 min.

> **WRITING FOCUS, page 175**
>
> Before students write their paragraphs, have them organize the information in their charts from exercise **2** into sentences containing transition words. For additional practice with transitions, provide pairs of students with a list of steps in a process; e.g., how to bake a cake. Have pairs order the steps and add a transition word in front of each.

- **Alternative Writing:** Suggest that students write about another process they know well; e.g., how to make a cup of coffee, how to paint a room, how to plant a garden, how to shop at a farmers market, etc.

UNIT 6 Homes and Communities
There Is/There Are

Unit Opener

Photo: Have students look at the photo. Ask, *What do you see in this photo?* Elicit: *houses, rocks, cliff, stairs, blue sky, a town.* Ask, *Do you want to live in this town? Why, or why not?* Have students read the caption with you. Find Greenland on the map.

Location: Uummannaq is in the northwestern part of Greenland. In 2013, it had fewer than 1300 residents. People there fish and hunt for a living. There is also a quarry and a canning factory.

Theme: Homes and communities are linked topics. Homes include apartments and houses. Communities can be physical places, like neighborhoods and towns. They can also be groups of people who have something in common, like clubs or social networks on the Internet.

Page	Lesson	Grammar	Examples
178	1	*There is/There are*	**There is/There's** a hospital on Main Street. **There are** two elevators in this building. **There is not/isn't** a lot of traffic on Elm Street. **There are not/aren't** any classes at night.
187	2	*Too Much/Too Many; Enough/Not Enough*	We have **too much** homework. He eats **too many** sweets. We have **enough** chairs. There is **not enough** time.
193	3	Indefinite Pronouns	There's **nothing** in the box. I don't see **anything** under the table. **Something** is on your desk. Kenji knows **everything** about cars.
201	**Review the Grammar**		
204	**Connect the Grammar to Writing**		

Unit Grammar Terms

count noun: a noun that names something you can count. They are singular or plural.
➢ *I ate an **egg**.*
➢ *I have twelve **carrots**.*

indefinite pronoun: a pronoun used to refer to people or things without specifically saying who or what they are. *Someone, something, everyone, everything, no one, nothing,* and *nowhere* are common indefinite pronouns.
➢ *There's **something** on your desk.*
➢ ***Everything** is in the car.*
➢ *There isn't **anyone** home.*
➢ *Does **everybody** understand?*

non-count noun: a noun that names something that cannot be counted.
➢ *Carlos drinks a lot of **coffee**.*
➢ *I need some salt for the **recipe**.*

LESSON 1	***There is/There are***

Student Learning Outcomes	• **Read** an online forum about travel in China. • **Talk** with a partner about things in different places. • **Ask** and **answer** questions with *There is/There are* and *How much/How many*. • **Find** and **edit** errors with *There is/There are*. • **Listen** about the city of Vancouver. • **Read** about the Galápagos Islands. • **Brainstorm** and **discuss** ideas about a city or town.
Lesson Vocabulary	(adj.) ancient (n.) canal (adj.) giant (n.) tortoise (n.) bridge (n.) coast (n.) scenery (n.) tourist

EXPLORE

1 READ, page 178   15 min.

- Have students read the title and look at the map and photo on the opposite page. Ask, *Where is Suzhou? What is nearby? What is interesting about the town in the photo?*
- Explain that side trips are short trips, often just a day, that travelers take from a central location.

Be the Expert

Suzhou is on both the Yangtze River and Taihu Lake. It is 2500 years old and has many beautiful pagodas, bridges, and canals. The gardens are a UNESCO World Heritage site.

2 CHECK, page 179   5 min.

1. There are ~~not~~ a lot of places to visit near Shanghai.
2. There are ~~25~~ 15 canals in Tongli.
3. There are 49 ~~roads~~ bridges in Tongli.
4. There is a ~~no~~ train from Shanghai to Suzhou.
5. There are not a lot of tourists in Tongli early in the day.

3 DISCOVER, page 179   5 min.

A 1. There are   3. There's no; there's
    2. there are   4. there aren't

B 1. there is   2. there are

- **Tip:** Show the answer by having students turn to Chart 6.1 on page 180.

LEARN

Chart 6.1, page 180   10 min.

- **Tip:** Emphasize singular and plural. Point to items and use *there is* or *there are*. (e.g., *There's a clock. There are two windows.*) Call on students and name something in the classroom to elicit a sentence with *there is* or *there are*.

> **REAL ENGLISH,** page 180
>
> *There* can have a meaning that is opposite to *here*. Illustrate this with examples: *Here, we have small buildings. My sister lives in New York. They have tall buildings there.*

4 page 180   10 min.

1. There are   5. There are   9. There is
2. There is   6. There are   10. There are
3. There are   7. There is   11. There is
4. There are   8. There are   12. There is

5 SPEAK, page 181   10 min.

- **Tip:** With books closed, call on students and name something in different locations (e.g., *a vending machine in the school*). Elicit affirmative and negative statements.

Chart 6.2, page 181   5 min.

- **Note:** *There* can cause problems for students because it is in the subject position, but the real subject actually comes after the verb. The verb agrees with the noun that follows it. However, because *there* is in the subject position, it follows the verb in *Yes/No* questions.

6 page 181   10 min.

1. aren't; Are there   5. aren't; Are there
2. isn't; Is there   6. are; Are there
3. 's; Is there   7. 's; Is there
4. 's; Is there   8. 's; Is there

7 page 182 — 10 min.

- **Expansion Tip:** Have students form two lines, A and B, facing each other. When you say *Start*, the two students across from each other alternate asking about things in different places as in exercise **7**. After 30 seconds, direct the first student in line A to move to the end of the line. Call *Start* again, and have students ask and answer questions with their new partners. Continue until students are very comfortable.

> **REAL ENGLISH, page 182**
>
> Point out that other numbers can also follow *There are.* (e.g., *There are two post offices near here.*) Ask questions to elicit answers with *There's (one)* and *There isn't (one)*. E.g., *Are there any restaurants in town?* (*Yes, there are three.*) *Is there an elevator in this building?* (*No, there isn't one.*)

Chart 6.3, page 182 — 5 min.

- **Note:** *How much* is used with non-count nouns and *is there*. *How many* is used with plural count nouns and *are there*. Point out that these questions do not include singular count nouns.
- **Tip:** To help students notice the word order in these questions, write sentences on the board, using a different color chalk or marker for each chunk of the sentence. To practice, write each word of the example questions and answers on separate cards. Shuffle and have students reorder them.

8 page 183 — 10 min.

1. many; are
2. much; is
3. many; are
4. much; is
5. many; are
6. many; are
7. many; are
8. much; is
9. many; are
10. many; are

PRACTICE

9 page 183 — 15 min.

A
1. How many students are there in this class?
2. How many tables are there in this room?
3. How many floors are there in this building?
4. How many windows are there in our classroom?
5. How much homework is there tonight?
6. How much money is there in your wallet?
7. How many train stations are there in your city?
8. How much furniture is there in your home?

- **Tip:** Have students work in pairs to make questions in exercise **9C** and then find new partners to take turns asking and answering.

10 EDIT, page 184 — 10 min.

Dan: They sure are. That's Santa Cruz Island over there.
Al: It looks like there ~~is~~ **are** some boats down there.
Dan: They're probably tour boats. There ~~is~~ **are** a lot of tourists at this time of year.
Al: Is this your first time in the Galápagos Islands?
Dan: No. I'm actually from here. I live on San Cristóbal. It's that island over there.
Al: Really? ~~Have~~ **Is** there a town on the island?
Dan: Yes, there**'s** ~~are~~ a small town and a few thousand people on the island. They live there.
Al: How about hotels? ~~There are~~ **Are there** any hotels on the island?
Dan: Yes, a few small ones, but there ~~haven't~~ **aren't** any big hotels on the island.

11 READ, WRITE & SPEAK, page 184 — 25 min.

Answers will vary. Possible answers:

B
1. There are many unusual animals on the Galápagos Islands.
2. There are giant tortoises on the islands.
3. There are over 25,000 people on the islands.
4. There are two airports.
5. There is an airport on Santa Cruz.
6. There are hotels in Puerto Ayora.
7. There are many tourists on Santa Cruz.
8. There is wildlife on Santa Cruz.

12 LISTEN & SPEAK, page 186 — 15 min.

A Check: open space; parks; mountains; scenery; highway; rain; traffic; water; snow

B Circle: rain; traffic

> **REAL ENGLISH, page 186**
>
> For additional practice, dictate sentences with *there*, *they're*, and *their* to the class. Have students write them on the board to check their spelling.

13 APPLY, page 186 — 15 min.

- **Expansion Tip:** Have students write sentences about a city they know but not identify the city. Students say their sentences to a group or the class. Their classmates ask *Yes/No* questions with *there* to guess the city.

LESSON 2	**Too Much/Too Many; Enough/Not Enough**
Student Learning Outcomes	• **Read** an advertisement about home design. • **Describe** homes using *too much/many* and *enough/not enough*. • **Write** and **speak** about things in your home. • **Listen** to a conversation about a home. • **Write** about a photo. • **Share** opinions about a room, office or home.
Lesson Vocabulary	(n.) art (adj.) comfortable (n. & adj.) expert (adj.) simple (adj.) basic (adj.) empty (adj.) round (adj.) straight

EXPLORE

1 READ, page 187   10 min.

- Direct students to the photo and ask, *Do you like this room? Does your home look like this? Are you interested in home design? Do you read articles or watch TV shows on this topic?*
- Read aloud the caption and ask for examples of basic colors. (*black, white*)
- Use the photo to elicit vocabulary: *straight, lines, basic, black, white, shapes, square, rectangle, chair, lamp, curtains, shelves.*
- Have students look at the photo of the living room on page 188 and read aloud the caption. Ask for examples of soft colors. (*cream, tan*) Ask, *Which living room do you like? Why?*

Be the Expert

Interior home design has become an increasingly popular profession in recent years. Many U.S. universities offer either a two-year or four-year degree in interior design. Career options include working in a design firm, for a home furnishings store, or at a residential building construction company.

2 CHECK, page 188   10 min.

Some people like: simple design, straight lines, empty space, basic colors

Other people like: round edges, comfortable furniture, soft colors

- **Tip:** Recycle the grammar from Unit 5 by having students identify the count and non-count nouns in the reading.

3 DISCOVER, page 188   10 min.

A 1. things   2. furniture
B 1. b   2. b   3. a

LEARN

Chart 6.4, page 189   10 min.

- **Note 1:** Students sometimes confuse *too* with *very*. Make sure they understand that using *too* indicates a problem.
- **Tip:** Point out that these expressions can be used with other verbs; they do not have to be in sentences with *There is/There are*.
- **Tip:** Illustrate the negative meaning of the expressions with examples. Try to put too many books in a bag, saying *There are too many books*. Put three chairs in front of the room and call up six students. Elicit the sentence: *There are too many students (for the chairs).*

4 page 189   10 min.

1. too much
2. too many
3. too many
4. too much
5. too much
6. too many
7. too much
8. too many
9. too much
10. too much

5 WRITE & SPEAK, page 189   5 min.

Answers will vary.

Chart 6.5, page 190 5 min.

- **Note 2:** Point out that *not enough* is the opposite problem from *too much* or *too many*. Remind students of the three chairs you put in the front of the room and the six students. Elicit: *There are not enough chairs.*
- **Note 3:** Remind students that they didn't use *too much* or *too many* with singular count nouns either.

6 LISTEN, page 190 15 min.

A **Enough:** 3, 4, 6, 7

Not Enough: 1, 2, 5, 8

B 1. There isn't enough furniture in the room.
2. There's not enough empty space.
3. We have enough chairs.
4. There are enough books for everyone.
5. We don't have enough money.
6. There's enough time.
7. We have enough food for dinner.
8. There isn't enough light in the kitchen.

- **Expansion Tip:** To recycle the grammar in Chart 6.4, have students rewrite the sentences using *too much* or *too many*.

PRACTICE

7 page 191 10 min.

1. too much furniture. There isn't enough space.
2. too many books; enough space
3. enough space for me
4. enough money
5. enough chairs
6. aren't too many books
7. is too much traffic
8. aren't enough parking spaces

- **Expansion Tip:** Have students work in pairs to write three additional statements using *enough, not enough, too much,* or *too many*. Have them exchange and discuss statements with another pair.

8 LISTEN AND SPEAK, page 191 15 min.

A 1. a   2. b

B

	Man	Woman
Neighborhood	N	P
Stairs	P	N
Windows	P	P
Size	N	N
Decor	N	P

- **Tip:** Have students write a paragraph about the neighborhood and apartment, and then exchange paragraphs with a partner to share and discuss their ideas.

9 WRITE, page 192 10 min.

- **Tip:** Ask students what they see in the photo. Describing the photo first will help them with the vocabulary used in the exercise.

1. He has too much work.
2. He doesn't have enough space on his desk to work.
3. He has too many things on his desk.
4. He doesn't have enough space for his coffee cup.
5. There are too many papers in his office.
6. He has too much furniture.
7. His office doesn't have enough space.
8. He doesn't have enough time to clean his office.

- **Expansion Tip:** Have students work in pairs to take turns saying statements about the photo. Their partner says whether the statement is true or false.

10 APPLY, page 192 10 min.

- **Expansion Tip:** Have students work in pairs to take turns asking *Yes/No* questions about the things in their partner's room, office, or home (e.g., *Do you have enough space in your office? Are there too many shelves in your apartment?*).

UNIT 6 LESSON 2 65

LESSON 3 | Indefinite Pronouns

Student Learning Outcomes
- **Read** about dune shacks.
- **Complete** sentences with indefinite pronouns.
- **Listen** to and **complete** a conversation about camping.
- **Plan** a camping trip.
- **Write** and **role-play** a conversation about a trip.

Lesson Vocabulary
(n.) campground (n.) fire   (n.) shack   (n.) spray
(n.) dune   (n.) luxury (n.) sleeping bag (n.) tent

EXPLORE

1 READ, page 193 — 10 min.

- Look at the photos. Ask, *What do you see? Do you want to stay here on vacation? Why, or why not?*
- Read the caption and find Massachusetts on the map. Point out that Cape Cod is the long thin "arm" that juts out into the Atlantic Ocean. Ask what other capes students know of (e.g., Cape of Good Hope, Cape Horn, etc.).

Be the Expert

This reading is an online forum about dune shacks, which are very basic shelters on the beach. Most have no electricity, indoor plumbing, or telephone landlines. Today, many vacationers find them a welcome escape from technology.

- After students listen to the reading, ask, *What are some good and bad things about dune shacks?* List their ideas on the board in a chart with the headings *Good things (+)* and *Bad things (-)*.

2 CHECK, page 194 — 5 min.

	Opinion
1. BW	N
2. BeachBunny	P
3. Traveler212	P
4. Birdy	N

3 DISCOVER, page 194 — 5 min.

A
1. Someone
2. anything
3. something
4. something
5. anything

B 1. b   2. a   3. b

- **Tip:** When you discuss the answers to exercise **B**, read the notes for Chart 6.6.

LEARN

Chart 6.6, page 195 — 10 min.

- **Note:** Indefinite pronouns can be either subjects or objects. They don't change form when they change function, unlike pronouns such as *I/me, he/him,* or *they/them.*
- **Note 2:** Remind students that we don't use two negatives in English (e.g., *I don't have nothing*). This means that when the statement is negative, we use *anything.*

> **REAL ENGLISH,** page 195
>
> Remind students that infinitives are *to* + base form of the verb. Provide or elicit other examples of this structure. (*There's always something to do/to see/to buy/to eat. I want something to eat/to wear/to do/ to read/ to watch on TV.*)

4 page 195 — 10 min.

1. b   6. a
2. a   7. a
3. a   8. a
4. b   9. a
5. a   10. b

5 page 196 — 5 min.

1. anything   5. anything/something
2. something   6. nothing

66 THERE IS/THERE ARE

3. something/everything
7. anything
4. everything
8. something/everything

Chart 6.7, page 197 — 10 min.

- **Note 1:** The endings *-body* and *-one* can be used interchangeably. Point out that these pronouns are all one word, except *no one*.
- **Tip:** Say sentences with a pronoun. Call on students to rephrase the sentence using the other pronoun that means the same thing.

6 page 198 — 10 min.

1. anyone
2. everyone
3. someone
4. somebody
5. Everyone
6. Someone
7. anybody
8. No one

7 page 198 — 10 min.

1. No one
2. Someone
3. anyone/someone
4. anyone
5. Everyone
6. everyone
7. No one

- **Tip:** To go over the answers, call on students to read the sentences aloud. Have them read the sentences again using the another correct pronoun (i.e., *nobody*, *somebody*, *anybody*, or *everybody*).

PRACTICE

8 page 198 — 15 min.

1. A: something — B: No one/Nobody
2. A: anything/something — B: nothing
3. A: someone/somebody — B: no one/nobody
4. A: ----- — B: everyone/everybody
5. A: something — B: anything

- **Tip:** After correcting their answers, have students practice reading the conversations in pairs. Encourage students to read the conversations with exaggerated emotions.

REAL ENGLISH, page 199

Someone else means another person. *Everyone else* means every other person.

A: I'm not going to the party.
B: Please come. *Everyone else* is coming.

We often use *Anyone else* as a question to ask if others should be included.

A: Jim and I want to eat pizza. *Anyone else*?
B: Yes, I want pizza, too.

9 LISTEN & SPEAK, page 199 — 15 min.

- **Tip:** Look at the photo. Ask, *What do you see? What do you think "glamping" means?*

A

1. T
2. F
3. F
4. F
5. F
6. T
7. T
8. F

B

1. everyone
2. anyone
3. anything
4. anything
5. nothing
6. Someone, everything
7. Someone
8. Nothing

10 page 200 — 10 min.

REAL ENGLISH, page 200

The phrase *or something* means that you are open to other ideas, especially when it is used in a suggestion.

A: Do you want to go out to eat *or something* tonight?
B: Let's go to the movies instead.

Ask pairs to write brief exchanges using *or something* to add a possibility. Check to ensure they use the structure appropriately.

1. everyone
2. everyone
3. something
4. anyone
5. everyone
6. anything
7. anyone/someone
8. something
9. everything

- **Tip:** Put students in groups of three. Ask them to read the conversation aloud a few times, so everyone can practice each role.

11 APPLY, page 200 — 15 min.

- **Tip:** Elicit ideas of interesting places to go and write them on the board. Encourage students to include places they have read about in earlier units.
- **Expansion Tip:** Have students present their group's ideas so the class can vote on the best plan.

Review the Grammar   UNIT 6

1 page 201   15 min.

1. much
2. There isn't
3. too much
4. something
5. There are
6. anyone
7. There's
8. Is there
9. there's
10. much
11. There aren't
12. Nobody

- **Expansion Tip:** Photocopy the completed conversation and cut it into strips so each of the 14 lines is on a different strip. Make enough sets so that each student gets a strip. Have students memorize their lines, and then stand and walk around the room to recite their lines and put themselves in order to recreate the conversation. If someone has the same line, the student must find another group. Alternatively, make enough sets of strips for each pair of students. Shuffle the strips and have students put them back in order.

2 EDIT, page 202   5 min.

Reporter: Welcome back to *WZCZ News*. Listen to this everyone! ~~There's~~ There are great white sharks near the beach in Cape Cod, Massachusetts. We're on the phone now with Tom Hardy. He's in our traffic helicopter over the beach. Tom, tell us, how ~~much~~ many sharks are there? ~~There is~~ Is there any danger?

Tom: Yes! ~~There are~~ There's a shark right below me. I see a lot more nearby. I'm glad I'm in a helicopter.

Reporter: Right. Are there many people in the water?

Tom: No, there ~~isn't~~ aren't. There's a shark warning, and everyone knows about the danger.

Reporter: OK, Tom. Thanks. How ~~many~~ much traffic is there today?

Tom: Usually, there ~~aren't~~ isn't a lot of traffic out here, but today there are a lot of cars on the roads. Everyone wants to see the sharks!

3 LISTEN, SPEAK & WRITE, page 202   25 min.

A Check: an elevator, 2 bedrooms, a laundry room

B 1. How many bedrooms are there?
2. Is there a washer and dryer?
3. Are there enough laundry rooms?
4. How many units are there?
5. How many buildings are there?
6. Is there an exercise room?
7. Does it have a swimming pool?
8. Is anyone in the apartment now?/Is there anyone in the apartment now?

4 SPEAK, page 203   10 min.

Answers will vary. Possible answers:

In picture A, there is a cat. There is nothing on the coffee table. There is one picture on the wall. There aren't any bookshelves. There isn't a rug in the room.

In picture B, there are three pictures on the wall. There are books and a cup on the coffee table. There are two floor lamps. There is a rug. There are bookshelves.

5 SPEAK, page 203   10 min.

- **Tip:** Suggest that students take notes on their ideas before they begin talking in pairs. Encourage them to use *enough, too many,* and *too much* in their notes and discussion.

- **Alternative Speaking:** Have students bring in photos of their own rooms or photos of rooms they like or dislike. Put them in pairs to share their ideas about the rooms.

Connect the Grammar to Writing

1 READ & NOTICE THE GRAMMAR,
page 204   25 min.

A • **Tip:** Before they read, have students look at the photo and the title. Ask, *What is the reading about? Do you think she likes her college? Why, or why not?*

B I like my college. It has a beautiful campus. <u>There are</u> about 1500 students. Everyone is very friendly. <u>There is</u> always someone to talk to. The classes are small. <u>There are no</u> large lectures, and the professors know all of their students' names. In my opinion, <u>there's</u> only one problem. <u>There's</u> too much homework!

   Unfortunately, the college is in a very small town. <u>There is</u> only one restaurant. <u>There are</u> only two small stores. <u>There's</u> no movie theater. <u>There isn't</u> anything to do on weekends. After college, I want to live in a big city.

C *Answers may vary. Possible answers:*

Positive Things	Negative Things
It has a beautiful campus.	There is too much homework.
Everyone is friendly.	It is in a small town.
There is always someone to talk to.	There is only one restaurant.
The classes are small.	There are only two small stores.
There are no large lectures.	There's no movie theater.
The professors know their students' names.	There isn't anything to do on weekends.

2 BEFORE YOU WRITE, page 205   10 min.

• **Tip:** To help students get started, brainstorm as a class places or communities that students could write about and write ideas on the board.

• **Tip:** After students complete the chart, have them share their ideas with a partner or a small group.

3 WRITE, page 205   25 min.

> **WRITING FOCUS, page 205**
>
> Make sure students understand which expressions can introduce both positive and negative opinions (*I think, in my opinion, personally*); which introduce only positive (*fortunately, luckily, happily*); and which only introduce negative opinions (*unfortunately*). Write a few sentences on the board for students to check and correct. For example: *Fortunately, it is raining outside, and I walk home from school.* (*Unfortunately, it is raining outside . . .*) *Unfortunately, I have a beautiful new car to drive.* (*Fortunately/Happily/Luckily I have a . . .*)

• **Alternative Writing:** Have students interview a partner about a place or community and write about that place.

UNIT 7 Extremes
Present Progressive

Unit Opener

Photo: Have students look at the photo. Ask, *What do you see?* Elicit: *ice, sky, a climber.* Ask, *Do you want to try this? Why or why not?* Have students read the caption with you. Find Iceland on the map.

Location: Myrdalsjokull Glacier is 230 square miles (595 square km). It is on top of the active volcano Katla. The volcano erupts every 40 to 80 years. It last erupted in 1918.

Theme: This unit is about extremes, especially in sports, weather, and careers. The people featured in this unit do risky activities, travel to hard-to-reach places, and pursue careers that sometimes put them in danger.

Page	Lesson	Grammar	Examples
208	1	Present Progressive: Statements	I **am**/I'**m reading**. They **are not**/They'**re not**/ They **aren't writing**.
218	2	Present Progressive: Questions	**Are** you **working**? **Is** she **sleeping**? Who **are** you **calling**? Where **are** they **going**? What **is** she **studying**? Why **are** you **running**?
228	3	Simple Present vs. Present Progressive; Non-Action Verbs	I **study** every day. *vs.* I'**m studying** right now. It **gets** dark early in winter. *vs.* It'**s getting** dark outside. I **know** the answer. (~~I am knowing the answer.~~) I don't **own** a car. (~~I am not owning a car.~~)
235	Review the Grammar		
238	Connect the Grammar to Writing		

Unit Grammar Terms

non-action verb: a verb that does not describe an action. Non-action verbs indicate states, sense, feelings, or ownership. They are not common in the progressive.
> I **remember** the party very well.
> They **have** a new car.

object: a noun or pronoun that receives the action of the verb. A sentence may have two objects: a direct object and an indirect object.
> I'm calling **Jack**.
> She's talking to **her brother**.

present progressive: a verb form that is used to talk about an action that is in progress now.
> The teacher **is talking** about grammar.

subject: the noun or pronoun that is the topic of the sentence.
> **Ann** is studying in the library.
> **They** ate breakfast.

LESSON 1 — Present Progressive: Statements

Student Learning Outcomes
- **Read** a conversation about highliners.
- **Talk** with a partner about photos using the present progressive.
- **Write** sentences about a photo.
- **Find** and **edit** errors with the present progressive form and spelling.
- **Complete** a Venn diagram.
- **Describe** what a classmate is doing.

Lesson Vocabulary

(v.) balance	(n.) cliff	(n.) edge	(n.) hang gliding	(n.) ice climber
(n.) belt	(n.) climb	(adj.) extreme	(n.) heights	(n.) valley

EXPLORE

1 READ, page 208 — 15 min.
- Have students read the title and look at the photo. Ask, *Where are they? What are they doing? Do you think this is safe? Why do people do this?* Then listen to the reading.

Be the Expert
- Highliners walk barefoot on a type of rope that is hollow and stretchy and use their arms for balance. The line swings and bounces when they walk on it. There are many videos available online to show students people highlining. Search *highlining video*.
- The highest highline record was set in Norway by Christian Schou in 2006. The line was 3281 feet (1000 meters) high.

2 CHECK, page 209 — 5 min.
1. T 2. F 3. F 4. T 5. F

3 DISCOVER, page 209 — 5 min.
A
1. 'm looking
2. 're walking
3. 're not wearing
4. 's standing

- **Tip:** Elicit the full forms of the verbs in exercise **A** before students do exercise **B**.

B c

LEARN

Chart 7.1, page 210 — 10 min.
- **Note 1:** Explain that some books may also use the term present continuous for this form.
- **Note 2:** Point out that this is an action that is taking place off and on during the present time. For example, he's teaching in Japan this year, but at the moment he is asleep.
- **Note 3:** In general, when a subject has more than one action, we don't repeat the subject or the helping verbs. (*I eat an apple and drink milk every day. She doesn't swim or ride a bike.*)
- **Note 4:** Contractions are used so often in conversation that students sometimes don't notice the use of *be*. Make sure they understand that this form always has two parts: *be* + verb + *-ing*.

4 page 210 — 5 min.
1. 're walking
2. 're wearing
3. is standing
4. 's taking
5. 's watching
6. 're doing
7. 're talking
8. 's looking; asking

5 page 211 — 10 min.
- **Tip:** Direct students' attention to the photo and elicit vocabulary. Write any unfamiliar words on the board. The Karakoram mountains are on the border of China, Pakistan, and India. The highest concentration of mountains over 26,247 feet (8000 meters) are found here.

1. is relaxing
2. is climbing
3. is wearing
4. is checking
5. is hanging
6. is looking
7. is thinking
8. are camping
9. are resting
10. is waiting

6 SPEAK, page 211 — 5 min.

Chart 7.2, page 212 — 5 min.

- After subject pronouns, speakers are more likely to use the contractions *'m*, *'s*, *'re* + *not*. With nouns, speakers are more likely to use *aren't* and *isn't*.

> **REAL ENGLISH, page 212**
>
> The sounds listed (*-s*, *-z*, *-ch*, *-sh*, soft *-g*) are similar to an /s/ sound. Speakers naturally separate the two sounds to be more comprehensible. Write on the board, *Louis's not reading.* Point out that the first sentence is difficult to say because of the ending sound on *Louis*. Write the correct statement, *Louis isn't reading.*

7 page 212 — 10 min.

1. We're not doing an exercise right now.
2. I'm not changing the sentences to questions.
3. She's not taking a test.
4. Our teacher isn't wearing a jacket.
5. We're not eating lunch.
6. He's not checking his e-mail.
7. Tom isn't reading a book in class.
8. My parents aren't working right now.
9. You're not teaching math.
10. They're not taking Greek this semester.

- **Tip:** Say the sentences from exercise **7** out of order and elicit the negative.

8 SPEAK, page 212 — 10 min.

- **Expansion Tip:** Have students walk around the room saying false statements about what they are doing. (e.g., *I'm eating Chinese food.*) Their partner corrects them. (e.g., *You're not eating Chinese food. You're practicing English.*) Encourage students to talk to ten classmates.

Chart 7.3, page 213 — 5 min.

- **Notes 3 & 4:** Make sure students can identify consonants and vowels. It is often easier to take note of the two-syllable words with the stress on the second syllable.

9 page 213 — 10 min.

1. playing
2. planning
3. trying
4. making
5. practicing
6. hitting
7. exercising
8. climbing
9. showing
10. entering

- **Tip:** Have students write sentences using the verbs and then share them in pairs.

10 LISTEN, page 213 — 10 min.

- **Tip:** Have students look at the photos on page 214. Elicit what they see.

1. is using
2. 's wearing
3. is jumping
4. 's standing
5. is trying
6. 's going
7. is flying
8. 's looking
9. are doing
10. 're having

PRACTICE

11 page 214 — 15 min.

1. I'm not spending
2. I'm studying
3. I'm not living
4. I'm staying
5. They're helping
6. I'm doing
7. I'm taking
8. We're learning
9. I'm sitting
10. enjoying
11. children are playing
12. having

- **Expansion Tip:** Have students write their own e-mails to a friend and then share in pairs.

12 page 215 — 10 min.

- **Tip:** Say true and false statements about the photo. Elicit if each sentence is true or false. Have students make the false sentences true.

1. Andy is not climbing in this photo.
2. He's doing something very dangerous.
3. He's jumping from a cliff to a rock.
4. He's carrying a rope.
5. He's not wearing a safety belt.
6. He's flying in the air right now.
7. The photographer is watching him.
8. He's taking some great photos.

13 EDIT, page 216 — 10 min.

I'm texting you from Arizona. I'm ~~visitting~~ visiting my sister Carol. Right now I'm ~~siting~~ sitting near a huge cliff. I **am/'m** enjoying the scenery. Carol is ~~takeing~~ taking lessons. She's climbing the cliff with her teacher today. I'**m/am** waiting for her. They ~~no~~ aren't climbing very high, but it's dangerous!

14 SPEAK & WRITE, page 216 — 25 min.

15 APPLY, page 217 — 10 min.

- **Tip:** Give students a two-minute time limit to describe a classmate. When time is up, call *Time*. Then they switch turns and describe another classmate.

LESSON 2 Present Progressive: Questions

Student Learning Outcomes	• **Read** an interview with a photographer. • **Ask** and **answer** questions using the present progressive. • **Write** and **speak** about people with dangerous jobs. • **Listen** to a conversation and **answer** questions. • **Ask** and **answer** questions about classmates.
Lesson Vocabulary	(n.) anchor (n.) cave (n.) geologist (adj.) steel (v.) attach (v.) drill (adj.) risk (n.) wind turbine

EXPLORE

1 READ, page 218   10 min.

- Use the photo to elicit vocabulary: *cliff, rope, camera, hang, strap, helmet, lamp*.

Be the Expert

- Stephen Alvarez has photographed a mummy high in the Peruvian Andes, rain forests in Costa Rica, and caves in Borneo, Mexico, and Canada.
- Majlis al Jinn is one of the largest known caves in the world. It is in a remote area of Oman, about 100 km (62 miles) from Muscat. It is about 310 meters (1017 feet) by 225 meters (738 feet). It can only be accessed by descending through one of three vertical entrances in the ceiling.

- **Tip:** After students have listened to and read the interview, have them work in pairs. One partner reads the interviewer's questions as the other answers from memory with the book closed. Encourage them to practice several times as they will remember more each time.

2 CHECK, page 218   5 min.

1. b   2. a   3. b   4. b   5. b

- **Tip:** Go over the answers by having pairs of students read the question and answers.

3 DISCOVER, page 219   5 min.

A after

LEARN

Chart 7.4, page 220   10 min.

- **Notes 1 & 2:** In most tenses, questions use a helping verb. In simple present and past, we add *do/does* or *did* to make questions and negatives. In the present progressive, there is already a helping, or auxiliary verb, *be*. Question order puts the auxiliary verb before the subject. Short answers to *Yes/No* questions consist of the subject + the auxiliary.

- **Tip:** Have students read the questions and answers from the chart aloud.

4 page 220   10 min.

1. a	6. a
2. a	7. b
3. b	8. b
4. b	9. a
5. a	10. a

5 page 221   5 min.

1. Is the scientist studying
2. Is he working
3. Is he standing
4. Is the shark swimming
5. Is the shark looking
6. Is the scientist doing
7. Is he putting
8. Is he wearing
9. Are the people in the boat helping
10. Are they watching

6 SPEAK, page 221   5 min.

Chart 7.5, page 222   10 min.

- **Note 1:** *Wh-* questions can be answered in complete sentences or with short answers.
- **Notes 2 & 3:** Although *why* is the question word most commonly used with negatives, *who* is also used (*Who isn't working on the assignment?*). We might use *where* and *who* in negative questions when we missed part of a speaker's comment. (e.g., **A:** *I'm not going to the lecture.* **B:** *Where aren't you going?*)

> **REAL ENGLISH, page 222**
>
> Suggest that students pay attention the next time they watch a television program or a movie and take note of how often speakers use the present progressive in greetings. Model additional appropriate answers to the greeting, for example:
> **A:** How's it going?
> **B:** Pretty good. How are you doing?
> **A:** Not bad.

7 page 222   10 min.
 1. What are you doing?
 2. Why are you crying?
 3. Who is she calling?
 4. Where are they living?
 5. What are you watching?
 6. Where is he working?
 7. What is she teaching this semester?
 8. Why aren't you working today?

8 SPEAK, page 222   10 min.
- **Expansion Tip:** Have students form two groups of equal numbers. One group forms an inside circle facing outward, and the other forms an outside circle facing inward so that each student is facing a partner. Students take turns asking and answering questions using the verbs in exercise **8**. After a minute, call *Time*. Have the outside circle move one place to the right and continue.

Chart 7.6, page 223   5 min.
- **Note 1:** In very formal English, students may also see or hear questions that begin with a preposition followed by *whom* (e.g., *To whom are you talking?*).

9 page 223   5 min.
 Subject: 1, 2, 5, 7, 10
 Object: 3, 4, 6, 8, 9
- **Expansion Tip:** Have students take turns asking and answering the questions using their own ideas.

10 page 223   5 min.
 1. Who are you studying with?
 2. Who's/Who is giving the lessons?
 3. Who's/Who is standing in the hallway?
 4. Who's/Who is he sitting behind?
 5. Who's/Who is writing on the board?
 6. Who's/Who is she living with?
 7. Who are you waiting for?
 8. Who's/Who is teaching the class?

11 SPEAK, page 224   5 min.

PRACTICE

12 LISTEN, page 224   10 min.
1. c	3. b	5. c	7. b
2. a	4. b	6. b	8. a

13 WRITE & SPEAK, page 225   15 min.
 A 1. What are those men doing?
 2. Who is standing on the cliff?
 3. Where are those men working?
 4. Are they working at night in this photo?
 5. What is the firefighter doing?
 6. Why is the firefighter doing this?
 7. Is the firefighter wearing special clothing?
 8. Is the firefighter sitting down?
 B a. 2   c. 3   e. 4   g. 7
     b. 1   d. 5   f. 6   h. 8
- **Tip:** Call on students to tell you what they see in the photos before they do the task.

14 LISTEN, WRITE & SPEAK, page 226   25 min.
- **Tip:** Ask students what they see in the photo. Making statements to describe the photo will help them with the vocabulary.
 A 1. c   2. a   3. b
 B 1. is calling
 2. is/'s Tay doing
 3. Is Evan living
 4. is/'s Evan doing
 5. Is he making
 6. is/'s Evan traveling
 7. Is Tay joking
 8. is/'s Evan working
- **Expansion Tip:** Have students role-play the interview with the worker.

15 APPLY, page 227   10 min.
- **Expansion Tip:** Have students write *Yes/No* questions for all the verbs in the box.

LESSON 3 Simple Present vs. Present Progressive

Student Learning Outcomes
- **Read** about storm chasers.
- **Complete** sentences with the simple present or the present progressive.
- **Identify** action and non-action verbs.
- **Listen** to and **complete** sentences about a conversation.
- **Find** and **edit** errors with action and non-action verbs.
- **Plan, write,** and **role-play** a weather report.

Lesson Vocabulary
| (v.) chase | (n.) hurricane | (n.) path | (n.) tornado |
| (n.) damage | (v.) measure | (n.) probe | (n.) tsunami |

EXPLORE

1 READ, page 228 — 10 min.
- Look at the photos. Ask, *What's in this photo? What do you see? Do you have this kind of storm in your city?* Read the caption and find Colorado on the map.

Be the Expert
- Storm chasers track tornadoes and hurricanes to find out more about them and give information to help people stay safe.
- Explain that tornadoes most often occur in the central part of the U.S. and in the springtime. The U.S. has the most tornadoes of any country in the world because it is large and doesn't have mountains to block the wind in the middle of the country.

- After students listen to the reading, ask, *What do most people do when a tornado approaches? What do storm chasers do? What kind of people become storm chasers?*

2 CHECK, page 229 — 5 min.
1. F   2. T   3. F   4. T

3 DISCOVER, page 229 — 5 min.
A
1. is standing
2. is getting
3. run
4. hear; try

B 1. 3, 4   2. 1, 2   3. a

- **Tip:** When you discuss the answers to exercise **B**, read the notes for Chart 7.7.

LEARN

Chart 7.7, page 230 — 10 min.
- If students ask, explain that we do use the present progressive for verbs such as *live, work,* and *study* to indicate that the situation is not permanent. (*We are living in Tokyo.*)
- **Note 3:** Review the frequency adverbs and other expressions of frequency that students have learned.

4 page 230 — 10 min.
1. is watching   6. 're learning
2. study   7. gives
3. he's listening to 8. is shining
4. It's raining! 9. 'm reading
5. gets   10. watch

5 page 231 — 5 min.
1. are having   6. rains
2. is moving   7. 's blowing
3. gets   8. checks
4. 's raining   9. wear
5. listens   10. 're not hiking

- **Expansion Tip:** Have students work in pairs to take turns making the sentences true for them. (e.g., *We aren't having a thunderstorm right now.*)

Chart 7.8, page 231 — 10 min.
- **Note 2:** Elicit additional examples for verbs in each category.
- **Tip:** Say a non-action verb and call on students to use it in a sentence.

UNIT 7   LESSON 3   75

REAL ENGLISH, page 231

Write the pairs of verbs on the board: *see/watch, hear/listen*. Have students choose which can take the present progressive and make sentences. Point out that some sensory verbs, such as *taste, feel,* and *smell,* have both an action and non-action meaning. For example: *The pizza tastes good* (this is a quality of the pizza), but *I'm tasting Ellen's cookies right now. This jacket feels soft. I'm feeling a little sick. The cake smells good. The dog is smelling the cat.*

6 page 232   10 min.

Action: 1, 2, 4, 8, 10, 13, 14

Non-Action: 3, 5, 6, 7, 9, 11, 12

- **Expansion Tip:** Have students rewrite the sentences to make them negative.

7 page 232   10 min.

1. gets
2. 'm listening
3. is talking
4. don't like
5. doesn't own
6. hear
7. is
8. belongs
9. 'm looking
10. see
11. isn't moving
12. 're checking

- **Tip:** To go over the answers, call on students to read the sentences aloud. Have them read again the sentences to make affirmative sentences negative and negative sentences affirmative.

PRACTICE

8 page 233   15 min.

1. is changing
2. is getting
3. is melting
4. is rising
5. use
6. is rising
7. is starting
8. know
9. need

9 page 233   10 min.

- **Tip:** Direct students' attention to the photo above. Ask, *What do you see? How do you think climate change affects islands like this?*

1. listen
2. hear
3. get
4. rains
5. causes
6. are listening
7. are talking
8. get
9. is moving
10. need
11. don't like
12. want

10 EDIT, page 234   10 min.

Right now I ~~look~~ 'm/am looking out the window of my house. I see a lot of dark clouds. A storm ~~comes~~ is coming. The sky ~~gets~~ is getting dark. Now I ~~am hearing~~ hear the wind. It's raining hard now. I ~~am not liking~~ don't like storms. ~~I'm being~~ I am afraid of them!

11 LISTEN & SPEAK, page 234   10 min.

A 1. a   2. b   3. b

B
1. is reporting — (b) from the coast.
2. is causing — (a) a lot of damage.
3. sees — (f) the waves.
4. hears — (g) the wind.
5. want — (h) to stay in their homes.
6. are asking — (d) people to leave their homes.
7. are burning — (c) in the fire.
8. feels — (e) safe.

11 APPLY, page 234   15 min.

- **Tip:** Elicit ideas about extreme weather events and write any new vocabulary on the board.
- **Tip:** Have students record their weather reports on their phones so they can revise as necessary before they role-play for the class.

UNIT 7 Review the Grammar

1 LISTEN, page 235   15 min.
1. b
2. a
3. a
4. b
5. a
6. a
7. a
8. b

- **Expansion Tip:** Have students create questions for each answer they didn't use in exercise **1**.

2 EDIT, page 235   5 min.
- Have students look at the photo and read the caption. Ask, *Do you think this is an easy or difficult marathon? Do you want to do this? Do you know any other difficult marathons?*

Tony: Wow. Look at this photo. This man ~~competes~~ is competing in a marathon. He ~~runs~~ 's/is running in the Sahara.

Kay: Why ~~are people wanting~~ do people want to run in the desert?

Tony: They ~~are liking~~ like the challenge. That marathon is very, very difficult. It lasts for five or six days. ~~Are you seeing~~ Do you see his backpack? He~~'s having~~ has all his food in there.

Kay: Do the runners stop at night to sleep?

Tony: That's a good question. I~~'m not knowing~~ don't know the answer.

3 WRITE & LISTEN, page 236   10 min.
1. how are you doing?
2. I'm doing
3. are you training
4. I'm training
5. do you like
6. I enjoy
7. I like
8. do you own
9. I have
10. I need
11. bicycles often break

4 SPEAK, WRITE & LISTEN, page 236   20 min.
A 1. b   2. b   3. b   4. a

B Answers will vary. Possible questions:
1. What is he doing?
2. What is he hanging from?
3. Why is he hanging from a plane?
4. How high is he flying?
5. Is he holding on tightly?

5 SPEAK & WRITE, page 237   10 min.
- **Tip:** Suggest that students look at more than one photo and jot down notes about what they could say for each before they choose one.
- **Alternative Activity:** Have students bring in photos of their own choosing. Have them write questions about their photos. Then they work with a partner to ask and answer questions about the photos.

Connect the Grammar to Writing

1 READ & NOTICE THE GRAMMAR,
page 238   25 min.

A The writer is at his university library in London. He is writing an e-mail.

B <u>I'm writing</u> to you from London! Right now <u>I'm sitting</u> in the university library. Some people <u>are studying</u>, but <u>I'm not</u>. I don't have any homework yet. Most people <u>are walking around and chatting</u>. It's not quiet at all.

<u>I'm not spending</u> all my time in the library. <u>I'm also playing</u> tennis and <u>singing</u> in the school choir. I already know a lot of people here. I like it here a lot, but I miss you!

- **Tip:** Point out that when we combine two ideas with *and*, we often don't repeat the subject and the auxiliary verbs if they are the same (e.g., *I'm also playing tennis and I'm singing . . .*). In addition, if there are two subjects but only one verb, we may not repeat the verb. (*Some people are studying but I'm not studying.*) Students will learn more about this in the Writing Focus.

C *Answers may vary. Possible answers:*

Right Now	Not Right Now
writing sitting in the library	playing tennis singing in the school choir

2 BEFORE YOU WRITE, page 239   10 min.

- **Tip:** After students complete the chart, have them talk about their activities with a partner. Partners can give feedback on what information is interesting, and ask additional questions.

3 WRITE, page 239   25 min.

> **WRITING FOCUS, page 239**
>
> Suggest that students practice combining sentence using their ideas from their charts, before they actually write their e-mails. Point out that sentence variety adds interest to writing. Have students identify how many sentences in the model e-mail use *and* to join two verbs. (two sentences)

- **Expansion Tip:** Have students exchange e-mail addresses in pairs, or give them your e-mail address, so they can actually e-mail their paragraphs. If they have e-mail partners, the partners should e-mail back. If they e-mail you, you can either e-mail back, or print their e-mails and bring to class. Distribute the e-mails and have students give feedback in class.

- **Alternative Writing:** Have students interview a partner about their activities. Then have them write an e-mail to another classmate about his or her activities.

UNIT 8 Travel

The Past: Part 1

Unit Opener

Photo: Have students look at the photo. Ask, *What do you see?* Elicit: *highway, ocean, rocks, lights/headlights, sunset.* Ask, *Do you want to go here? Why, or why not?* Have students read the caption with you. Find Oregon on the map.

Location: Highway 101 runs along the West Coast of the United States through California, Oregon, and Washington. It is more than 1500 miles (about 2500 km) long. The highway runs right next to the ocean in parts. It also goes through redwood forests and across the Golden Gate Bridge in San Francisco.

Theme: This unit is about travel and includes information about the Amazon, the Antarctic, Lake Victoria, Iceland, and Machu Picchu.

Page	Lesson	Grammar	Examples
242	1	Simple Past of *Be:* Statements	He **was** in Miami yesterday. You **weren't** in Tokyo yesterday. I **was** at home last night.
249	2	Simple Past of *Be:* Questions	**Was** the information helpful? Yes, it **was**. **Were** the guides interesting? No, they **weren't**. **Where was** Barbara yesterday? **When were** you in Norway?
256	3	Simple Past: Affirmative Statements	He **started** his trip in August. They **planned** their trip. I **studied** Japanese before my trip.
265	4	Simple Past: Negative Statements	It **didn't come** last Monday. We **saw** some beautiful scenery. Meg **cut** her hair last week.
272	**Review the Grammar**		
274	**Connect the Grammar to Writing**		

Unit Grammar Terms

auxiliary verb: (also called *helping verb*) a verb used with the main verb. *Be, do, have,* and *will* are common auxiliary verbs when they are followed by another verb. Modals are auxiliary verbs.
➢ I **am** working.
➢ He **didn't** play soccer yesterday.
➢ I **can** play the drums.

irregular verb: a verb form that does not follow the rules for regular verbs. Many verbs in English are irregular in the past.
➢ *swim* → *swam*
➢ *have* → *had*

LESSON 1	**Simple Past of *Be*: Statements**			
Student Learning Outcomes	• **Read** a travel blog about the Atlas Mountains. • **Make** affirmative and negative statements with the simple past of *be*. • **Find** and **edit** errors with the past of *be* and past time expressions. • **Listen** to a conversation and **write** sentences. • **Speak** about your own experiences on a trip. • **Write** about a place you have visited.			
Lesson Vocabulary	(adj.) fresh (n.) guide	(v.) hire (n.) honey	(n.) range (n.) ruins	(n.) scenery (n.) village

EXPLORE

1 READ, page 242   20 min.

- Have students read the title and look at the photo. Ask, *Where is this? What is the climate like? Do you want to visit this place? Why, or why not?*

Be the Expert

- The Atlas Mountains stretch across northwestern Africa, forming a barrier between the Sahara Desert and the coastline of the Mediterranean Sea. The highest mountain in the range is Toubkal at 13,665 feet (4165 meters). The people who live in the mountainous villages are Berbers. They have lived there for thousands of years.
- The Djemaa el Fna Square in Marrakech dates back to the 11th century. It is surrounded by restaurants, stands, and public buildings. In the square, people meet, tell stories, play music, tell fortunes, and give henna tattoos among other activities. UNESCO declared it a World Heritage cultural site in 2001.
- Marrakech, Rabat, Fez, and Tangier are cities in Morocco. Seville is a city in Spain.

- **Tip:** After students listen and read, play the audio again and have students make a slash (/) in the text every time the speaker pauses slightly. This will help students notice thought groups, or word chunks.

2 CHECK, page 243   5 min.

1. T   2. F   3. F   4. F   5. T

3 DISCOVER, page 243   5 min.

A 1. 'm   2. wasn't   3. were   4. are   5. was

B Present: 1, 4

Past: 2, 3, 5

- **Tip:** Remind students that this is a travel blog. Ask, *When you describe your travels and adventures, do you usually talk about the present, the future, or the past?* (the past)

Chart 8.1, page 244   5 min.

- **Note 1:** Point out that although in simple present *I* uses a form of *be* that is different from the other pronouns, in simple past it uses the same form as *he, she* and *it*.
- **Tip:** Call on students and say a subject pronoun, eliciting the affirmative and negative statements in the chart.

4 page 244   5 min.

1. was	6. was
2. was	7. were
3. was	8. were
4. were	9. were
5. was	10. were

5 SPEAK, page 244   5 min.

- **Expansion Tip:** After students finish, have them work individually to write two affirmative statements and two negative statements using the past of *be*. One partner reads a statement aloud. The other listens and then changes it to be affirmative or negative.

Chart 8.2, page 245   10 min.

- **Notes 1 & 5:** Generate additional expressions with *last, yesterday,* and *ago* and write them on the board.
- **Note 2:** Write example sentences on the board or display them with a projector. Use a different color for the time expressions, so students will remember their placement.

80 THE PAST: PART 1

6 page 245 — 10 min.

1. last
2. ago
3. yesterday
4. ago
5. ago
6. last
7. ago
8. ago
9. last
10. yesterday

- **Tip:** Say the sentences from exercise **6** out of order, and elicit the negative. For greater challenge, add new affirmative sentences, eliciting the negatives.

PRACTICE

7 LISTEN, page 246 — 5 min.

Present: 2, 4, 6
Past: 1, 3, 5, 7, 8

8 READ, WRITE & SPEAK, page 246 — 10 min.

- **Tip:** Have students look at the photo and read the caption. Lake Atitlan is the deepest lake in Central America. The lake basin was formed by a volcanic eruption 84,000 years ago. The Toliman volcano is on the southern shores of the lake. The people who live in nearby villages still wear Mayan clothing and observe Mayan customs.

- **Tip:** Have students look at the travel plan. Ask: *How many days was her trip? What places are on her visit to Guatemala? What notes are next to Day 3? Day 6?*

A Answers may vary. Possible answers:

The bus ride was short.

The hotel was very nice, but the food wasn't very good.

The ruins of Antigua were beautiful.

The food at the restaurant was delicious.

The scenery at Lake Atitlan was amazing.

The villages were beautiful and interesting.

The drive wasn't fun because the road was very narrow.

The bus driver was friendly, but the bus ride was scary.

In Chi Chi, the prices were very good.

The weather wasn't good.

Tikal was crowded. On the last day, I was tired, but it was a great trip!

9 SPEAK, page 247 — 10 min.

- **Tip:** Model the activity. Say and write example sentences. (e.g., *My parents were here last week; It was rainy and cold three days ago. My favorite band was in Mexico City last month.*)

- **Alternative Writing & Speaking:** Have students write sentences with each time expression. Give them a topic, such as studying English or the weather, to write sentences about. Then have them share their sentences in pairs.

10 EDIT, page 247 — 10 min.

Greetings from Italy! We were in Rome ~~before~~ two days ago. Now we're in Florence. We're having a great time! Yesterday the weather ~~is~~ was rainy, so it was a good day to visit the Uffizi. The Uffizi is a huge art museum. We ~~was~~ were there for five hours. I was really tired ~~yesterday~~ last night. ~~The~~ Last week we were in Venice. There weren't many tourists, so it ~~weren't~~ wasn't very crowded. It's a beautiful city. Have a great summer, and please say hello to your family.

11 LISTEN & SPEAK, page 247 — 25 min.

A
1. camping
2. a month ago
3. was
4. wasn't

B page 248

1.	terrible - N	fun - S
2.	warm	wet - N & S
3.	sunny - S	wet
4.	terrible - N	not bad - S
5.	easy - S	difficult - N
6.	amazing - N	incredible - S

C Answers will vary. Possible answers:

Selena: The camping trip was fun. The weather on Friday was wet. The hike was easy.

Nick: The camping trip was terrible. The hike was difficult. The views were amazing.

- **Tip:** After completing exercise **D**, call on students to role-play for the class.

12 APPLY, page 248 — 10 min.

- **Tip:** Have students complete exercise **A** in pairs. If your students are better at writing than speaking, do exercise **B** before exercise **A**.

UNIT 8 LESSON 1 81

LESSON 2 | Simple Past of *Be*: Questions

Student Learning Outcomes	• **Read** a conversation about Iceland. • **Ask** and **answer** questions using the simple past of *be*. • **Speak** with a partner about a vacation you took. • **Listen** to a conversation and **answer** questions. • **Ask** and **answer** questions about a special past event.
Lesson Vocabulary	(n.) daylight (n.) giraffe (n.) safari (n.) tribe (n.) falls (n.) relative (v.) set (n.) zebra

EXPLORE

1 READ, page 249 — 5 min.

- Elicit from students what they know about Iceland and the Northern Lights.
- If possible, show additional photos of the Northern Lights. Many slide show images can be found online by searching for the keywords *Northern Lights images*.

Be the Expert

- The Northern Lights are also called aurora borealis in the northern hemisphere and aurora australis in the southern hemisphere. The dancing lights are formed by collisions between the electrically charged particles from the sun with Earth's atmosphere. There are many colors, but green and pink are the most common. The lights appear over the north and south poles. Generally, the best time to see them is during the winter when there is little daylight. The lights peak about every 11 years.

- Read the caption. Explain that beaches near volcanoes often have black sand because of the bits of lava contained in it. Iceland has many active volcanoes.
- Use the photo to elicit the vocabulary: *ice*, *beach*, *sea*, and *sky*.

2 CHECK, page 250 — 5 min.

1. two years ago
2. wasn't
3. cold
4. in July
5. great

- **Tip:** Suggest students complete the activity without looking back at the conversation. Then they check their answers by rereading.

3 DISCOVER, page 250 — 5 min.

A
1. was
2. Were you
3. Were you
4. was
5. were you
6. Was

B after

Chart 8.3, page 251 — 5 min.

- **Tip:** Write sentences on the board using the past of *be* and different subjects. (e.g., *I was in Geneva last year./She was interesting./It was fun./They were in the same class./We were on vacation.*) Have students come to the board and write *Yes/No* questions for each statement.

> **REAL ENGLISH, page 251**
>
> Adding more information keeps the conversation going and lets the other person know that you want to continue. To help students practice this, after they complete exercise **4**, have them ask and answer the questions in pairs and add more information.

4 page 251 — 10 min.

1. A: Was he — B: he wasn't
2. A: Was he — B: he was
3. A: Were they — B: they weren't
4. A: Was — B: it was
5. A: Were there — B: there were
6. A: Was it — B: it was
7. A: Were you — B: we weren't
8. A: Were the Northern Lights — B: they were

82 THE PAST: PART 1

Chart 8.4, page 252   10 min.

- **Tip:** Have students work in pairs to take turns asking and answering the questions in the chart using different answers.
- **Notes 1, 2 & 3:** These notes are reminders: Students learned and practiced these in the simple present.
- **Note 3:** Write examples of mistakes in written English on the board. Ask, *Which is correct?* For example:
  The market is interesting. Because it is very old.
  (*The market is interesting because it is very old.*)

5 page 221   5 min.

1. How	5. Where	8. How
2. When	6. Why	9. What
3. Why	7. Why	10. How
4. Where		

- **Expansion Tip:** Have students choose one of the questions to memorize. Then have students stand and walk around the room to ask ten students their question. Students can use answers in the exercise or their own ideas to respond.

6 page 253   10 min.

1. When was he in China?
2. Why was the tour bus late?
3. How was the weather in India?
4. Was the tour interesting?
5. When was your last vacation?
6. Where were you two hours ago?
7. Where were you last summer?
8. Why were our classmates absent?
9. Were you on vacation last week?
10. Where were you born?

7 SPEAK, page 253   10 min.

- **Tip:** Encourage students to provide more information after short answers to keep their conversations going.

PRACTICE

8 LISTEN, page 253   10 min.

1. b	6. b
2. a	7. a
3. c	8. b
4. b	9. c
5. a	10. a

9 page 254   10 min.

- **Tip:** Have students work in pairs to complete the conversation and practice it to reinforce their understanding of the grammar point.

1. Where were	7. was
2. Were	8. Were
3. I wasn't	9. I was
4. Why were	10. Were
5. was	11. wasn't
6. Where were	

10 READ, WRITE & SPEAK, page 254   15 min.

A
1. Who was David Livingstone?
2. Where was he from?
3. What was he interested in?
4. Where was his first trip?
5. When was his most famous trip?
6. Where was this trip?
7. What was the name of the falls?
8. Why was the English name Victoria?

- **Tip:** Direct students' attention to the photo and caption. Victoria Falls is the largest falls in the world because it is both wide and tall, so it is the largest sheet of falling water. It is about 5577 feet wide and varies between 262–304 feet high.
- **Alternative Writing & Speaking:** Assign each student a famous person. Have students research and write about the person using the paragraph about David Livingstone as a model. Have them underline the sentences that answer the *Wh-* questions in the box and then share their paragraphs in groups.

11 LISTEN & SPEAK, page 255   25 min.

A
1. e	5. a
2. f	6. g
3. b	7. h
4. c	8. d

- **Tip:** When students do exercise **B**, allow one student to look at the book to ask the questions while the partner answers with book closed. Then they switch roles.

12 APPLY, page 255   10 min.

- **Expansion Tip:** Have students write a paragraph about the special event. Then have them exchange paragraphs in pairs and provide feedback.

LESSON 3	**Simple Past: Affirmative Statements**			
Student Learning Outcomes	• **Read** an article about a trip to Antarctica. • **Spell** past tense regular and irregular verbs. • **Pronounce** past tense endings of regular verbs. • **Find** and **edit** errors in the simple past. • **Listen** and **speak** about trips to Machu Picchu. • **Write** about a visit to a place.			
Lesson Vocabulary	(adj.) digital (v.) follow	(n.) Internet (adj.) local	(n.) nomad (v.) plan	(v.) post (v.) spend

EXPLORE

1 READ, page 256   10 min.

- Ask, *What do you see in this photo? Do you want to visit here?* After students listen to the reading, ask, *Do you read travel posts such as this?*

> **Be the Expert**
>
> - It is almost 9000 miles (about 14,500 km) from Washington D.C. to Antarctica.
> - The Salar de Uyuni is the world's largest salt flat with an area of 4000 square miles (about 10,582 square km). The salt flat is a crust of salt several meters thick. It is very flat. Under the salt flat is a pool that contains lithium, about 50 to 70 percent of the world's supply. Pink flamingoes live here.
> - Andrew Evans continues to take trips and post blogs. Students can find out more about his Antarctic trip or other trips on the National Geographic website. They may enjoy reading other posts for reading practice.

2 CHECK, page 257   5 min.

1. T   2. F   3. F   4. F   5. T

- **Tip:** Have students underline the sentences in the text where they find the answers.

3 DISCOVER, page 257   5 min.

A 1. wanted   2. traveled   3. followed

B They all end in *-ed*. This shows the past.

LEARN

Chart 8.5, page 258   5 min.

- **Note 1:** Emphasize that if actions are still happening, even if they began in the past, the simple past is not used. The past time expressions that students learned in Lesson 1 are cues for using the simple past.

4 page 258   5 min.

Present: 2, 3, 7, 9, 10

Past: 1, 4, 5, 6, 8

- **Expansion Tip:** Have students rewrite each sentence using the other tense.

Chart 8.6, page 259   10 min.

- **Notes:** Point out that some of these spelling rules are similar to the rules for *making plurals* (e.g., changing *y* to *i* and doubling consonants).

5 page 259   5 min.

1. carried   7. called
2. posted   8. shared
3. ordered   9. stayed
4. stopped   10. enjoyed
5. climbed   11. loved
6. tried   12. visited

6 PRONUNCIATION, page 260   10 min.

- **Notes 2 & 3:** Have students put their fingers on their throats and say the verbs in the chart. They should notice that their throats do not vibrate for the verbs in 2, in either the base or past tense form, but do vibrate with the verbs in 3.
- **Tip:** When going over the answers to exercise **A**, have students identify the number of the rule in the chart that applies to each answer.

A

1. /əd/   5. /t/
2. /t/   6. /d/
3. /əd/   7. /t/
4. /t/   8. /d/

Chart 8.7, page 261 — 5 min.

- **Note:** Tell students that there are no definite rules or patterns for irregular verbs. They need to memorize them.
- **Tip:** Say a verb in its base form and elicit the past form, then switch. Have students practice in pairs.

> **REAL ENGLISH,** page 261
> Have students write sentences for the expressions in the box in simple present and simple past, and then share their sentences in pairs.

7 page 261 — 10 min.

1. went; go
2. took; take
3. bought; buy
4. came; come
5. got; get
6. had; have
7. left; leave
8. rode; ride
9. did; do
10. heard; hear

- **Tip:** Have students rewrite the sentences to use the simple present. Remind them to change the time expressions.

8 page 261 — 10 min.

1. left
2. went
3. made
4. had
5. got
6. bought
7. spent
8. taught

- **Expansion Tip:** Have students write a paragraph about a trip they took, using all of the words in exercise **8**.

9 SPEAK, page 262 — 5 min.

- **Expansion Tip:** Divide the class into two groups. Group 1 compiles and writes on the board six verbs, different from those in the Student Book. Group 2 compiles and writes six past time expressions on the board. Then all the students use the cues on the board to write new sentences.

PRACTICE

10 LISTEN, page 262 — 15 min.

A Present: 3, 5, 7
Past: 1, 2, 4, 6, 8

B
1. went
2. came
3. travels
4. stayed
5. make
6. left
7. want
8. enjoyed

11 page 263 — 10 min.

1. had
2. needed
3. carried
4. had
5. went
6. crossed
7. decided
8. followed
9. traveled
10. took
11. tried
12. learned
13. made
14. called

- **Tip:** Have students work in pairs to take turns reading the completed paragraph aloud, focusing on correct pronunciation of the -ed endings.

12 EDIT, page 263 — 5 min.

Hiram Bingham ~~studyed~~ studied South American history. In 1908, he ~~get~~ got a job at Yale University in the United States and ~~tought~~ taught history. In 1908, he went to Santiago, Chile, and learned about the lost cities of the Incas. He ~~was~~ visited the ruins of an ancient Incan city in Choquequirao. In 1911, he ~~go~~ went to Peru. There he ~~heared~~ heard about more ruins called "Machu Picchu." He traveled with two Peruvians along the Urubamba River near Cusco. There some people ~~showwed~~ showed them the way to some very old ruins. It was Machu Picchu!

13 LISTEN & SPEAK, page 264 — 10 min.

- **Tip:** Direct students' attention to the photo. Ask, *What do you see? Do you want to go there? Why or why not?*

A 1. was   2. is   3. wasn't

B Ana and Sudie: 1, 2, 5, 6, 7
Don: 1, 3, 4, 8

14 APPLY, page 264 — 15 min.

- **Tip:** Brainstorm details to include about the trip and write them on the board (e.g., *when, who, what*).
- **Tip:** Model the activity on the board. Write sentences for each of the three headings and then tell the class about it.
- **Alternative Activity:** Have students work in pairs to research and prepare a presentation about a historical site such as Machu Picchu.

LESSON 4 | Simple Past: Negative Statements

Student Learning Outcomes	• **Read** an article about a journey down the Amazon. • **Complete** negative statements with the simple past. • **Speak** about yourself using the simple past. • **Find** and **edit** errors in the simple past. • **Listen** to and **talk** about an experience with bears. • **Write** and **talk** about travel problems.
Lesson Vocabulary	(adv.) backwards (n.) cub (adj.) foreign (n.) journey (v.) continue (adj.) dangerous (v.) join (n.) path

EXPLORE

1 READ, page 265   10 min.

Be the Expert

- Ed Stafford holds the world record for being the first person to walk the entire length of the river.
- The Amazon is the second longest river in the world and the largest. When it is low, it is one to six miles (1.6 to 10 km) wide. During the rainy season it can be 30 miles or 48 km wide. 2.5 million species of insects live in the Amazon region as well as 40,000 species of plants. It has the highest biodiversity in the world. Some of the animals are dangerous, including jaguars, piranha, and the poison dart frog. Some diseases that are common there are malaria, yellow fever, and dengue fever.

- Look at the photo. Ask, *What do you see? Does this look like fun?*
- Have students trace the Amazon on a map. Ask, *What countries did Ed walk through?*
- After students listen to the reading, ask, *Why do you think he did this?*

2 CHECK, page 266   5 min.

1. Peru   4. difficult
2. with a friend   5. Atlantic
3. two years

3 DISCOVER, page 266   5 min.

A 1. didn't go   2. didn't travel   3. didn't want
B 1. past   2. negative

- **Tip:** Look back at the sentences in exercise 2. Elicit true negative statements, e.g., *Ed Stafford's journey did not begin in Brazil.*

LEARN

Chart 8.8, page 267   5 min.

- **Note 1:** Point out that as in the simple present, in negative statements the auxiliary is inflected, not the main verb. The main verb is always in the base form in these negative statements.

4 page 267   5 min.

1. started; didn't start   5. took; didn't take
2. went; didn't go   6. bought; didn't buy
3. traveled; didn't travel   7. wanted; didn't want
4. had; didn't have   8. stayed; didn't stay

- **Expansion Tip:** Have students write three other sentences about Ed Stafford's trip that are either true or false. They take turns saying their sentences to a partner. Their partner says if each is true or false and corrects the false statements.

Chart 8.9, page 267   5 min.

- **Tip:** Call on students and say a word from the chart, eliciting either the past or present form.

5 page 268   10 min.

1. saw   5. drank   9. rode
2. began   6. knew   10. won
3. wrote   7. met   11. felt
4. ate   8. gave   12. lost

Chart 8.10, page 268   5 min.

- **Note:** Suggest that students pay attention to the time expressions and other verbs in a sentence to identify the tense. Call on students to identify the time expressions in the example sentences. Elicit additional examples with these expressions.

6 page 268 — 10 min.

Present: 1, 3, 9
Past: 2, 4, 5, 6, 7, 8, 10

7 SPEAK, page 269 — 5 min.

- **Tip:** Call on students to tell the class about their partners.

PRACTICE

8 page 269 — 15 min.

1. wrote	6. drank	11. lost
2. put	7. shut	12. knew
3. became	8. sold	13. met
4. hurt	9. gave	14. began
5. read	10. ate	15. told

- **Tip:** Have students work in pairs to practice saying one of the words from exercise **8** in random order and elicit the word in simple past from their partner.

9 WRITE & SPEAK, page 269 — 10 min.

> **REAL ENGLISH,** page 269
>
> Suggest that students practice extending their conversations in exercise **B** to use *really* and add information or ask a question. Have students perform their conversations for the class.

10 page 270 — 15 min.

A
1. didn't travel
2. didn't visit
3. began
4. didn't have
5. didn't travel
6. didn't go
7. rode
8. saw
9. wrote
10. sold
11. wrote
12. didn't let
13. became

B
1. F 3. F 5. F 7. F
2. T 4. T 6. F 8. F

11 EDIT, page 271 — 10 min.

I ~~make~~ made reservations six months ago for a trip to my cousin's wedding. The night before my trip I called a taxi company for a 6:00 a.m. pick-up. The day ~~begin~~ began with a terrible rainstorm. The taxi didn't ~~came~~ come at 6:00 a.m. I ~~was call~~ called the company. Nobody answered the phone, so I got in my car and drove to the airport by myself. Unfortunately, they didn't ~~had~~ have any parking places at the parking garage. I parked six miles from the airport. I ~~not~~ didn't get my flight. They put me on a flight to another city, and I rented a car. It ~~costed~~ cost more, but I didn't miss the wedding. I even arrived an hour early!

12 LISTEN & SPEAK, page 271 — 10 min.

- **Tip:** Have students look at the photo. Ask: *What animal is this? Where do they live? What do people do when they see bears?* (Black bears live throughout North America, from Canada to Mexico. Mothers are very protective of their cubs and take care of them for about two years.)

1. took
2. went
3. didn't listen
4. didn't stay
5. saw
6. saw
7. didn't run
8. didn't take

13 APPLY, page 271 — 15 min.

A *Answers may vary. Possible answers:*

1. I got sick.
2. I lost my passport/wallet.
3. Someone took my passport/wallet.
4. I missed my plane/train/bus.
5. I got on the wrong plane/train/bus.
6. I didn't bring/pack the right clothes.
7. My luggage didn't arrive.

- **Alternative Writing:** Have students write a paragraph about a bad day they have had, explaining what went wrong. Encourage them to give details using the simple past. If they have trouble with ideas, tell them they can make up events to tell a funny story. Have students read their final paragraphs to each other in small groups. Encourage listeners to ask follow-up questions using the simple past.

Review the Grammar — UNIT 8

1 page 272 — 10 min.

1. were
2. had
3. lived
4. was
5. left
6. traveled
7. didn't return
8. was
9. left
10. traveled
11. took
12. stayed
13. didn't travel
14. wrote
15. read
16. became

- **Expansion Activity:** Have students create Venn diagrams to compare and contrast the two famous travelers.

2 EDIT, page 272 — 5 min.

- **Tip:** Before doing the activity, have students look at the illustration. Ask: *Who is this? When did he live? Why is he famous?* Elicit what students know about the famous explorer.

True or *false*? Ferdinand Magellan ~~is~~ was the first person to travel around the world.

False. Magellan ~~planed~~ planned the trip, but he didn't complete it. Magellan ~~leaved~~ left Spain in 1519 with 216 men on five ships. Only one of his ships went all the way around the world. It ~~returnned~~ returned to Spain in 1522. Eighteen men ~~are~~ were on the ship. Magellan himself ~~was~~ did not finish the journey. He ~~was~~ died in the Philippines in 1521.

3 LISTEN AND SPEAK, page 273 — 10 min.

A 1. T   2. T   3. F

B

	Jason Lewis	Colin Angus
1. He started in England.	✓	
2. He started in Canada.		✓
3. He left in 2004.		✓
4. He went to Alaska.		✓
5. He went to Australia.	✓	
6. He started the trip with a partner.	✓	✓
7. He rowed a boat from Alaska to Russia.		✓
8. His fiancé joined him on the trip.		✓
9. He crossed the Equator.	✓	
10. He finished his trip in 2007.	✓	
11. He finished first.		✓
12. He rode a bicycle from Costa Rica to Canada.		✓

- **Alternative Listening:** Recreate and distribute the chart above with the verbs missing from the sentences. Have students first listen and fill in the past tense verbs before listening for the answers.

4 SPEAK & WRITE, page 273 — 10 min.

- **Alternative Activity:** Have students work in pairs to research a trip one or more people took to an interesting place. Suggest they search for the key words *famous traveler* on the Internet. Have students give a presentation on their research to a group or the entire class.

Connect the Grammar to Writing

1 READ & NOTICE THE GRAMMAR, page 274

25 min.

A • **Tip:** Suggest that students put a (+) by sentences that talk about good things and a (–) by sentences that talk about bad things. (Overall, the trip was a good experience.)

B page 275

Today <u>was</u> an exciting day. We're in Canada! We <u>reached</u> the end of the Pacific Crest Trail this afternoon. We <u>started</u> at the Mexican border five months ago. We <u>hiked</u> every day, and now here we are!

This <u>was</u> an amazing experience. The scenery <u>was</u> beautiful. We <u>hiked</u> on trails high up in the mountains. It <u>was</u> difficult sometimes, especially when it <u>rained</u>. That <u>wasn't</u> fun at all!

Our friends from California <u>met</u> us at the Canadian border. We are having a great time tonight!

C page 275

Answers may vary. Possible answers:

	Information about the Trip
Place	started at the Mexican border; reached the end of the Pacific Crest Trail in Canada
Events and activities	reached the end today; hiked every day; friends met at the Canadian border
Description of the trip	amazing, beautiful scenery, high in the mountains, difficult, wasn't fun when it rained

2 BEFORE YOU WRITE, page 275

10 min.

• **Tip:** To give students more ideas to write about, model the activity by briefly talking about one or more trips you took. Then elicit several examples of ideas students are thinking about.

3 WRITE, page 275

25 min.

> **WRITING FOCUS,** page 275
>
> Suggest that students go back to the blog in exercise **1** and circle the subjects in each sentence. As they have already underlined the verbs, this will encourage them to notice sentence patterns.

• **Tip:** Have students exchange paragraphs with a partner, so they can edit for the elements of a complete sentence, i.e., capital letters, ending punctuation, and subject and verbs.

• **Alternative Writing:** Have students interview a partner about a trip they took. Have them create and fill in a chart such as the one in exercise **2**, and write a paragraph about his or her trip.

UNIT 9 Achievements
The Past: Part 2

Unit Opener

Photo: Ask, *What do you see in the photo?* Elicit: *mountains, snow, climbers, rope, top, peak.* Ask, *Do you like to climb mountains? Does this look hard?* Read the caption together. Find Pakistan on the map.

Location: Gasherbrum II is part of the Gasherbrum group of mountains in the Karakoram range between Pakistan and China. It has the 13th highest peak in the world. A British lieutenant and surveyor first saw these peaks in 1856, and he named them K1, K2, K3, K4, and K5 after Karakoram. Only K2 still has its original name.

Theme: This unit is about achievements and gives information about the achievements of famous people, including Wangari Maathai, Neil Armstrong, Ernest Shackleton, Jacques Cousteau, and Tenzing Norgay.

Page	Lesson	Grammar	Examples
278	1	Simple Past: Questions	**Did** she **help**? Yes, she **did**./No, she **didn't**. **Where did** you **go**? **Who went** with you?
288	2	Past Time Clauses	She finished school **before she moved to Seoul**. I made dinner **when I got home**.
297	3	Past Progressive	She **was studying** in Mexico City in 2011. You **weren't living** in Berlin in 2009. Junko **was riding** her bike when it **started** to rain.
303		**Review the Grammar**	
306		**Connect the Grammar to Writing**	

Unit Grammar Terms

auxiliary verb: (also called *helping verb*) a verb used with the main verb. *Be, do, have*, and *will* are common auxiliary verbs when they are followed by another verb. Modals are also auxiliary verbs.
 ➤ I **am** working.
 ➤ He **won't** play soccer this afternoon.
 ➤ I **can** play the drums.

non-action verb: a verb that does not describe an action. Non-action verbs indicate states, sense, feelings, or ownership. They are not common in the progressive.
 ➤ I **remember** the party very well.
 ➤ She **smelled** the fire before she **saw** it.
 ➤ They **have** a new car.

past progressive: a verb form used to talk about an action that was in progress at a specific time in the past.
 ➤ He **was watching** TV when the phone rang.

time clause: a clause that tells when an action or event happened or will happen. Time clauses are introduced by conjunctions such as *when, after, before,* and *while*.
 ➤ I'm going to call my parents **after I eat dinner**.
 ➤ I called my parents **when I got home**.

LESSON 1	**Simple Past: Questions**
Student Learning Outcomes	• **Read** a conversation about Wangari Maathai. • **Ask** and **Answer** *Yes/No* questions in the simple past. • **Write** questions in the simple past. • **Listen** to an interview and complete questions. • **Find** and **edit** errors with simple past questions. • **Listen** for specific information about an explorer. • **Ask** and **answer** questions to find out more about classmates.
Lesson Vocabulary	(v.) copy (n.) firewood (n.) movement (n.) resource (adj.) entire (v.) give up (n.) professor (adj.) rural

EXPLORE

1 READ, page 278   15 min.

- Use the photo to teach the meaning of *forest* and *rural*.
- **Tip:** Use the photos on pages 278 and 279 to elicit ideas about what life and culture in Kenya is like (e.g., colorful clothing, head scarves, rural, forested areas).

Be the Expert

- Wangari Maathai was born in Kenya. She attended college in Kansas, and then received her master's in biology from the University of Pittsburgh. In was in Pittsburgh that she first learned about environmental restoration. She became a professor when she returned to Kenya, and she was the first East African woman to receive a Ph.D. in veterinary anatomy. She married a man who was involved in politics, and she became interested in the problem of unemployment. Planting trees was a way to restore the environment while providing jobs. She encouraged women to plant seedlings of trees native to the area and paid them a small stipend. This was the beginning of the Green Belt Movement. Maathai worked for women's right for many years. She also served in parliament.
- The Green Belt Movement works to combat climate change and deforestation. It also helps to empower people and promote democracy as well as preserve traditional values. More information can be found on their website. Have students find out one thing the organization does, one fact about Maathai, and one way people can get involved.
- Of 101 people who have won the Nobel Peace Prize, 15 were women, including Mother Teresa and Aung San Suu Kyi.

2 CHECK, page 279   5 min.

    1. b   2. a   3. a   4. a

- **Tip:** To review simple past forms, have students underline the verbs in the simple past in the conversation.

3 DISCOVER, page 279   5 min.

A   1. did; get   3. did; plant
     2. did; help   4. did; start

B   1. b   2. b

- **Tip:** Ask students to identify the *Yes/No* question and the *Wh-* questions. Suggest that students write the questions in exercise **A** in the simple present to notice the ways in which question formation is similar.

LEARN

Chart 9.1, page 280   10 min.

- **Tip:** On the board, contrast the formation of simple present questions with simple past questions and point out the note below.
- **Note:** Explain that *did* works in the simple past in much the same way as *do/does* work in the present. However, we use *did* for all subjects. There is no change for third person. Remind students that the verb *be* is also an exception in the present tense.

> **REAL ENGLISH,** page 280
>
> Call on students and ask them *Yes/No* questions in the simple past. Have them give a *yes/no* response first, and then a response without *yes* or *no*.

4 page 280 — 5 min.

- **Tip:** Read the questions and answers aloud and have students repeat. When students have completed the activity, have them practice asking and answering in pairs.

  1. d 2. c 3. f 4. a 5. b 6. e

5 page 281 — 10 min.

- **Tip:** Have students underline the verb in the simple past first to note the regular and irregular forms.

  1. A: Did she win a prize? B: Yes, she did.
  2. A: Did they plant a lot of trees? B: Yes, they did.
  3. A: Did she live in Kenya? B: Yes, she did.
  4. A: Did he read the book? B: No, he didn't.
  5. A: Did you know about her? B: No, we didn't.
  6. A: Did she grow up in Nairobi? B: Yes, she did.
  7. A: Did he finish the book? B: Yes, he did.
  8. A: Did they learn about the Green Belt Movement? B: No, they didn't.

6 SPEAK, page 281 — 5 min.

- **Expansion Tip:** Have students make three more questions using their own ideas to ask about last night, and then find new partners to take turns asking and answering their questions.

Chart 9.2, page 282 — 5 min.

- **Note 1:** With students' help, identify the specific type of information each question word elicits.
- **Note 2:** Use tactile or kinesthetic activities to reinforce word order in questions. For example, students write each word of a question on cards, then shuffle and reorder to practice. Or give one card to each student and have them put themselves in order to ask a question.

REAL ENGLISH, page 282

Explain that *What for* means *for what purpose*, which is not always the same as *Why*. To help students understand the difference, say sentences and elicit either *Why* or *What for*. For example:
I went to the post office. [Why?/What for?]
The car hit a tree. [Why?]
My back hurts. [Why?]
My teacher called me last night. [Why?/What for?]

---

7 page 282 — 5 min.

  1. b   3. a   5. a   7. a
  2. a   4. b   6. a   8. a

- **Expansion Tip:** Have students write questions for the other answer. For example, for question 1, students might write *How long did she live in Africa?*

8 page 283 — 10 min.

- **Tip:** Have students look at the photo and read the caption. The *Apollo* program was the third space program carried out by NASA. The first program, Project *Mercury*, sent one man at a time into space; Project *Gemini* (1962–1965) sent up a two-man spacecraft. *Apollo* was designed for three men with a goal of landing on the moon.

  1. Where did Neil Armstrong's family live?
  2. Where did he go to college?
  3. What did he love?
  4. What did he do in 1962?
  5. How did he get to the moon?
  6. Who did he travel to the moon with?
  7. When did they start their trip?
  8. When did they land on the moon?
  9. What did Neil Armstrong do on July 20, 1969?
  10. What did millions of people do?
  11. Why did Neil Armstrong win awards?
  12. When did he die?

9 WRITE & SPEAK, page 283 — 5 min.

- **Tip:** Point out that when *did* is followed by *you* in a question, the second *d* in *did* is often pronounced as /dz/ or /dj/. *You* is often pronounced *ya*. *Did you study for the test?* becomes *Didja study for the test?*
- **Expansion Tip:** Have students form two circles—an inside circle facing out, and an outside circle facing in. Students take turns asking and answering their questions. When you call *Switch*, the outside circle moves one position to the right. Continue for several more turns. Call on students to tell the class about one of their partners.

Chart 9.3, page 284 — 5 min.

- **Note 2:** To practice, write a few sentences on the board: *Alan came late to class, My parents took me to dinner, A package arrived in the mail.* Call volunteers to the board to change the statements to questions with *who* or *what*.

10 page 284   5 min.

    Subject: 1, 2, 4, 5, 7
    Object: 3, 6, 8

11 page 284   5 min.

1. Who lived in that house?
2. Who did she ask?
3. Who were his parents?
4. What did she do?
5. Who didn't go?
6. What changed your life?
7. What did they say?
8. Who helped them?

PRACTICE

12 LISTEN, page 285   5 min.

| 1. b | 3. a | 5. b | 7. a |
| 2. a | 4. a | 6. a | 8. b |

- **Expansion Tip:** Have students write questions for the other answer choices.

13 page 285   10 min.

1. where	6. Who
2. Why	7. When
3. Did	8. How
4. What	9. Why
5. Were	10. Did

14 SPEAK, page 286   5 min.

- **Alternative Writing:** Have students write a paragraph about Mr. Nash based on the interview.

15 EDIT, page 286   5 min.

1. A: Did you grow up in South Africa?
   B: Yes, I did.
   A: Did you ever ~~saw~~ see Nelson Mandela?
   B: Yes, I went to hear him speak many times.
   A: Did you read the new book about him?
   B: No, I didn't. Who ~~did write~~ wrote it?
   A: I don't remember, but it was really good.

2. A: When ~~they did~~ did they win the prize?
   B: Last week.
   A: How did they feel?
   B: They were very happy, of course.

3. A: ~~Were~~ Did you meet the president?
   B: No, I didn't. How about you?
   A: I saw her, but I didn't meet her.
   B: Who ~~she met~~ did she meet with?
   A: Photographers and news reporters.

16 WRITE & SPEAK, page 286   10 min.

A   1. Where did you grow up?
    2. Did you come from that city?
    3. Where did you go to school?
    4. What did you study?
    5. How did you do in school?
    6. Who helped you?
    7. Who did you live with?
    8. Where did you go last year?

17 LISTEN, SPEAK & WRITE, page 287   20 min.

A   1. F   2. T

B   Lived: Hong Kong
    Explored: Rivers
    In the 1980s: Led expeditions
    In 1985 and 2005:   Yangtze River
    Started: An exploration and research society

18 APPLY, page 287   15 min.

- **Expansion Tip:** Have students use their questions to interview one partner. Students write the answers on a piece of paper but don't use the name of their partner. Collect the papers and redistribute. Call on students to read the sentences as the class guesses who it is.

UNIT 9   LESSON 1

LESSON 2 | Past Time Clauses

Student Learning Outcomes	• **Read** an article about Ernest Shackleton's expedition. • **Identify** the time order of actions. • **Write** sentences with time clauses. • **Listen** to information and **put** the events in order. • **Listen** to conversations and **write** sentences with time clauses. • **Find** and **edit** errors with commas. • **Write** and **talk** about a personal challenge.
Lesson Vocabulary	(v.) crush (n.) goggles (n.) navy (v.) surround (n.) destination (n.) lifeboat (v.) rescue (v.) survive

EXPLORE

1 READ, page 288   15 min.

Be the Expert

- Ernest Shackleton was born in Ireland in 1874 and led three British expeditions to the Antarctic. He was knighted by King Edward VII after the Nimrod expedition in 1909.
- About 98 percent of Antarctica is covered by ice, and it is the coldest, driest, windiest continent. In the early 1900s, a number of expeditions tried to reach the geographic South Pole. Shackleton's Nimrod expedition was the first to get as far south as they did, but they did not reach the geographic South Pole. Norwegian Roald Amundsen's group was the first to reach the pole in 1911. One month after his success, British explorer, Robert Scott's group reached the pole, but the entire party died on their way back.
- **Tip:** Suggest that students research the Amundsen or Scott expedition and compare it to Shackleton's.

- Use the photo to teach the meaning of *ice* and *surround*. Elicit ideas about what life on the ship might have been like.
- **Tip:** After students read and listen, have them write three questions in the simple past to ask and answer with a partner.

2 CHECK, page 289   5 min.

1. F   2. F   3. T   4. F   5. T

3 DISCOVER, page 289   5 min.

A Check (✓): 1, 2, 4, 5

B Tip: As an explanation, go over the information in the Real English box on page 290 during your discussion of the answers for exercise **A**.

LEARN

Chart 9.4, page 290   10 min.

- **Note 3:** Adding words such as *before* and *after* to a clause shows that the idea is not complete. Write sentences on the board with one clause (e.g., *We finished class, She called me, The car stopped*). Call students to the board to add *before* clauses to each sentence, then call on different students to add *after* clauses to the original sentences.

> **REAL ENGLISH**, page 290
>
> Have students rewrite the example sentences in Chart 9.4 to use preposition + noun combinations instead of time clauses, e.g., *They ate lunch before us.*

4 page 290   5 min.

- **Expansion Tip:** Have students rewrite the sentences to put the clauses in reverse order. Remind them to use correct punctuation.

1. 1; 2   5. 2; 1
2. 2; 1   6. 1; 2
3. 1; 2   7. 1; 2
4. 2; 1   8. 1; 2

5 page 291   10 min.

- **Tip:** Have students look at the time line. To make sure they read it correctly, ask questions about events (e.g., *Which is first—ice surrounded the ship or ice began to crush the ship?*).

1. before   5. before
2. Before   6. before
3. After   7. after
4. Before   8. after

6 SPEAK, page 291 — 3 min.

Chart 9.5, page 292 — 10 min.

- **Note 2:** Copy the sample sentences on the board. Write *1* and *2* over the correct clause.
- **Note 3:** Write the example sentence on the board in reverse order (*He called us when he got to Chicago.*) and point out that a comma is not necessary with this order.

7 page 292 — 10 min.

- **Tip:** Have students write the sentences on the board using different colored chalk or markers for the time clauses if possible.

1. When their team won the World Cup, they celebrated.
2. When my sister graduated, we had a party.
3. When he reached the top of the mountain, he took a photo.
4. When I had a problem, Lisa helped me.
5. When Neil Armstrong landed on the moon, my parents were very happy.
6. When he finished the race, Bob texted us.
7. When I heard the good news, I called my mother.
8. When they moved to Ohio, they bought their first house.

PRACTICE

8 page 293 — 5 min.

1. when she ran in a race last year (past time clause)
2. After her injury
3. Before the next big race
4. before the race
5. After she ran the first mile (past time clause)
6. After the fifth mile
7. When she won the race (past time clause)
8. After she won the race (past time clause)

9 page 293 — 5 min.

1. when
2. When
3. After
4. When
5. After
6. When
7. Before
8. After

10 LISTEN & WRITE, page 294 — 15 min.

- **Tip:** Point out the photo and caption. Elicit how students think the saucer was used. Students can learn more about it on the Cousteau Society website.

A 1. b   2. c   3. a   4. d

B 2; 4; 9; 1; 7; 8; 3; 5; 6

C 1. after he got married
2. Before he designed the aqualung
3. after he helped to design an underwater camera
4. After/When he bought a ship
5. After he wrote a book
6. Before his book became a film
7. When his book became a film
8. When he had a TV show

11 EDIT, page 295 — 5 min.

Before Jacques Cousteau wrote *The Silent World*⁀he wasn't famous. After the book became a movie⁀Cousteau led many expeditions to study the ocean. When he led expeditions⁀a film crew went with him on his boat, the *Calypso*. He made a one-hour television show. It was very popular. When people watched this TV show⁀they learned about the ocean. He had the TV show for nine years. Before it ended⁀Cousteau began to see many changes and problems in the ocean. After he saw these problems⁀he wanted to help the ocean. He started the Cousteau Society and made special television shows about problems in the ocean. Many people joined the Cousteau Society after they saw the television shows. Jacques Cousteau died in 1997 after a long career as an explorer, an inventor, and a friend of the ocean.

12 LISTEN & WRITE, page 295 — 15 min.

A Conversation 1: 1, 3, 5

Conversation 2: 2, 3, 4, 6

B 1. In conversation 1, Max was nervous before he started his presentation.
2. He was not nervous when he started the presentation.
3. Max practiced a lot before his presentation.
4. His dog fell asleep before he finished.
5. In conversation 2, Sidney felt sick when he was playing the game.
6. He left the game before half-time.
7. His team scored a goal after he left the game.
8. His stomach did not hurt after the game.

13 APPLY, page 296 — 10 min.

- **Alternative Speaking:** Have students give a presentation to a group about their challenges.

UNIT 9   LESSON 2   95

LESSON 3 | Past Progressive

Student Learning Outcomes
- **Read** an article about Tenzing Norgay.
- **Complete** sentences with the past progressive.
- **Discuss** an event with a group.
- **Listen** to information and **complete** sentences.
- **Write** about an event.

Lesson Vocabulary
(n.) attempt (n.) expedition (n.) porter (n.) warning
(n.) disability (n.) iceberg (n.) voyage (n.) wheelchair

EXPLORE

1 READ, page 297 — 15 min.

- Use the photo to teach the meaning of *peak*.
- **Tip:** Suggest that students use context to guess the meaning of important vocabulary: *attempt, porter, rescue*.
- **Expansion Tip:** Have students work in pairs to discuss the qualities that Norgay and Hillary probably had that helped them reach the top of the mountain.
- **Expansion Tip:** Suggest that students research one of these topics related to Mount Everest and report to a group or the class—pollution on Everest, the role of oxygen and special equipment in helping climbers, the work conditions of Sherpas.

Be the Expert

- Tenzing Norgay and Edmund Hillary were the first two individuals known to have reached the top of Mt. Everest. Jamling Norgay and Peter Hillary, the sons of the two climbers, climbed Mt. Everest on the 50th anniversary of the first climb. Mount Everest, at nearly 9000 meters, is the highest mountain on Earth. Nearly four thousand people have made it to the summit of Mount Everest on more than 5000 ascents; however, many people have died attempting the climb.
- Sherpas are an ethnic group in Nepal known for their climbing ability. They are well adapted to living at a high altitude with lower levels of oxygen. The term is sometimes used to refer to any porter who helps guide climbers up the mountain. Have students discuss in pairs or small groups the ways in which living in high mountains is different from living at sea level.

2 CHECK, page 298 — 5 min.

1. T 2. T 3. F 4. T

3 DISCOVER, page 298 — 5 min.

A 1. was living   3. were climbing; rescued
   2. got   4. reached

B 1. a, c   2. d

- **Tip:** Have students look at the photo and caption. Ask, *What are the men doing? How do you think they feel?*
- **Tip:** As you go over the answers to exercise **3**, have students look at the chart on page 299 to name the form for *a* and *c*.

LEARN

Chart 9.6, page 299 — 10 min.

- **Note 1:** Point out that we also use the present progressive to talk about a specific time—this moment in the present.
- **Note 2:** The past progressive can be used for an action that was interrupted by another. (e.g., *I was sleeping when he called.*) The action may or may not continue after the interruption. Elicit ideas from students of activities of theirs that were interrupted and not continued. Have volunteers write sentences on the board.

4 page 299 — 5 min.

1. were trying   7. were waiting
3. were climbing   8. were hoping
5. was living

- **Tip:** Have students rewrite the sentences to make them negative.

5 page 299   5 min.

1. were climbing
2. was working
3. were traveling
4. were living
5. was not paying attention
6. was sleeping
7. were waiting
8. was driving
9. were talking
10. were studying

Chart 9.7, page 300   10 min.

- **Note 1:** Actions that are very short in duration are often in the simple past. Provide examples of such verbs. Include *start, begin, stop, end, ring, fall, hit, find,* and *lose*.
- **Note 2:** Again, point out that the shorter action is in the simple past. If actions are of the same duration, then we can use past progressive for both. (e.g., *I was sleeping while Jack was watching TV.*)
- **Note 3:** To review, elicit non-action verbs from students. Write a past progressive sentence with a non-action verb on the board and draw a large *X* through it.

6 page 300   10 min.

1. started
2. got; was helping
3. had
4. didn't know
5. didn't understand; called
6. gave
7. came; was teaching
8. wanted; had

- **Tip:** Have students rewrite the sentences to make affirmative clauses negative and negative clauses affirmative.

PRACTICE

7 page 301   5 min.

1. began
2. were living
3. was working
4. wanted
5. organized
6. were
7. liked
8. took

8 LISTEN & SPEAK, page 301   20 min.

A 1. England; New York
2. 2000
3. 20
4. April
5. reports

B 1. was crossing
2. had
3. needed
4. knew
5. was having
6. was going
7. didn't believe
8. sank
9. died
10. was

- **Alternative Speaking:** Have students research the *Titanic* to find out 3–5 new facts. Then have students retell the story of the *Titanic* disaster to a partner, adding their new information.

9 APPLY, page 302   15 min.

- **Expansion Tip:** Have students look online for articles about the past event they write about. Suggest that they print an article, underline all examples of past progressive, and then share with a partner.
- **Alternative Activity:** Find an article about an event such as the first moon landing. Distribute copies to students and ask them to underline the past progressive verbs.

Review the Grammar — UNIT 9

1 WRITE & SPEAK, page 303 — 10 min.
- **Tip:** Model the activity. Complete the sentences about yourself.
- **A** *Answers will vary.*

2 WRITE, LISTEN & SPEAK, page 303 — 20 min.

A
1. were trying
2. were
3. died
4. were traveling
5. wanted
6. was
7. was preparing
8. reached
9. ended
10. began
11. were planning
12. had
13. wanted

- **Tip:** Point out the photo and caption. Ask, *What do you think this photo shows?* (Amundsen being the first to reach the South Pole.)

C page 304
- **Tip:** Divide the class into two teams. With books closed, the teams take turns asking each other their questions. Each correct answer earns a point.

3 EDIT, page 304 — 10 min.

Q: Who was the first man ~~was~~ to the North Pole?
A: No one really knows. In 1909, two men from the United States, Robert Peary and Fredrick Cook, both said, "I was the first."

Q: Why did so many explorers want ~~wanted~~ to reach the poles first?
A: They ~~were wanting~~ wanted to be famous.

Q: Did expeditions ~~continued~~ continue after explorers reached the North and South Poles?
A: Yes, they did.

Q: Why ~~they continued~~ did they continue?
A: Many explorers were scientists. They wanted to learn many things about the poles. When they ~~were~~ returned, they ~~were having~~ had a lot of new information.

- **Tip:** Point out the photo of Robert Peary and ask students what they know about him. Peary was a U.S. Navy engineer. On April 6, 1909, he and his team were the first to reach the North Pole.

4 LISTEN & WRITE, page 304 — 25 min.

A

	Dana	Allen
Lives in Oklahoma		✓
Is married	✓	✓
Has two daughters		✓

B

Allen		Dana
2	Graduated from high school	1
5	The tornado happened	3
4	Graduated from college	2
1	Got a job	4
3	Got married	5
6	Had a child	6

D Answers will vary. Possible answers:
1. Allen was living in Oklahoma when Dana saw him.
2. Allen got a job before he graduated from high school. / Allen got married before he graduated from college.
3. Allen graduated from college after he got married.
4. Dana was visiting Oklahoma when the tornado happened.
5. Dana graduated from college before she got married.
6. Dana got a job after she visited Oklahoma.

5 WRITE & SPEAK, page 305 — 15 min.
- **Tip:** Model the activity. On the board, write a time line about events in your life. Say sentences about the time line. Allow students to ask you questions.
- **Expansion Tip:** Have students interview a partner and write a paragraph about his/her life events.

Connect the Grammar to Writing

1 READ & NOTICE THE GRAMMAR, page 306

20 min.

B   Florence Nightingale lived in the 1800s. <u>When she was 24</u>, Nightingale studied nursing. <u>After she finished school</u>, she got a job in a hospital. She became the director of the hospital after only three years. <u>When she was 34</u>, Nightingale took a group of nurses to help injured soldiers in Crimea. <u>Before the nurses arrived</u>, the hospital was very dirty. Many soldiers got diseases. <u>After Nightingale arrived with her nurses</u>, the number of deaths went down by 66 percent.

   <u>When she returned to England</u>, Nightingale wrote a book about ways to improve hospital care. Her book changed the nursing profession. Her knowledge saved many patients' lives.

C 1. Lived in the 1800s.

   2. Studied nursing

   3. Got a job

   4. Became

   5. Took a group of nurses to . . .; . . . went down 66 percent

   6. Wrote a book

- **Expansion Tip:** Have students underline past time clauses in the article on Tenzing Norgay on page 297. Which structure is more common, the time clause first or second?

2 BEFORE YOU WRITE, page 307

15 min.

- **Tip:** If students do research on their topic, suggest that they search for a time line of the person's life.
- **Tip:** Tell students that they can write about a person they know or a famous person. Suggest that they look through the unit for names of famous people they would like to know more about.

3 WRITE, page 307

15 min.

WRITING FOCUS, page 307

Give students a paragraph such as the one below from Lesson 3, exercise **7**. Have students read the paragraph, and then write sentences about the information using time clauses. Then have them compare sentences with a partner.

   The Paralympic Games are international competitions for athletes with disabilities. The idea for the games began in 1948. At that time, many former soldiers were living in England with disabilities from the war. Dr. Ludwig Guttmann was working at a London hospital, and he wanted to help the soldiers. He organized an archery competition for people in wheelchairs. Soon there were many sport competitions for people with disabilities. Many people likes Guttmann's idea, and the first Paralympics took place in 1960.

Answers may vary. Possible answers:

Before the Paralympic Games began, there were not any games for people with disabilities.

After Guttman organized the first archery competition, people started many games for people with disabilities.

- **Alternative Writing:** Have students write about an important event in history rather than about a person.

UNIT 10 Human and Animal Encounters

Adjectives and Adverbs

Unit Opener

Photo: Ask, *What do you see in the photo?* Elicit or teach: *diver, whale, tank, mask, flippers.* Ask, *Do you dive? Are you interested in whales? Does this look scary?* Read the caption together. Find New Zealand on the map. Southern right whales were once nearly extinct, but their population has been recovering in recent years.

Location: The Auckland Islands are an archipelago in the Sub-Antarctic region. No humans live on the island, but feral cats, pigs, and mice live there, as do many birds including penguins, and seals. An estimated 1000 Southern right whales live near the islands.

Theme: This unit is about encounters between humans and animals. It gives information about fennec foxes, gorillas, chimpanzees, and Iberian lynx among others.

Page	Lesson	Grammar	Examples
310	1	Adjectives; Using Nouns as Adjectives	The article is **interesting**. **How tall** is your brother? She is a **tour guide**.
320	2	Adverbs of Manner and Adjectives	I drive **carefully**. Jonathan **looks tired**. He runs **fast**.
329	3	Adjectives and Adverbs with *Too, Very,* and *Enough*	I don't want to go outside. It's **too cold**. The people were **very friendly**. It's **cold enough** for gloves and a hat today.
336	Review the Grammar		
338	Connect the Grammar to Writing		

Unit Grammar Terms

adjective: a word that describes or modifies a noun or pronoun.
➢ She is a **good** teacher.
➢ He is **friendly**.

adverb: a word that describes or modifies a verb, an adjective, or another adverb.
➢ He eats **quickly**. (modifies the verb *eat*)
➢ That's an **incredibly** big TV. (modifies the adjective *big*)
➢ The student speaks **very** softly. (modifies the adverb *softly*)

adverb of manner: an adverb that describes the action of the verb. Many adverbs of manner are formed by adding *-ly* to the adjective.

➢ She sang the song **beautifully**.

irregular adjective: an adjective that does not change form in the usual way.
➢ *good* → *better*   *bad* → *worse*

irregular adverb: an adverb that does not change form in the usual way.
➢ *well* → *better*   *badly* → *worse*

linking verb: a verb that connects, or links, subjects and adjectives. The adjective modifies the subject. *Be, become, feel, get, look, seem, smell, sound, stay,* and *taste* are linking verbs.
➢ We **are** hungry.
➢ He **feels** happy.

LESSON 1	**Adjectives; Using Nouns as Adjectives**		
Student Learning Outcomes	• **Read** an article about the fennec fox. • **Write** about animals using adjectives. • **Ask** and **answer** questions with *How* and *What*. • **Read** a paragraph and **identify** adjectives and the nouns they modify. • **Listen** to information and **answer** questions. • **Write** and **role-play** an interview.		
Lesson Vocabulary	(adj.) active (n.) assignment	(n.) den (adj.) excellent	(adj.) nocturnal (adj.) rare	(adj.) saltwater (adj.) thick

EXPLORE

1 READ, page 310   15 min.

- **Tip:** Use the photos on pages 310 and 311 to elicit ideas about the fennec fox's habitat, and the reasons it may look the way it does. This will help students anticipate the content of the article.
- Use the photo to teach the meaning of *fox* and *den*. Have students use context cues to guess the meaning of *nocturnal, thick,* and *active*.

Be the Expert

- One of the most effective ways for animals to survive is through natural camouflage, or an appearance that allows it to blend in with its surroundings. This hides the animals from predators as well as from prey. The fennec fox is the same color as the desert sand. Elicit other animals that use camouflage as protection (e.g., polar bear, deer, walking sticks, chameleon).
- The Sahara is the world's hottest desert, and the third largest desert. Only the Antarctic and the Arctic deserts are larger. It is 3.6 million square miles (9.4 million square km). Some other animals that live in the Sahara include gazelles, cheetahs, lizards, snakes, ostriches, and crocodiles. One type of antelope, the addax, can go a year without drinking. The temperature during the day is usually very hot (30–50 degrees Celsius), but can go down to 4 degrees at night.

2 CHECK, page 311   5 min.

    1. c   2. b   3. d   4. e   5. a

- **Tip:** Have students match the sentences without referring to the article. Encourage students to check their answers by scanning for key words (e.g., sandy color, ears, thick fur, excellent hearing, water).

- **Expansion Tip:** Have students research the answers to the questions under "Related Articles." Or, provide the information in the *Be the Expert* box, and have students take turns asking and answering the questions in pairs.

3 DISCOVER, page 311   5 min.

A   1. small   4. excellent
     2. large   5. helpful
     3. thick

B   c

LEARN

Chart 10.1, page 312   10 min.

- **Notes 1-4:** These notes are review from Unit 1, Lesson 3.
- **Note 5:** Provide other phrases such as *interested in, good at, tired of,* and *happy about*.
- **Note 6:** Adverbs such as *very, really, pretty,* and *quite* modify adjectives. Place the adverbs on a continuum to show their degree and elicit example sentences.
- **Tip:** Write sentences on the board with the first pattern. (e.g., *The student was clever. Our homework was difficult.*) Have students write sentences using the adjectives before the nouns. (e.g., *The clever student won a prize.*)

> **REAL ENGLISH, page 312**
>
> *Very* can be used before adjectives and adverbs. *Really* can be used before adjectives, adverbs, and verbs. Write sentences on the board: *I am _____ tired. She _____ enjoys action movies. We worked _____ slowly.* Elicit which sentences can be completed with *very* and which with *really*.

4 page 312 — 5 min.

Arabian camels live in the sandy desert. They are perfect animals for life in this difficult climate. Long eyelashes protect them from blowing sand. They have large feet, so they don't sink into deep sand. They can go for a long time without food or water. They truly are desert animals.

- **Expansion Tip:** Have students use the adjectives to write a paragraph about something else.

5 page 313 — 10 min.

Answers may vary. Possible answers:

1. tall
2. friendly
3. a small
4. huge
5. a nice
6. beautiful
7. interesting
8. an intelligent
9. scary
10. a strong

- **Tip:** Have students write sentences for any adjectives in the box that they didn't use.

6 WRITE & SPEAK, page 313 — 5 min.

- **Expansion Tip:** Have students write sentences about the photo at the top of page 313 and share in pairs.

Chart 10.2, page 314 — 10 min.

- **Note 1:** Explain that questions with *How + be* and *What . . . like* are open-ended. The answer can address any aspect. Questions with *How + adjective* are asking about a specific quality or aspect of something. Ask questions of each type to elicit appropriate answers.
- **Note 2:** Explain that in questions with *What do/does . . . like*, the word *like* is a verb. In questions with *What + be . . . like*, *like* is not a verb. Ask questions about students in the class to elicit appropriate answers.

REAL ENGLISH, page 314

Have students work in pairs to brainstorm nouns that can be categorized (e.g., *music, fruit, street food, art*). Then have students find new partners to ask and answer questions that begin with *What kind of . . . ?*

7 page 314 — 5 min.

- **Tip:** Look at the photo on page 315. Ask questions to practice the grammar, e.g., *What are meerkats like?*

1. a
2. a
3. a
4. a
5. a
6. b
7. b
8. b
9. b
10. b
11. b
12. a

8 page 314 — 5 min.

- **Tip:** Have students write three new adjective with *how* and *what* questions to ask their partners.

Chart 10.3, page 316 — 10 min.

- **Note 1:** Explain that an answer to a question that begins with *What kind of a (noun) is it*, includes a noun used as an adjective (e.g., *What kind of a ball is it? It's a soccer ball*).
- **Note 2:** Write examples on the board, e.g., *He's a math teacher.* Point out that the second noun is the one that functions as a noun in the phrase.
- **Tip:** Point out objects in the classroom that have nouns used as adjectives (e.g., *coat closet, file cabinet, window shade, wall clock, computer screen, phone case*). Elicit more from students.

9 page 316 — 5 min.

1. desert
2. pencil
3. apartment
4. English
5. biology
6. swimming
7. math
8. shoe

10 page 316 — 10 min.

1. an animal trainer
2. a wildlife park
3. a baby elephant
4. a taxi driver
5. a science teacher
6. a weather report
7. college students
8. a homework assignment
9. government workers
10. an exercise room

- **Tip:** Have students use the phrases in exercise **10** in original sentences. (e.g., *An animal trainer works with all kinds of animals.*)

PRACTICE

11 page 317   5 min.

- **Tip:** Ask questions about the photo: *What are the people doing? What is the crocodile like?*

(Saltwater) crocodiles are large dangerous crocodiles. On the Adelaide River, near Darwin, Australia, they are also a (tourist) attraction. (Tour) boats take people along the river. The (tour) guides hang small pieces of meat above the side of the boats, and the crocodiles jump up and eat the meat. Fifty years ago, (crocodile) hunters killed almost all of the crocodiles. The Australian government passed a strict law to protect the crocodiles, and crocodiles are now common in Australia.

12 WRITE & SPEAK, page 317   10 min.

A
1. an exciting
2. a boat
3. huge
4. small
5. nervous
6. tour
7. close
8. scary

- **Alternative Writing:** Have students write an e-mail about a trip they took. Encourage them to use 6–10 noun modifiers and adjectives. Students exchange e-mails with a partner and respond.

13 LISTEN & WRITE, page 318   20 min.

- **Tip:** Elicit adjectives to describe the sharks in the photos.

A 1. He's an underwater photographer.
    2. He enjoys it.

B
1. c   3. g   5. f   7. d
2. a   4. h   6. e   8. b

C page 319

Answers may vary. Possible answers:
1. What kind of photographer is Skerry?
2. What is his job like?
3. How dangerous was the shark?
4. How big was the shark? / What was the shark like?
5. What were his photographs like?
6. How close was the shark?
7. How rare are whitetip sharks?
8. What was the water like?

- **Expansion tip:** Suggest that students use the adjectives and nouns from exercise **C** to write original sentences that use verbs other than *be*. (e.g., *An underwater photographer uses special equipment.*)

14 APPLY, page 319   15 min.

- **Expansion Tip:** Have students find new partners and take turns interviewing for each other's job.
- **Alternative:** Have students write a description for an interesting job, describing the qualities needed for the job, but not saying what it is. Students read their descriptions aloud as their classmates guess the job. (e.g., *My job is very important. I am helpful and I like people. I don't mind sick people. I know a lot about medicine.*) (a doctor)

5. One of the gorillas touched his hair lightly.

6. King sat quietly.

7. I read the news article quickly.

8. We did the exercise carefully.

5 page 322 — 10 min.

1. loudly	5. silently
2. quickly	6. calmly
3. carefully	7. rudely
4. well	8. clearly

- **Tip:** Have students work in pairs to identify adjectives that mean the opposite of the underlined words (quiet/soft, slow, careless, poor, noisy, nervous, polite, unclear). Then have students say the sentences using the opposite adjectives and adverbs. Point out that sometimes it sounds better to say "in a(n) . . . way" rather than to use an adverb.

6 SPEAK, page 323 — 3 min.

- **Expansion Tip:** Have students use all of the adverbs in sentences about themselves or someone they know.

Chart 10.5, page 323 — 10 min.

- **Note 2:** Explain that when the verb is about perception, it is a linking verb. (e.g., *The blanket felt soft* vs. *I felt the blanket*.) Say sentences with the verbs given. Elicit whether the verbs are used as linking or action verbs.

> **REAL ENGLISH, page 323**
>
> Provide adjectives that students *can* use before a noun that mean something similar to *afraid*, *asleep*, *alone* (e.g., *the sleeping baby*, *the scared tourists*, *the solitary hiker*).

7 page 323 — 10 min.

- **Tip:** Have students write the sentences on the board using different colored chalk or markers for the adjectives and adverbs if possible.

1. The gorillas were interested in the photographer.

2. He didn't seem afraid. In fact, he acted bravely.

3. She looked happy as she looked at the photographs.

4. I love these flowers. They smell wonderful.

5. I had a headache last night. I felt fine this morning.

6. Most people feel nervous when they make presentations.

7. Please taste this soup. Does it taste OK?

8. I need to buy some warm clothes. The weather is getting cold.

9. You sound upset. Did something happen?

10. I'm very tired today. I didn't sleep well last night.

8 SPEAK, page 324 — 5 min.

- **Expansion Tip:** Have students work in pairs to role-play conversations in which they use as many linking verbs as they can. Encourage them to be dramatic.

Chart 10.6, page 324 — 5 min.

- **Note 1:** There are a limited number of these irregular adverbs. Suggest that students memorize them. Elicit examples for each word used as an adjective and then as an adverb.

> **REAL ENGLISH, page 324**
>
> Encourage students to use the *-ly* form for the adverb. It is correct in every situation. Search online for examples of *slow* and *slowly* used as adverbs and bring them to class.

9 page 324 — 5 min.

- **Tip:** Go over the example with the class. Elicit how they know *hard* is an adjective (it follows *be*, a linking verb). Remind students to look at the verb to determine if it is action or linking, as well as to look at the form of the word.

Adjectives: 1, 2, 7, 8, 10, 11, 12

Adverbs: 3, 4, 5, 6, 9

PRACTICE

10 page 326 — 5 min.

1. quickly	6. easy
2. curious	7. high
3. hungry	8. well
4. loud	9. carefully
5. good	10. intelligent

UNIT 10 LESSON 2

11 page 326   5 min.

Answers may vary. Possible answers:

1. walk fast
2. yell loudly
3. swim quickly
4. study hard
5. read carefully
6. speak softly
7. arrive early
8. drive slowly

- **Tip:** In pairs, have students discuss how true the statements are for them.

12 EDIT, page 326   5 min.

Welcome to our Wildlife Park. Stay ~~safely~~ **safe**. There are a lot of wild animals in this area. Here are some important safety tips:

- Carry a can with rocks in it. Shake ~~loudly~~ the can **loudly**. Wild animals usually stay away when they hear people.
- During a wild animal encounter, do not look directly at the animal. Look down.
- Do not run. Walk ~~quiet~~ away **quietly**.
- Do not climb a tree. Many animals climb trees ~~good~~ **well**.
- When you see baby animals, do not stand between them and their mothers.
- Speak softly.
- On a tour, follow ~~closely~~ your guide **closely**.
- Try to stay ~~calmly~~ **calm**.
- If an animal runs ~~direct~~ **directly** at you, try to look large and tall. Hold your arms and a jacket above your head.

13 LISTEN & SPEAK, page 327   15 min.

A 1. b   2. b

B
1. F
2. T
3. T
4. F
5. T
6. F
7. F
8. F

- **Alternative Speaking:** Have students describe an unusual animal encounter that they know about from a movie, TV program, or book. Encourage them to use adjectives and adverbs of manner.

14 APPLY, page 328   15 min.

- **Alternative Activity:** Have students present their encounters to the class or small group as if they are reporters on a news program.
- **Expansion Tip:** Have students write a description of the animal and its actions without naming the animal. Call on students to read their descriptions to the class as the other students try to guess the animal.

LESSON 3	**Too, Very, Enough + Adjective**
Student Learning Outcomes	• **Read** an article about the Iberian lynx. • **Talk** about general topics using *too* or *very*. • **Write** sentences with *enough* or *not enough* and an adjective. • **Find** and **edit** errors with *too, very,* and *enough*. • **Listen** to conversations and **complete** sentences. • **Write** about and **share** feelings about animals and zoos.
Lesson Vocabulary	(n.) countryside (adj.) extinct (n.) habitat (adj.) native (v.) expand (n.) forest (n.) lynx (n.) property

EXPLORE

1 READ, page 329   15 min.

- Use the photo to teach the meaning of *lynx* and *collar*. Ask how the collar can help researchers. (Tracking collars with GPS allow experts to monitor movements of wildlife to aid in conservation efforts.)

- **Tip:** Suggest that students use context to guess the meaning of important vocabulary: *expand, habitat, native, extinct, remove.*

- **Expansion Tip:** Have students work in small groups to discuss reasons people might want to save animals from becoming extinct.

Be the Expert

- The Iberian lynx is the most endangered of all cat species. There are now only two populations—both living is small areas in southern Spain. The Iberian lynx is small (10–13kgs; 88–100cm), with spots. The lynx eats small animals, especially rabbits. There are several reasons why it is endangered: There are fewer rabbits to eat, the habitat is smaller, hunters kill lynx, and cars hit the animals on roads and highways.

- Some animals are threatened, which means their numbers are declining and they may become extinct. Some animals are endangered, which means they will soon be extinct if we don't do something to save them. Animals that have become extinct during the 20th century include the Bali and Caspian tigers, the Arabian ostrich, the Japanese sea lion, the western black rhinoceros, and a deer in Thailand.

2 CHECK, page 330   5 min.

1. b   3. b
2. a   4. a

- **Tip:** Have students write three more questions about the information in the article. Then, in pairs, students practice asking and answering the questions.

3 DISCOVER, page 330   5 min.

A   1. very quickly   3. too late
      2. too close   4. big enough

B   a. too

- **Tip:** Have students look at the photo and the map. Ask questions: *What is the lynx like? Are its ears very big? Why is it spotted? Is its habitat in Spain big enough?*

LEARN

Chart 10.7, page 331   10 min.

- **Note 1:** Remind students that they used *too* in Unit 6 to talk about problems. (e.g. *There are too many students in this class. There is too much noise on my street.*)

- **Note 2:** In some languages, *too* and *very* are conveyed by the same word. Elicit examples of adjectives or adverbs that are unlikely to be used with *too* (e.g., friendly, nice, well, kind, helpful).

4 page 331   5 min.

1. too   3. too   5. very   7. too
2. very   4. very   6. very   8. very

- **Tip:** Suggest that students revise the sentences with *very* to make *too* more appropriate. (e.g., *The Iberian lynx is too beautiful. Hunters kill it for its coat.*)

5 SPEAK, page 331 — 5 min.

Chart 10.8, page 332 — 10 min.

- **Note 1:** Remind students that they learned about *enough* in Unit 6. (e.g., *There are enough chairs for everyone.*)
- **Note 2:** *Enough* goes before nouns but after adjectives.
- **Note 3:** The structure *adjective/adverb + enough + infinitive* is used to talk about qualities that are sufficient to complete a task. (e.g., *I'm smart enough to pass the test.*) Write several adjectives and adverbs on the board. Have students work in pairs to write sentences that use the structure.

6 page 332 — 10 min.

1. not big enough
2. loudly enough
3. clearly enough
4. well enough
5. carefully enough
6. not warm enough
7. not loud enough
8. cold enough
9. old enough
10. not old enough

- **Tip:** Have students choose three sentences to rewrite to say the opposite action. (e.g., *Our classroom is too small for all the students.*)

7 page 332 — 3 min.

- **Expansion Tip:** Provide additional prompts such as *This book is . . ., The weather today is . . .*, etc.

PRACTICE

8 page 333 — 5 min.

1. g	5. a
2. f	6. b
3. d	7. e
4. h	8. c

- **Alternative Speaking:** Have students work individually to write questions for which each item in Column A is an answer. (e.g., *Why is he failing English? He's not studying hard enough.*) Have students ask and answer their questions with a partner.

9 page 333 — 10 min.

1. very interesting
2. very sad
3. big enough
4. too large
5. close enough
6. very true
7. too far
8. big enough
9. very expensive
10. too expensive

10 EDIT, page 334 — 15 min.

The City Zoo is planning to expand. Right now, the zoo isn't ~~enough~~ large enough for all of the animals. Many animal exhibits are too small. There isn't enough land to expand on this site. The zoo tried very hard to buy more land in the city, but the land was ~~enough~~ too expensive. Last week, the zoo bought the old Cherry Hill Farm. "We are ~~too~~ very happy about this," says the Zoo Director. "The Cherry Hill Farm is ~~too~~ very large. The property is big enough for us to build a new zoo." Plans for the new exhibits are ~~too~~ very exciting. They include natural habitats. These are ~~enough~~ big enough for the animals.

- **Tip:** Call on students to describe the photo. To generate discussion, explain that polar bears live in five countries: the USA (Alaska), Canada, Russia, Greenland, and Norway. Polar bears do not live in Antarctica. Norway is the only country where polar bears are protected from all hunting. The polar bear is endangered because of global warming and the destruction (melting) of its habitat.

11 LISTEN & SPEAK, page 334 — 15 min.

A 1. c   2. b   3. a

B Answers may vary. Possible answers:
1. too windy; too hard; warm enough
2. very interesting; too dark; dark enough; too hot; very crowded; too slowly
3. too huge; big enough; too small

12 APPLY, page 335 — 15 min.

- **Tip:** Remind students that we often use *because* in answers to *Why* questions. Suggest that students write a first sentence that states whether they like or dislike zoos, and then write three or four more statements giving reasons and/or details.
- **Alternative Speaking:** Divide the class in half. One side works in pairs to prepare arguments in favor of zoos, the other side against zoos. Then each pair joins a pair from the other side to debate the issue of zoos.

UNIT 10 Review the Grammar

1 page 336 — 10 min.

- **Tip:** Have students look at the photo of the king cobra and elicit how they feel about it.

  1. beautiful
  2. quietly
  3. dangerous
  4. quick
  5. good
  6. quickly
  7. good
  8. directly
  9. close
  10. dangerous
  11. quick
  12. well
  13. amazing

2 EDIT, page 336 — 5 min.

I had an ~~amaze~~ amazing day today. I saw a dugong. It was huge! The water was ~~clearly~~ clear and quiet. It wasn't very ~~deeply~~ deep. I saw ~~perfectly~~ the dugong perfectly. It was moving slowly along the bottom and eating the seagrass. Every few minutes it swam up and ~~quick~~ quickly put its nose out of the water. It seemed very ~~gently~~ gentle. No one was afraid of it. There aren't many dugongs anymore. They're endangered. I was ~~luckily~~ lucky to see one!

- **Expansion Tip:** With a partner, have students discuss reasons why the dugong might be endangered. This will set them up for the next exercise.

3 LISTEN, WRITE & SPEAK, page 337 — 15 min.

A 1. the supply of seagrass
3. hunters
5. nets on large fishing boats
6. the number of baby dugongs

B 1. The supply of seagrass is not large enough.
2. Seagrass grows too slowly.
3. Hunters catch and kill them very easily because dugongs swim too slowly.
4. Fishing boats kill dugongs very frequently because dugongs aren't fast enough.
5. The number of dugongs does not grow very quickly.

4 READ & SPEAK, page 337 — 10 min.

- **Expansion Tip:** Have students read their passage aloud to their partner as their partner takes notes. The partners then retell the information from their notes.

Connect the Grammar to Writing

1 READ & NOTICE THE GRAMMAR, page 338   20 min.

- **Tip:** Write the example sentences from Grammar Focus on the board. Use colored chalk or markers to connect the adjectives and adverbs to the words they modify. For example, you might write the noun and its modifier in blue and one verb and its modifier in red and the other in green.

B   I am <u>afraid</u> of snakes. In my hometown, there are a lot of <u>huge</u> snakes. They are very <u>dangerous</u>. One time, I almost stepped on a snake when I was walking in my yard. I was walking (slowly), so I didn't step on it, so it was very <u>scary</u>. Another time, I went on a camping trip, and a <u>big</u> snake crawled into our tent. (Fortunately), I saw it before it got dark. Of course, I screamed (loudly), and my father ran (quickly) to help. That was my <u>last</u> camping trip.

C

What is the topic of the paragraph?	The writer's feelings about snakes.
How does the writer feel about them?	The writer doesn't like them/is scared of them.
Why? What encounters or experiences did the writer have with snakes?	The writer almost stepped on one. One crawled into the tent on a camping trip.

2 BEFORE YOU WRITE, page 339   15 min.

- **Expansion Tip:** Have students interview each other using the questions, and then write a paragraph about their partners.

3 WRITE, page 339   15 min.

> **WRITING FOCUS, page 339**
>
> Have students rewrite the text of *A Dangerous Situation* on page 336. Ask them to take out all adjectives and adverbs. Then have students read the two versions aloud in pairs. Elicit which version is more interesting and why.

- **Expansion Tip:** Have students work individually to write a paragraph about one of the topics in the unit without using any adjectives or adverbs. Students exchange paragraphs with a partner. The partner adds adjectives and adverbs to make the paragraphs more interesting.

- **Alternative Writing:** Have students write about a favorite sports star or sports team. Encourage them to use adjectives and adverbs to describe why the team or player(s) are so good.

UNIT 11 Challenges and Abilities

Modals: Part 1

Unit Opener

Photo: A BASE jumper is someone who jumps, not from an airplane, but from a fixed object, in this case a very high bridge over a river. Explain that every year on a special holiday in October, people jump off the bridge using parachutes. It is the largest gathering of BASE jumpers in the world.

Location: The bridge Daisher is jumping from is 876 feet (267 meters) high. The New River Gorge in West Virginia is also popular for whitewater rafting and rock climbing.

Theme: Students will read about unusual people who overcame challenges and difficulties.

Page	Lesson	Grammar	Examples
342	1	Can/Could	I **can** speak Spanish. I **can't** speak German. I **couldn't** speak German before this class. **Can** he **swim**? Where **can** we **get** some coffee? How far **could** he **fly**?
352	2	Be Able To; Know How To	I'm **able to** swim. We **weren't able to** finish the assignment. I **know how to** swim. I **knew how to** read before I started school.
359	3	And, But, and So; Contrasts after But	He was a very fast runner, **so** he won a lot of races. Larry ran very fast, **but** he didn't win the race. I **was** there, **but** she **wasn't**. We **can't** speak Korean, **but** they **can**.
367	**Review the Grammar**		
370	**Connect the Grammar to Writing**		

Unit Grammar Terms

clause: a group of words with a subject and a verb.
  ➢ *We watched the game.* (one clause)
  ➢ *Mia works hard, and she always does well on exams.* (two clauses)

independent clause: (also called main clause) a clause that can stand alone as a sentence. It has a subject and a verb.
  ➢ *I'm listening, but my classmate is talking.*
  ➢ *She likes to watch movies, and she loves to read.*

modal: an auxiliary verb that adds additional meaning to a verb such as ability or possibility. *May, might, can, could, will, would,* and *should* are common modals.
  ➢ *Julie can speak three languages.*
  ➢ *He may be at the office. Call him.*

LESSON 1 — Can/Could

Student Learning Outcomes	• **Read** about a man who can fly using a special jet wing. • **Express** ability and inability in the present and past using *can* and *could*. • **Complete** sentences about people's abilities. • **Pronounce** the affirmative and negative forms of *can* correctly. • **Ask** *Yes/No* and information questions about ability using *can* and *could*. • **Find** and **edit**, errors with *can, can't, could,* and *couldn't*. • **Listen** to and **write** information about cars that can fly.
Lesson Vocabulary	(n.) engine (n) helicopter (n.) parachute (n.) pollution (n.) fuel (v.) imagine (n.) passenger (n.) wing

EXPLORE

1 READ, page 342   10 min.

- If possible, introduce this article by showing a video of Rossy flying around Mount Fuji. Do an Internet search for *"Jetman"* or *"Yves Rossy"*.
- Use the photos to teach the meaning of *fly*, *wing*, and *jet engine*.

Be the Expert

- Yves Rossy always dreamed of flying. He became a pilot, but he really wanted to fly himself! After flying with wing suits, he got the idea of developing a special wing with jet engines that he can steer with movements of his body. In addition to flying over the Swiss Alps, he has flown across the English Channel and around Mount Fuji in Japan.
- Rossy gave a TED Talk about his wing. (A TED Talk is a short, powerful talk sponsored by the non-profit originally named for a "Technology, Entertainment, and Design" conference.) Search the TED website to watch this talk.

2 CHECK, page 343   5 min.

1. T   3. F   5. T
2. T   4. F

3 DISCOVER, page 343   5 min.

A   1. can fly   2. can't fly   3. couldn't open
B   1. a   2. b   3. b

- **Tip:** Write *can fly* and *can't fly* on the board. Write *modal* and arrows pointing to *can* and *can't*. Explain that a modal adds meaning to the other verb. Show Chart 11.1.

LEARN

Chart 11.1, page 344   10 min.

- **Note 1:** Write a few verbs on the board (e.g., *eat, sleep, play an instrument*, etc.). Elicit original sentences using *can, can't, could,* and *couldn't* with each.
- **Tip:** Students may be familiar with the use of *could* in requests, which is not an example of past ability. If students ask, confirm that this is another use of this modal and they will study this soon. The use of *can* and *could* in requests and offers is taught in 13.6 and 13.7.

4 page 344   5 min.

1. can fly   5. couldn't travel
2. can't stay   6. couldn't leave
3. can learn   7. can go
4. couldn't open   8. couldn't see

5 PRONUNCIATION, page 345   15 min.

- **Tip:** After going over the chart, write on the board: *I can talk now. I can't talk now.* Ask students to listen as you say both sentences. Stress *now* in the first sentence. Stress *can't* in the second sentence. Explain that the negative is more important, so it is stressed more. The vowel is longer and clearer. The affirmative *can* in sentence 1 is not important, so it is not stressed. The vowel is short and pronounced as a schwa.

Write 1 and 2 above the sentences. As you say the sentences, ask, *Am I saying sentence 1 or sentence 2?*

A   Can: 2, 6, 10   Can't: 1, 3, 4, 5, 7, 8, 9
B   Answers will vary.

- **Tip:** Ask students to tell the class what they learned about their partners.

112   MODALS: PART 1

Chart 11.2, page 346

- **Note 1:** Say a few sentences with *can* and *could*. Ask students to change the sentences into questions. (e.g., *Joe can drive. Can Joe drive?*).
- **Notes 2 & 3:** This is the first time students have seen questions with *How far* and *How fast*, but they are familiar with *How much*. Another question following this model is *How long*. Write examples of these questions on the board to point out the similar structure.

6 page 346   10 min.

1. A: Can you ice skate?   B: Yes, I can.
2. A: Can you ski?   B: No, I can't.
3. A: Could you understand the article?   B: No, we couldn't.
4. A: Can she play the piano?   B: Yes, she can.
5. A: Could he sing very well?   B: No, he couldn't.
6. A: Can you drive a car?   B: Yes, I can.
7. A: Can your brother cook?   B: Yes, he can.
8. A: Could they swim?   B: No, they couldn't.

7 page 347   10 min.

1. How far can a marathon runner run?
2. How fast can that plane fly?
3. What can astronauts do?
4. Who can help you?
5. How many languages can you speak?
6. What can you play?
7. Where can you see the Northern Lights?
8. When/What time can they meet?
9. How can they get to Paris?
10. How far could he swim when he was younger?

8 SPEAK, page 347   10 min.

- **Tip:** Model this activity. Show that students can only write a student's name if he or she says *Yes*.
- **Expansion Tip:** If you know of students who have special talents, put this activity into a handout and add items to include those abilities.

PRACTICE

9 page 348   10 min.

- **Tip:** Before doing this activity, ask students: *Can you drive your car in the water? Can cars fly?* Search for *amphicar video* or *flying car video* to find videos of cars that can float or fly. Show them to the class if possible.

1. can travel   5. could buy
2. could go   6. can't buy
3. could, go   7. couldn't pass
4. could do   8. can drive

10 EDIT, page 348   5 min.

Dad: Here's an interesting ad. It says, "Yes, cars can ~~flies~~ fly!"

Daughter: That's crazy. Cars can't ~~to~~ fly!

Dad: Well, I saw a flying car when I was a child.

Daughter: Really? Could it ~~flies~~ fly?

Dad: Yes, but it couldn't ~~goes~~ go very fast.

Daughter: Where can you ~~can~~ drive it? You can't drive a car with wings on the highway.

Dad: Sure you can. The wings fold up, and you can ~~to~~ drive it on the highway.

11 page 349   15 min.

1. Can cars really fly?
2. Could companies build flying cars more than fifty years ago?
3. Where can the flying cars travel?
4. Can they take off from the highway?
5. How fast can the cars go?
6. How many people can the cars carry?
7. How many suitcases can you fit?
8. Where/How can I learn more about them?

12 LISTEN, WRITE & SPEAK, page 350   30 min.

A & B

1. Name: Transition
   Air speed: 115
2. Name: PAL-V
   Air speed: 110
   Distance: 350
   Passengers: 2
3. Name: Skycar
   Passengers: 2

13 APPLY, page 351   20 min.

- **Alternative Speaking:** Ask students to discuss the capabilities of a bicycle, a car, and a motorcycle.
- **Expansion Tip:** Have students describe their favorite app or device. Ask, *What couldn't you do before you got this device/app? What can you do now?*

LESSON 2	**Be Able To; Know How To**	
Student Learning Outcomes	• **Read** the true story of a dolphin that lost its tail and got an artificial tail. • **Use** *be able to* to express ability in the present and past. • **Write** sentences with *know how to* for abilities acquired through practice or experience. • **Ask** and **answer** questions about abilities using *be able to* and *know how to*. • **Find** and **edit** errors with *be able to* and *know how to*. • **Listen** to a story about one of the first women mathematicians. • **Discuss** differences in women's lives over time.	
Lesson Vocabulary	(n.) aquarium (adj.) artificial	(n.) physics (v.) save	(n.) secret (n.) tail	(n.) trap (v.) wrap

EXPLORE

1 READ, page 352 — 15 min.

Be the Expert

- This article tells the true story of a dolphin that lost its tail when it got caught in a crab trap. Prosthetic specialists who had only worked with artificial limbs for humans made an artificial tail for the dolphin. The story was made into a movie called *Dolphin Tale*.
- Winter still lives at the Clearwater Marine Aquarium and can be viewed online through a webcam. She is known around the world through TV programs and news reports.

- Use the photo to teach *aquarium*, *tail*, and *artificial tail*.
- **Expansion Tip:** Search online for *video Cieran Winter tale*. Show a video of Cieran, an eight-year old boy who is a double amputee as he learns how to swim with Winter. Have students discuss the story of Cieran and Winter.

2 CHECK, page 353 — 5 min.

2, 5, 1, 3, 4

3 DISCOVER, page 353 — 5 min.

A 1. wasn't able to
2. weren't able to
3. was able to

B 1. b   2. a

- **Tip:** Rewrite the sentences from exercise **A**, filling in the blanks with *could* and *couldn't*. Explain that these words add the same meaning of past ability and inability.

LEARN

Chart 11.3, page 354 — 5 min.

- It may be helpful to tell students that *be able to* is a "semi-modal." It is different from the modals because students need to change *be* and include *to* before the other verb.
- **Note:** Students sometimes wonder why they need to study *be able to* when it has the same meaning as *can* or *could*. *Be able to* is important because they can use it with a modal. (e.g., *When I save enough money, I'll be able to buy a car. Students should be able to choose their teachers.*)

4 page 354 — 5 min.

1. wasn't able to swim
2. was able to help
3. weren't able to save
4. were able to make
5. was able to move
6. were able to see
7. was able to swim
8. weren't able to see

5 page 355 — 10 min.

1. A: When you were a child, were you able to swim?
   B: Yes, I was.
2. A: Were you able to understand that question?
   B: No, I wasn't.
3. A: Were you able to finish your homework?
   B: Yes, I was.
4. A: Were the students able to finish the test?
   B: No, they weren't.
5. A: Was Fred able to go to the movies?
   B: No, he wasn't.
6. A: Were your parents able to go with you?
   B: Yes, they were.
7. A: Were you able to fall asleep last night?
   B: No, I wasn't.

8. A: Were you able to hear the bell?
   B: No, I wasn't.
9. A: Were they able to do the exercise?
   B: Yes, they were.
10. A: Was she able to find her book?
    B: Yes, she was.
11. A: Was Oleg able to talk to his teacher?
    B: No, he wasn't.
12. A: Were you able to see anything?
    B: No, I wasn't.

6 WRITE & SPEAK, page 355   10 min.

- **Expansion Tip:** This is a good point to review time clauses (Unit 9). Have students write one of their sentences on the board and then change the order of the clauses. Remind them to add a comma if necessary.

Chart 11.4, page 356

- **Notes 2 & 3:** Explain that *know how to* is also a semi-modal. It is different from the modal *can* because students need to change the verb *know* and use *to* before the verb.

- **Note 4:** Show additional contrasts between *can* and *know how to*. Write on the board:

  <u>can</u>

  see   read   swim   stand
  add   speak   speak English

  Elicit sentences with *can* and the verbs: *I can see, I can read,* etc. Then write, *I know how to. . .* to the left of the verbs. Ask, *Which verbs can I use to complete this sentence?* Circle the correct ones as they tell you: *read, swim, add, speak English.*

> **REAL ENGLISH,** page 356
>
> *Learn how to* follows naturally from *know how to.* Use the circled verbs on the board, and ask, *When did you learn how to read,* etc.?

7 page 356   10 min.

1. They don't know how to play tennis.
2. I don't know how to fly a plane.
3. He doesn't know how to speak Chinese.
4. We don't know how to solve the problem.
5. She doesn't know how to cook.
6. I didn't know how to swim.
7. They didn't know how to help.
8. We didn't know how to find the answer.
9. Ted doesn't know how to fix your computer.
10. Lori didn't know how to get there.

8 page 357   10 min.

1. Do you know how to fly a plane?
2. Does your son know how to ride a bicycle?
3. Do they know how to dance the tango?
4. Do you know how to play the guitar?
5. Does he know how to scuba dive?
6. Do they know how to take good photographs?
7. Do I know how to play golf?
8. Does she know how to fix a car?
9. Does he know how to make cookies?
10. Do you know how to use this vending machine?

9 SPEAK, page 357   10 min.

- **Expansion Tip:** Have higher-level students ask follow-up questions such as *When did you learn? How did you learn?* or *Do you want to learn? Do you want to do that some day?*

PRACTICE

10 page 357   10 min.

| 1. b | 3. h | 5. f | 7. g |
| 2. a | 4. e | 6. c | 8. d |

11 EDIT, page 358   10 min.

Q: When people were sick in the old days, were doctors able to help them?

A: In the past, many people died because doctors ~~didn't~~ weren't able to save them. Doctors didn't know how to help very sick people.

Q: Were women able to ~~being~~ be doctors?

A: In some countries, they were, but in most countries, women weren't able to be doctors. They ~~wasn't~~ weren't able to go to medical school.

12 LISTEN & SPEAK, page 358   25 min.

A 1. c   2. a

B 2, 4, 6, 7, 8

13 APPLY, page 358   15 min.

- **Alternative Speaking:** Have students discuss how life is different for people in their families now than it was for their grandparents.

- **Expansion Tip:** Write this prompt on the board: *Technology is both positive and negative. What are students/doctors/criminals/advertisers able to do now that they couldn't do ten years ago?* Divide the class into groups to discuss each topic and report to the class.

LESSON 3	***And, But,* and *So***
Student Learning Outcomes	• **Read** about challenges for athletes. • **Combine** ideas in sentences with *and* and *so*. • **Talk** about contrasting ideas in sentences with *but*. • **Complete** sentences with *and, but,* or *so*. • **Find** and **edit** errors with *and, but,* and *so*. • **Listen** to information about people who overcame challenges. • **Write** about people who overcame challenges
Lesson Vocabulary	(v.) amputate (n.) gymnastics (adj.) normal (n.) table tennis (n.) archery (n.) medal (adj.) physical (n.) telescope

EXPLORE

1 READ, page 359   15 min.

- Look at the photo. Ask, *What is unusual about this athlete?* (She has no legs.) Show the word *Paralympics* in the caption.

Be the Expert

- The first Paralympic Summer Games in 1960 were held in Italy. The first Winter Games were held in 1976 in Sweden. Since 1988, they have been held in the same locations as the Olympics. Initially, the games were only open to athletes in wheelchairs, but now athletes with many different types of disabilities compete.
- The word *Paralympic* combines the Greek word *para* that means *beside* and *Olympics*.

- **Tip:** Suggest that students search the Paralympics official website to view videos of the athletes and competitions. The website also includes biographies of the athletes.

2 CHECK, page 360   5 min.

  1. F   2. F   3. T   4. F   5. T

3 DISCOVER, page 360   5 min.

A 1. but   2. so   3. and
B 1. a   2. b   3. c

- **Tip:** Write the sentences from Chart 11.5 on the board. Elicit how each illustrates the rules in exercise **B**.

LEARN

Chart 11.5, page 361   5 min.

- **Note 1:** Remind students that they learned about independent clauses in Unit 9 when they studied time clauses.
- **Note 2:** In American English, we use a comma after the first independent clause.
- **Note 5:** If students ask, point out this is just one of several ways that *so* is used in English.

> **REAL ENGLISH,** page 361
>
> Students often make mistakes in writing with *so* and *but*. (e.g., *I like pizza. So I eat it a lot.*) Write sentences such as these on the board. Have students rewrite them correctly.

4 page 361   5 min.

- **Tip:** Have students complete these sentences orally.
  1. He didn't win, but he did very well.
  2. He had an artificial leg, so he could walk.
  3. He was in an accident, and he lost his leg.
  4. She had an artificial leg, but she could run very fast.
  5. She entered the race, and she won.
  6. The Games were very popular, so tickets sold fast.
  7. Ava is strong, but she's not fast.
  8. They were very fast, so they won a lot of races.

5 page 362   10 min.

1. but   3. and   5. so   7. so
2. and   4. so   6. but   8. but

6 SPEAK, page 362 — 10 min.

- **Alternative Speaking:** Give students small pieces of paper. Have them think of complete sentences with *and*, *but*, and *so*. Have them write the first clause with the conjunction on one piece of paper, and the second clause on the second piece of paper. Have them mix the papers and give to another student to match.

Chart 11.6, page 362 — 10 min.

- **Note:** Explain that this construction is very common in conversation, but it is not often used in writing, particularly academic.

7 page 363 — 5 min.

1. can't
2. don't
3. didn't
4. does
5. aren't
6. were
7. was
8. does
9. didn't
10. isn't

- **Tip:** Ask higher-level students to close their books and listen as you read the sentences and they complete them.

8 page 363 — 5 min.

1. is
2. 'm not
3. can
4. don't
5. can
6. didn't
7. don't
8. did

9 SPEAK, page 363 — 10 min.

- **Expansion Tip:** Have students talk about differences with their siblings, spouses, or housemates. Ask, *Do these cause any problems, or are they a good thing?*

PRACTICE

10 page 364 — 10 min.

1. d
2. c
3. i
4. a
5. b
6. j
7. h
8. e
9. g
10. f

11 page 364 — 15 min.

1. but
2. and
3. so
4. so
5. but
6. and
7. but
8. so
9. so
10. so
11. but
12. but

12 EDIT, page 365 — 10 min.

When Aimee Mullins was born, she didn't have bones in part of her legs, ~~but~~ so she couldn't walk. The doctors talked to her parents, ~~so~~ and they decided to amputate part of her legs. Some people have trouble with artificial legs, ~~and~~ but Mullins doesn't. She learned to walk with them, ~~but~~ and they were a normal part of her life. In high school Aimee played softball, and in college she competed in many track and field events. In the Paralympics, she ran 100 meters in 17.01 seconds, ~~so~~ and she jumped 3.14 meters in the long-jump. Aimee Mullins has a physical disability, ~~and~~ but that doesn't slow her down.

- **Tip:** Aimee Mullins also gave a TED Talk that can be viewed online.

13 LISTEN & WRITE, page 365 — 25 min.

A couldn't hear: Beethoven
couldn't see: Bruce Hall
had very little money: Walt Disney
artist and business person: Walt Disney
underwater photographer: Bruce Hall
music composer: Beethoven

B *Answers will vary. Possible answers:*

1. Walt Disney's family was poor, so got a job. He wasn't a good student, and he left high school after one year. He started a company, and he did very well.
2. Bruce Hall is blind, but he's a photographer. He heard about stars, but he couldn't see them. He learned how to scuba dive, so he takes underwater photographs.
3. Beethoven was a great musician, so he wrote music. He became a composer, but he lost his hearing. He became deaf, but he continued to write music.

14 APPLY, page 366 — 10 min.

- **Tip:** Bring in photographs of people who have or had challenges. Have students write sentences about them.

- **Alterative Writing:** Are your students thinking about careers? Have them write about different options and list the differences between the professions. For example:

A nurse can work part time, and a nurse can make a good salary, but it's a stressful job.

My parents want me to be a teacher, but I don't. I like to cook, so I want to be a chef.

Review the Grammar — UNIT 11

1 page 367   10 min.

1. Can you/Do you know how to
2. can't/don't know how to
3. can't/don't know how to
4. can't
5. can't
6. Can you/Do you know how to
7. can't
8. can/know how to
9. Can you/Do you know how to
10. can't/don't know how to
11. can't/don't know how to

2 READ & SPEAK, page 367   25 min.

A   Alison Wright is a photographer and writer. She travels to *remote* villages, places far away from cities and airports. She takes photographs of the people there and writes about their lives. Several years ago, she was traveling on a bus on a remote mountain road in Laos when a truck hit the bus. She was able to get out of the bus, but she had a broken back and many other injuries. She couldn't move, and she wasn't able to breathe very well. No one could help her because she was very far away from any doctors or hospitals. She waited for 10 hours. Finally, someone came by in a small truck and saw her. He put her in the back of his truck and drove for eight hours to a small hospital in Thailand. A doctor there was able to save her life, but she had serious injuries. She returned to her home in the United States and had more than 20 operations. When she left the hospital, she couldn't walk very well, and she wasn't able to travel. However, she didn't give up. She became stronger and exercised every day because she had a dream: she wanted to climb Mount Kilimanjaro. Four years later, she did it. She was able to climb Mount Kilimanjaro!

- **Tip:** Search an online news site for *"overcame challenges"* to find recent stories about people who overcame challenges. Show the story in class and ask students to discuss the challenge using the target structures in this unit.

3 EDIT, page 368   10 min.

Bethany Hamilton grew up in Hawaii, ~~but~~ and she was an excellent surfer. She won many competitions, ~~but~~ and she was the number 1 surfer for the 13-year-old age group. One day, she was on her surfboard with one arm in the water, ~~but~~ and a shark bit her. People nearby took her to the hospital, ~~so~~ but doctors couldn't save her arm. She lost her arm, ~~so~~ but she got back on her surfboard one month after the shark attack. Most people can't surf with one arm, ~~and~~ but Bethany can. She entered a competition four months after the attack, ~~so~~ and she won fifth place. A year later, she entered a national competition, and she won! Bethany faced a huge challenge when she lost her arm, ~~and~~ but she didn't give up.

4 LISTEN & SPEAK, page 369   15 min.

A
1. they couldn't
2. this wave did
3. he wasn't
4. she couldn't
5. Richard didn't/it was very difficult
6. Tami did
7. she couldn't
8. Tami did

B
1. Tami wanted to see the world, so she helped people sail their boats across the ocean.
2. A hurricane was coming, but Tami and Richard didn't know.
3. The hurricane was moving toward them, so they changed direction.
4. A huge wave turned the boat over, and it caused a lot of damage to the boat.
5. Tami looked for Richard, but she didn't find him.
6. Tami's trip to Hawaii took 41 days, but she survived.
7. It was a terrible experience, but Tami still likes to sail.
8. Tami is a brave woman, and she's a good sailor.

Connect the Grammar to Writing

1 READ & NOTICE THE GRAMMAR,
page 370   15 min.

B   My cousin got very sick when she was 14 years old. She was in the hospital for two weeks, and she couldn't go to school for a month. She <u>wasn't able to</u> sit up, so she <u>couldn't</u> do any homework. When she finally went back to school, she <u>didn't know how to</u> do any of the math problems, and she was behind in all her courses.

   Before my cousin got sick, she wasn't really a very good student, but she decided to change. She studied every weekend, and she also studied with a tutor after school. Finally, she <u>was able to</u> catch up with the other students. She studied hard every day, and after high school she went to a very good university. I was very surprised.

C

My Cousin's Challenge	
Challenges	**Actions**
got sick; was in the hospital; couldn't go to school for a month; wasn't able to sit up; couldn't do any homework; didn't know how to do math problems; was behind in all her courses	decided to change; studied every weekend; studied with a tutor after school; caught up with the other students; studied hard every day; went to a very good university

2 BEFORE YOU WRITE, page 371   15 min.

- **Alternative Activity:** Students may want to write about challenges that they faced academically or difficulties that their parents had in their lives. Have students brainstorm by asking, *Think of a situation when you couldn't do something that you wanted to do. Why couldn't you? What did you do instead?* Then have students fill in the chart.

- **Tip:** This topic is often asked in applications for college or jobs. If this is relevant for your students, suggest that they write about themselves rather than someone else.

3 WRITE, page 371   20 min.

> **WRITING FOCUS, page 371**
>
> Show students a paragraph that has no time clauses or compound sentences with *and, but,* or *so.* (You could choose and rewrite one of the paragraphs in this lesson as an example.) Discuss the paragraph. *Does it make sense? How does it sound?* Then have students rewrite the paragraph using more complex sentences.

- **Expansion Tip:** Write this prompt on the board: *Tell about a difficult situation or challenge. What happened, and how did you handle it?*

   Have students role-play answering this question in an interview for a job or school.

UNIT 11   CONNECT THE GRAMMAR TO WRITING   **119**

UNIT 12 Amazing Places
Comparative and Superlative Adjectives

Unit Opener

Photo: Ask students to read the caption. Ask, *Why is the name Horseshoe Bend? What's a horseshoe?* Ask, *What are some amazing places? What makes them amazing? Did you visit any of these places? What is your favorite place in the world?*

Location: The Colorado River runs from the Rocky Mountains in the United States to the Gulf of California in Mexico. The river has cut through many layers of rock and created beautiful canyons, including the Grand Canyon. Page, Arizona, is a small town in the desert. Many popular movies have been filmed there including *Hulk*, *Planet of the Apes*, and *Superman 3*.

Theme: Students will learn about many amazing places such as Mount Everest, the National Museum of Anthropology, and the Pyramids of Giza.

Page	Lesson	Grammar	Examples
374	1	Comparative Adjectives	Ted is **older than** his brother. The new store is **more expensive than** the old store.
383	2	Superlative Adjectives	That's **the newest** building in the city. This is **the most beautiful** park in Paris. Is that store **the best** place to shop? What is **the best** place to shop?
391	3	Possessive Pronouns; *Whose*	That car is **hers**. The book is **mine**. **Whose car** did you take?
399	**Review the Grammar**		
402	**Connect the Grammar to Writing**		

Unit Grammar Terms

comparative adjective: the form of an adjective used to talk about the difference between two people, places, or things.
➤ I'm **taller** than my mother.
➤ Canada is **larger** than Mexico.

comparison: a statement of the similarities or differences between things, ideas, or people.
➤ Mexico City is **more crowded than** Buenos Aires.

possessive pronoun: a pronoun that shows ownership or relationship: *mine, yours, his, hers, its, ours, theirs*. Possessive pronouns are used in place of a possessive adjective + noun.
➤ My sister's eyes are blue. **Mine** are brown. What color are **yours**?

superlative: the form of an adjective or adverb used to compare three or more people, places, or things.
➤ Mount Everest is **the highest** mountain in the world.
➤ Evgeny is **the youngest** student in our class.

LESSON 1 Comparative Adjectives

Student Learning Outcomes	• **Read** about the differences between Mount Everest and K2. • **Describe** differences between two people, places, and things using the comparative form of adjectives. • **Ask** *Yes/No* and information questions using the comparative form of adjectives to find out differences. • **Find** and **edit** errors with comparatives of adjectives. • **Listen** to information about two travel destinations. • **Compare** two destinations and **explain** a choice using the comparative form of adjectives.
Lesson Vocabulary	(n.) airfare (adj.) challenging (n.) length (adj.) steep (n.) attraction (n.) jungle (adj.) off season (adj.) tropical

EXPLORE

1 READ, page 374   10 min.

- Direct students to the photo. Ask, *What are they doing? What mountain are they climbing?* Discuss the caption and review the word *expedition* (from Unit 9).
- **Tip:** Before reading, have students test their knowledge by trying exercise **2** on page 375. Then have them read the article to check their answers.

Be the Expert

Mount Everest and K2 are both in the Himalayan Mountain Range. Everest is on the border of Nepal and China. K2 is about 800 miles away, on the border of Pakistan and China. Mount Everest is 29,035 feet high, and K2 is 28,250 feet high. The death rate among climbers on Everest is 4.4 percent whereas the death rate on K2 is 19.7 percent. Even so, Everest is very dangerous. In 2014, 16 Sherpas were killed in an avalanche. At that time, 39 expedition teams with almost 400 foreign climbers were waiting to attempt to climb Mount Everest.

2 CHECK, page 375   5 min.

Mount Everest: higher, more famous

K2: more difficult, more challenging, steeper, more dangerous

3 DISCOVER, page 375   5 min.

A 1. more famous than
2. more difficult; more dangerous
3. more challenging than
4. worse than

B 1. T   2. F

- **Tip:** Explain that showing how two things are different and similar is to *compare* them. Refer to the article and explain that we use the *comparative* form of adjectives to compare two things. Have students look at Chart 12.1.

LEARN

Chart 12.1, page 376   10 min.

- This chart shows the comparative form of one-syllable adjectives. The comparative of longer adjectives is dealt with in Chart 12.2.
- **Tip:** With higher-level students, you can expand on Notes 4 & 5 with pronunciation tips related to short words that end in VC and VCV. Explain that in a word ending with VCV such as *tape*, the first vowel is usually pronounced as a long vowel sound. Contrast this with the VC word *tap*.

> **REAL ENGLISH, page 376**
>
> To give additional examples of *one*, point to your book and a student's book. Ask, *Which book is older?* The student points and says, *That one is older.* Use other adjectives to point and compare objects in your room: e.g., desk – clean; book – new. (*This desk is cleaner than that one. My book is newer than that one.*)

4 page 376   5 min.

1. higher than   5. better than
2. lower than   6. shorter than
3. steeper than   7. harder than
4. worse than   8. longer

5 SPEAK, page 377   5 min.

- **Tip:** After students practice comparing other students, have them make sentences about themselves, using the adjectives in the box.

Chart 12.2, page 377

- **Notes 1 & 2:** The comparative of long adjectives with *more* + adjective is much easier for students than the adjectives ending in *y* that require a change in form. Spend extra time on Note 2.

> **REAL ENGLISH, page 377**
>
> The *-er* form of these comparatives is the preferred form, but sometimes people say *more* + these adjectives. Have students repeat the forms in the box. Then ask students to use them to compare these things: a cat and a dog (quiet); English and Chinese (simple); a hallway and a street (narrow).

6 page 377   10 min.

1. more interesting than
2. more expensive than
3. quieter than
4. more beautiful than
5. sunnier than
6. more crowded than
7. more relaxing than
8. busier than
9. noisier than
10. scarier than

- **Expansion Tip:** Say some adjectives (e.g., *easy*). Students write the comparative (*easier*). Then have students generate new sentences with two or three of the adjectives.

7 WRITE & SPEAK, page 378   10 min.

- **Tip:** Have students write their comparisons on the board after they finish speaking.

Chart 12.3, page 378

- **Tip:** Write comparative statements on the board. Elicit the questions. (e.g., write: *Boston is smaller than Chicago.* Elicit: *Which is smaller, Boston or Chicago?*)

8 page 378   10 min.

1. Which mountain is higher?
2. Which hotel is cheaper?
3. Which course is more difficult?
4. Is your new apartment bigger?
5. Is your new apartment farther away?
6. Which is worse, rain or snow?
7. Which bus stop is closer to your house?
8. Which neighborhood is safer?

- **Tip:** As you go over the answers, add specific questions to ask students about places or things they know about.

9 page 379   10 min.

1. Which is smaller, Monaco or Grenada?
2. Is Australia bigger than Russia?
3. Which is more convenient, the bus or the subway?
4. Which is nicer, your parents' house or your apartment?
5. Who is older, your brother or your sister?
6. Is your city larger than New York?
7. Which is more difficult, English or your language?
8. Which is more fun, shopping online or shopping in a store?

10 SPEAK, page 379   5 min.

- **Tip:** Have students think of additional choice questions to ask each other.

PRACTICE

11 page 380   10 min.

A
1. better
2. lower
3. cheaper
4. more crowded
5. quieter
6. colder
7. rainier
8. more interesting

122   COMPARATIVE AND SUPERLATIVE ADJECTIVES

12 EDIT, page 380 — 10 min.

- **Q:** I'd like to visit Edinburgh, Scotland. Air fares are ~~more good~~ **better** in the winter. Is the winter a good time to visit?

- **A:** Edinburgh is a great place to visit any time of the year! Of course, the temperatures in the winter are ~~cold~~ **colder** than in the summer, but it's usually not very cold. One big difference in the winter is the amount of daylight. In the winter, the days are ~~more short~~ **shorter** than in the summer.

- **Q:** Which is a better place to stay, a hotel or a bed and breakfast?

- **A:** It's usually ~~easyer~~ **easier** to meet people in a bed and breakfast, and they are often ~~cheap~~ **cheaper** than hotels. Sometimes, they are ~~more far~~ **farther** from the center of the city than hotels, so be sure to look on a map.

- **Tip:** Ask, *What do you think? Which is a better place to stay, a bed and breakfast or a hotel?* Note to students that a bed and breakfast is often called a "B and B."

13 READ, WRITE & SPEAK, page 381 — 25 min.

- **Tip:** Have students write sentences in their notebooks. After they compare their sentences with one partner, have them switch partners to ask another student their questions.

- **Alternative Writing & Speaking:** Have students write questions instead of statements and ask other students. As a follow-up, have them write a paragraph comparing the two mountains.

- **Expansion Tip:** Choose two local places that students can climb or hike (e.g., a tower, a trail, a mountain). Have them research the differences between the two places or choose one to visit and report on. As a follow-up, have students write reviews of the places.

14 LISTEN & SPEAK, page 381 — 30 min.

A *Answers will vary.*

B

	Phuket	Prague
Average rainfall each year	**62** inches (160 cm)	**20** inches (50 cm)
Average high temperature	**92** F (33C)	**80** F (27C)
Tourists	5.3 million each year	4.9 million each year

C *Answers will vary. Possible questions and answers:*

- **Q:** Which place is more interesting?
- **A:** Prague, because I like historic places.
- **Q:** Which place is more historic, Phuket or Prague?
- **A:** Prague.
- **Q:** Is Prague rainier than Phuket?
- **A:** No, it isn't.
- **Q:** Which place is closer to the mountains?
- **A:** Phuket is.

D *Answers will vary.*

15 APPLY, page 382 — 20 min.

- **Alternative Activity:** Have students make advertisements for a travel website, (e.g., *Visit Rome! It's the most beautiful place in the world. Our prices are cheaper than any others on the web*).

LESSON 2	**Superlative Adjectives**
Student Learning Outcomes	• **Read** about one of the most interesting museums in the world. • **Use** the superlative form of adjectives to describe people, places, and things. • **Ask** and **answer** questions to discover how one thing is different from others. • **Find** and **edit** errors with the superlative. • **Discuss** geography trivia. • **Listen** and **discuss** places that are the best in some way. • **Write** a "Top-ten" list for a visitor to your city.
Lesson Vocabulary	(adj.) ancient (n.) artifact (n.) exhibit (n.) mask (n.) anthropology (n.) collection (adj. & n.) jade (n.) region

EXPLORE

1 READ, page 383 — 15 min.

Be the Expert

- The National Museum of Anthropology has an outstanding collection of archaeological and anthropological artifacts that span the time from Mayan civilization to the arrival of the Spanish in Mexico. The artifacts show ancient cultures from what is now Mexico, Guatemala, Belize, and Honduras: the Teotihuacan, Toltec, Aztec, Mixtec, Zapotec, Olmec, and Maya.
- The Stone of the Sun (on page 384) has carvings on it that depict the Aztec sun god Tonatiuh and the passage of the sun god through the calendar.

- Use the photos to teach *museum, artifact, ancient,* and *jade*.
- **Tip:** Ask, *What are some museums near here? What kinds of things are in the museums? Do they have paintings? Do they have historical things?*
- **Tip:** For a higher-level class, ask, *How is this museum different from museums you know?*

2 CHECK, page 384 — 5 min.

1. Yes   2. Yes   3. Yes   4. No

3 DISCOVER, page 384 — 5 min.

A 1. the largest
2. the most interesting
3. the biggest

B 1. F   2. T

- **Tip:** As students say the answers to exercise **B**, emphasize the phrase *the way something is different from others*. Show Note 1 in Chart 12.4 and point out that the superlative is used for people, places, and things.

LEARN

Chart 12.4, page 385 — 5 min.

- **Note 1:** Students sometimes think of the superlative as a way to compare three or more things. Explain that it is really a way to describe one person, place, or thing in relation to others.
- **Tip:** Use a non-verbal gesture for "small word" to remind students if they forget to use *the* when forming superlatives.

REAL ENGLISH, page 385

To illustrate, write *I am one of the best students in the class* with the final *s* on *students* very large. Elicit and have students write additional examples with both regular and irregular plurals on the board.

4 page 385 — 5 min.

1. the largest	5. The cheapest
2. the best	6. the smallest
3. the biggest	7. the nicest
4. the oldest	8. The fastest

Chart 12.5, page 386 — 5 min.

- **Tip:** Have students quiz each other. One student says an adjective, and the other supplies the superlative form.

REAL ENGLISH, page 386

Give students a list of phrases containing the superlative + infinitive and have them provide the first part of a sentence e.g., *best place to eat, easiest language to learn.*

124   COMPARATIVE AND SUPERLATIVE ADJECTIVES

5 page 386   10 min.

1. the most modern
2. the most expensive
3. the most beautiful
4. the most interesting
5. the most famous
6. the most crowded
7. the most helpful
8. the most exciting

6 SPEAK, page 387   10 min.

- **Expansion Tip:** Ask several students to say their opinions. Ask the others, *Do you agree?* (No, I think X is the most famous place. I think X is more beautiful than Y.) Discuss why the comparative is appropriate (comparing two places).

Chart 12.6, page 387   5 min.

- Questions with the superlative are often used to ask for recommendations, e.g., *What's the best place for lunch near here?*
- **Tip:** As a follow-up, have students change question 8 using these cues: cheap, large, famous, close, expensive. (e.g., *What is the cheapest restaurant?*)

7 page 387   10 min.

1. Who is the oldest person
2. What is the best place
3. Is this supermarket the cheapest? / Is this the cheapest supermarket?
4. What is the most interesting museum
5. Who is your best friend
6. Which city is the biggest
7. Are you the youngest
8. What is the nicest restaurant

8 SPEAK, page 387   5 min.

- **Tip:** Have students report on interesting things they learned from each other.

PRACTICE

9 page 388   10 min.

1. the oldest
2. the longest
3. the earliest
4. The most important
5. The busiest
6. the newest
7. The best
8. The most popular

10 EDIT, page 388   10 min.

Every year National Geographic asks some of **the** most adventurous explorers for their ideas about the best places to have exciting experiences. Here are some of their favorites:

- The ~~better~~ **best** place to surf in the world is the Mentawai Islands in Indonesia.
- **The** most challenging place to kayak is the Yarlung Tsangpo River in the Himalayan Mountains.
- The ~~more~~ **most** difficult downhill ski race is Hahnenkamm in Austria.
- One of the hardest ~~trip~~ **trips** is across the entire Sahara Desert in North Africa.
- The most amazing place to scuba dive is in the Galápagos Islands in Ecuador.
- The ~~taller~~ **tallest** mountain in South America is Aconcagua in Argentina.
- **Expansion Tip:** Have students conduct a similar poll. They write questions to find out about other students' favorite places to go.

11 SPEAK, page 389   15 min.

B Biggest art museum: Metropolitan Museum

Highest waterfall: Angel Falls (in Venezuela)

Driest place: the Atocama Desert in Chile

Smallest country: the Vatican

Longest river: the Nile

- **Expansion Tip:** Have students write a trivia quiz about your city or country.

12 LISTEN & SPEAK, page 389   25 min.

A Conversation 1: c

Conversation 2: a

Conversation 3: b

B 1. b   2. a   3. c

C *Answers may vary. Possible answers:*

1. has some of the best museums in Europe
2. is the most famous museum in the world
3. is one of the biggest museums
4. have some of the most unusual wildlife in the world
5. has the most expensive streets to shop on
6. The richest people

13 APPLY, page 390   15 min.

- **Expansion Tip:** Have students share their "Top-ten" lists and create a poster, brochure, or slide show of information for new students or visitors. Organize the information by category (shopping, entertainment, dining, etc.), and assign each to a group of students.

LESSON 3 — Possessive Pronouns; *Whose*

Student Learning Outcomes
- **Read** about an architect's unusual buildings.
- **Use** possessive pronouns to avoid repetition of nouns.
- **Identify** referents in sentences with possessive pronouns.
- **Ask** and **answer** questions with *whose* to determine possession.
- **Find** and **edit** errors with possessive pronouns and questions with *whose*.
- **Listen** and **discuss** personal preferences about modern architects using possessive pronouns.
- **Discuss** classmates' original designs using possessive pronouns.

Lesson Vocabulary
(v.) agree	(adj.) curved	(v.) spot	(adj.) unusual
(n.) campus	(n.) opinion	(n.) style	(adj.) unique

EXPLORE

1 READ, page 391 — 15 min.

- To introduce the reading, look at the photos. Ask, *Do you like this building? Do you know who designed it?* Introduce the words *architect* and *architecture*. Ask, *Do you like modern architecture?*

Be the Expert

- There are also Gehry buildings in the Czech Republic, Germany, Switzerland, the UK, Australia, and Panama. Most are tourist attractions because they are so unusual.
- His most famous buildings include the Walt Disney Concert Hall in Los Angeles, CA; the Dancing House in Prague; and the Opus Hong Kong Tower in China. His design has also been chosen for the future Dwight D. Eisenhower Memorial in Washington, D.C.
- Adding to their unique design, Gehry buildings are often composed of unusual materials such as corrugated metal and chain link.

- **Tip:** Find photos of Gehry buildings online using the keywords *slides Gehry building*.
- **Tip:** Ask students to complete these sentences with their opinions: *Gehry is the (__est / most ___) architect I know of. His buildings are some of the ___ buidings in the world.*

2 CHECK, page 392 — 5 min.

Gehry's buildings: curved lines, bright colors, surprising colors

Other buildings: soft colors, straight lines

- **Tip:** For a higher-level class, have students make sentences with information from the chart.

3 DISCOVER, page 392 — 5 min.

A 1. b   2. c

- **Tip:** Look at these sentences in the reading and discuss why the writer uses these pronouns (to avoid repetition of *Gehry's buildings*, *Gehry's colors*, or *Gehry's*). Then have students look at the form for additional possessive pronouns in Chart 12.7.

LEARN

Chart 12.7, page 393 — 5 min.

- If necessary, review possessive adjectives in Unit 1.
- *Its* (possessive adjective) is not listed because it is not common to use a possessive pronoun for this form.
- **Tip:** Take several students' pens or books. Give back the wrong ones. Say, *This isn't Patrick's book. It isn't his. This one isn't Cally's book. It isn't hers. Is this one his book? Is it his? Is this one Cally's book? Is it hers?*

> **REAL ENGLISH,** page 393
>
> Make some comparisons with students in the class, e.g., say, *Alice's bag is bigger than my bag.* Then say, *Hers is bigger than mine.*

4 page 393 — 5 min.

1. Their buildings are traditional, but (his) are not.
2. His colors are bright and surprising, but (theirs) are different.
3. Our architecture is very different from (theirs).
4. San Francisco is my favorite city. What's (yours)?
5. His apartment is bigger than (hers).

6. That notebook isn't *his*. He took my notebook by mistake.

7. Is that my phone or *yours*?

8. Please call me on John's phone. I left *mine* at home. Here's his number.

5 page 394 5 min.

1. theirs
2. mine
3. yours
4. hers
5. theirs
6. mine
7. ours
8. yours

Chart 12.8, page 394 5 min.

- **Tip:** Point to things in the classroom. Ask, *Whose book is this?* Students answer with a possessive noun or possessive pronoun (e.g., *It's Jackie's. It's mine*).
- **Note 3:** Exercise 6 will help students work on the differences between *Whose* and *Who's*.

6 page 395 5 min.

1. Whose
2. Whose
3. Who's
4. Whose
5. Whose
6. Who's
7. Who's
8. Who's
9. Whose
10. Whose

7 page 395 5 min.

1. Whose idea was it?
2. Whose glasses are those?
3. Whose notebook is it?
4. Whose apartment is closer?
5. Whose turn is it?
6. Whose pen is that?
7. Whose phone is that?
8. Whose car is behind ours?
9. Whose computer did you use?
10. Whose book did you borrow?

8 SPEAK, page 395 10 min.

- **Expansion Tip:** Have students put some of their possessions in a pile. Have them take turns holding up objects from the pile and asking, *Whose . . . is this?* Other students answer, *It's Jane's. It's mine.*

PRACTICE

9 page 396 10 min.

1. Our
2. whose
3. our
4. Mine
5. yours
6. your
7. our
8. our
9. their
10. their
11. your
12. mine
13. whose

10 EDIT, page 396 15 min.

Meg: I just finished the design for our architecture class a few minutes ago. Did you finish ~~your~~ yours yet?

Toshi: Yes, I finished mine last night. Juan and Tony finished ~~their~~ theirs last week. They're always ahead of everyone else.

Meg: Did they show you theirs?

Toshi: No, they didn't want to show it to me because ~~my~~ mine wasn't finished yet.

Meg: I'm sure ~~their~~ theirs is good. Their designs are always really good. ~~Who's~~ Whose design is that over there?

Toshi: Oh, that's Ana's.

Meg: ~~Whose~~ Who's Ana?

Toshi: She's Diana's roommate. Her designs are always very unusual.

11 LISTEN & SPEAK, page 397 25 min.

A 1. b 2. a 3. c

B 1. Their 4. his
2. her 5. theirs
3. Hers 6. their

- **Expansion Tip:** Have students bring in photos of buildings by these architects or others. Have them compare the designs of the buildings and give opinions of which they like best and why.

12 APPLY, page 398 20 min.

- **Expansion Tip:** Show two famous paintings, one by a man and one by a woman. Have students discuss which one they like better, using possessive pronouns.
- **Alternative Writing & Speaking:** Have students prepare a presentation about a new building or development project (e.g., a park or shopping center) in their area. Have them answer these questions: *Where is this? How is it different from other buildings? Is the area different because of this building? What do you think about it?*

UNIT 12 LESSON 3

Review the Grammar UNIT 12

1 READ, WRITE & SPEAK page 399   15 min.

A
1. the most famous
2. the largest
3. the tallest
4. smaller
5. taller
6. most popular
7. betterf
8. farther
9. the oldest
10. the smallest

B *Answers will vary.*

2 EDIT, page 400   10 min.

 Mesa Verde National Park in Colorado has the most interesting ruins in the United States. They are ancient cliff dwellings—homes in cliffs. They belonged to the Anasazi people. The Anasazi were Native Americans. They were some of the ~~earlyest~~ earliest people in North America. They lived in the Mesa Verde area from 600 to 1300. The Mesa Verde Park has 600 cliff dwellings. There were two types of rooms in the dwellings. *Kivas,* or round rooms, were for families so they were ~~largest~~ larger than the other kind of room.

 Next to Mesa Verde National Park is the Ute Mountain Tribal Park. Mesa Verde is more crowded than the Ute Park, so Ute Park is sometimes a ~~best~~ better park to visit. It also has beautiful cliff dwellings. It's one of the most interesting ~~place~~ places to visit in North America.

3 LISTEN, WRITE & SPEAK, page 400   15 min.

A 1. b   2. b

B

Type	Length	Cost	Other Information
Bus Tour	4 hours	$50 each	air conditioned
Van Tour	full day	$145	lunch
Jeep Ride	NI	$100 a person	hot
Car Rental	NI	$75	NI

C *Answers will vary. Possible answers:*
1. The van tour is longer than the bus tour.
2. A car rental is cheaper than the bus tour. It's the cheapest.
3. The bus tour is more comfortable than the jeep ride. The bus tour is the most comfortable.
4. The jeep tour is the most fun. It's more fun than the other tours.
5. The van tour is the most educational. It's more educational than renting a car.
6. The van tour is more expensive than the car rental. It's the most expensive.

- **Expansion Tip:** Have students research places to visit in their city. Have them write alternative plans for making a visit there (by bus, walking, etc.). Have them present their ideas to their classmates and discuss the ideas they think are the best.

4 APPLY, page 401   25 min.

- **Tip:** Assign students different historical or well-known sites in your area for question 2 and have them report to the class.
- **Alternative Activity:** Plan a field trip in your area or assign exploration of various neighborhoods or areas in your city to groups of students. Have students plan the best time, best way to get there, etc. Have them take photos and report back to the class on their experiences.

Connect the Grammar to Writing

1 READ & NOTICE THE GRAMMAR, page 402 15 min.

A The writer compares Waikiki Beach and Waimea Beach.

B   I like to go to two different beaches in Hawaii, Waimea and Waikiki. Waimea is my favorite. It is <u>farther</u> from my home <u>than</u> Waikiki is, but it is one of <u>the most beautiful</u> beaches on the whole island.

   Sometimes the waves in Waimea are very big. Then I go to Waikiki because it's a <u>safer</u> place to swim. The waves at Waikiki are always <u>smaller than</u> the waves at Waimea. Waikiki Beach is <u>more crowded than</u> Waimea, but it is <u>closer</u> to my home, so it's <u>more convenient</u>. I'm very lucky to live in Hawaii.

C

Waimea	Waikiki
farther from home bigger waves the most beautiful	safer smaller waves more crowded closer more convenient

2 BEFORE YOU WRITE, page 403 15 min.

Answers will vary.

3 WRITE, page 403 20 min.

- **Alternative Writing:** Have students write about a travel destination. Have students read each other's descriptions and compare the places using cues, such as *interesting, easy to reach, convenient to visit,* etc.
- **Alternative Speaking:** Have students interview people outside of class about their favorite places. Have them write reports about what people told them.
- **Expansion Tip:** Have students conduct a survey of people outside of your class to find the most popular places to spend time, to visit on a holiday, and so on.

> **WRITING FOCUS,** page 403
>
> Have students close their books. Say, *Listen to two paragraphs. How are they different? Which one sounds better?* Then read the paragraph with no pronouns and the one with pronouns aloud.

- **Expansion Tip:** Choose a paragraph from this unit or elsewhere in the book. Rewrite the paragraph without pronouns and distribute a copy to each student. Have students rewrite the paragraph with the correct pronouns.
- **Expansion Tip:** Have students turn their writing from exercise **2** into a presentation with slides of the places they are comparing.

UNIT 13 Customs and Traditions

Modals: Part 2

Unit Opener

Photo: Yee Peng (or Yi Peng) is a festival of lights celebrated in Northern Thailand. Near Chiang Mai, Yee Peng is celebrated with more than a thousand lighted lanterns released in the sky. In other places in Thailand, people float lanterns on water.

Location: Chiang Mai is the name of a mountainous province in northern Thailand. It is also the name of the largest city in the province, located in a valley between mountains.

Theme: This broad theme includes a look at doing business internationally, celebrating special occasions such as weddings, and the impact of tourism and technology on disappearing cultures.

Page	Lesson	Grammar	Examples
406	1	Should/Shouldn't	You **should study** for the test. You **shouldn't go** to a party the night before a test. **Should** she **try** again?
413	2	May and Can; Have To/Don't Have To	They **can** enter now. We're ready. **May** I sit here? We **have to** leave at six-thirty. We **didn't have to** work yesterday. **Do** you **have to** work this weekend?
422	3	Can/Could/Would: Polite Requests and Offers	**Can** you open the door? **Could** you carry this for me? **Would** you like another piece of cake?
428	**Review the Grammar**		
430	**Connect the Grammar to Writing**		

Unit Grammar Terms

auxiliary verb: (also called *helping verb*) a verb used with the main verb. *Be, do, have,* and *will* are common auxiliary verbs when they are followed by another verb. Modals are also auxiliary verbs.
➢ I **am** working.
➢ He **won't** be in class tomorrow.
➢ She **can** speak Korean.

modal: an auxiliary verb that adds additional meaning to a verb such as ability or possibility. *May, might, can, could, will, would,* and *should* are common modals.
➢ You **should** eat more vegetables.
➢ Julie **can** speak three languages.
➢ He **may** be at the office. Call him.

LESSON 1 Should/Shouldn't

Student Learning Outcomes
- **Read** advice about doing business in another country.
- **Use** *should* and *shouldn't* to give advice.
- **Ask** *Yes/No* and information questions using *should*.
- **Complete** conversations with advice.
- **Listen** to information about customs in different countries.
- **Read** about intercultural interactions and **discuss** advice.
- **Write** advice about business customs in your country.

Lesson Vocabulary
(n.) advice	(n.) custom	(adv.) in the meantime	(v.) present
(n.) client	(v.) exchange	(adv.) informally	(adj.) punctual

EXPLORE

1 READ, page 406 — 10 min.

- Have students look at the photo. Ask, *What does Tokyo look like? What are the people doing in the photo on page 407? Why are they bowing to each other?*
- Elicit the meaning of *client* from the context. Ask for examples of professions who have clients (e.g., lawyers, accountants, architects).

Be the Expert

- The Tokyo Tower on the left in the photo looks very tall, but it is not the tallest tower in Japan. The Tokyo Skytree is 2080 feet (634 meters), twice the height of the Eiffel Tower. There are observation decks on both of these towers, and they also function as telecommunications towers.
- People who do business internationally try to learn about customs in the countries they travel to. In the United States, it is not necessary to take gifts when you are doing business together, but it is customary in Japan. In the USA, people are very casual about exchanging business cards. In Japan, business cards are very important, and they are treated respectfully. When people receive a business card, they hold it on the top two corners and are careful not to cover the printing on the card. They study the name and title. When they place the cards on the table, they place the card of the person highest in rank on top and put it on their card holder higher than the others.

- **Expansion Tip:** Have students role-play exchanging business cards and introducing themselves. If they are from different countries, have them share information about customs regarding business meetings in their countries.

2 CHECK, page 407 — 5 min.

Good idea: 1, 4, 5

Bad idea: 2, 3

3 DISCOVER, page 407 — 5 min.

A
1. should take
2. shouldn't keep
3. should hold
4. should place

B 1. b   2. b

- **Tip:** Remind students that modals add meaning to another verb. *Should* and *shouldn't* add the meaning of advice.

LEARN

Chart 13.1, page 408 — 5 min.

- Point out to students that there are no changes in *should* for any of the subjects and the main verb is always in the simple form.
- **Tip:** Write *good* and *should* on the board and have students say them. Check their pronunciation to make sure these words rhyme.

4 page 408 — 5 min.

1. should buy	5. shouldn't be
2. should have	6. should read
3. shouldn't keep	7. should ask
4. should bring	8. should learn

5 WRITE & SPEAK, page 408 — 5 min.

- **Tip:** To summarize exercise **5**, ask, *What is good advice for everyone?*

Chart 13.2, page 409 — 5 min.

- **Note:** There are many ways to ask someone's advice. *What should I do?* is the easiest, but we often say, *What do you think I should do?* Or *What do you think? What should I do?*

6 page 409 — 10 min.

1. Should I bring
2. Should we shake hands?
3. When should I be there?
4. What should he wear?
5. Should they call the office?
6. Who should she ask?
7. How should we get there?
8. Where should we meet?
9. Should she be on time?
10. Why should we arrive early?

- **Tip:** Provide cues for problems (e.g., *I feel sick*). One student asks for advice and another gives advice. (e.g., Student A: I feel sick. *What should I do?* Student B: You should stay home.) Additional cues: have a headache, can't sleep, have a test tomorrow, don't understand the homework, etc.

PRACTICE

7 page 410 — 10 min.

1. You shouldn't be
2. I should be
3. Should I take
4. You should ask
5. should I ask
6. should you wear
7. should I call
8. You should look
9. I should buy
10. we should hurry

8 READ, WRITE & SPEAK, page 411 — 10 min.

A
1. Should she explain his mistake?
2. How should she greet them?
3. Should they say "No, thank you"?
4. When should they talk about business?
5. Should she say something?

B Answers will vary.

- **Tip:** Ask students, *What customs are different in Canada and the country Chris is visiting? Are customs in your country similar to Canada or the other country?*

9 LISTEN & WRITE, page 411 — 10 min.

A

	South Africa	Thailand	USA
1.			✓
2.	✓		
3.	✓		
4.		✓	
5.		✓	
6.		✓	

B Answers will vary. Possible answers:

1. you should be exactly on time or early for a meeting
2. you shouldn't talk business too soon
3. you shouldn't put someone's business card in your pocket
4. you shouldn't use your left hand to give something
5. you shouldn't touch someone's head or pass anything above someone's head
6. you shouldn't show the bottom of your foot

10 APPLY, page 412 — 20 min.

- **Tip:** Suggest that students think about actions and also nonverbal gestures, e.g., standing with hands in their pockets, crossing their arms in front of them, slouching, eye contact, and so on.
- **Alternative Writing & Speaking:** Have students write situations similar to those in exercise **8**. Have them show the situations to other students and ask students to give advice about the situations.
- **Expansion Tip:** Have students look online for cultural customs around the world and report back to the class two interesting things they learned.

LESSON 2   May and Can; Have To; Don't Have To

Student Learning Outcomes
- **Read** a blog about unusual laws.
- **Use** *can, can't,* and *may* to express or ask for permission.
- **Use** *have to* and *don't have to* to express necessity or lack of necessity.
- **Ask** and **answer** questions about customs, laws, and rules.
- **Find** and **edit** errors with *can* and *have to*.
- **Listen** to information about wedding customs in India.
- **Write** about and **discuss** wedding customs in different countries using *can, can't, have to,* and *don't have to.*

Lesson Vocabulary
(n.) approval	(adj.) dirty	(p.) in between	(n.) reason
(v.) arranged	(adj.) historic	(n.) law	(adj.) upside down

EXPLORE

1 READ, page 413   20 min.
- Point out the photo on page 413. Ask, *Is it OK for women to do this in every (your) country?*

Be the Expert
- Sometimes laws are passed and then never reviewed for relevance as times change. Other laws are appropriate in certain countries, but seem extreme to people in different cultures. For example, in a town in Connecticut, it's illegal to walk backwards on a street after dark. In movie theaters in Thailand, everyone has to stand up for the national allegiance before the film starts. In a beach town near Venice, Italy, people can't take shells or build sandcastles. In Paraguay, it's apparently legal to duel, but the duelers have to be registered blood donors.

- **Tip:** Search for more unusual laws on the Internet. Have students comment on the laws. Write typical comments on the board: *That makes/doesn't make sense. That's funny/crazy/interesting. Is that still true? That's not true. Really? I don't believe that.*
- **Expansion Tip:** Look at the photo on page 414. Discuss the types of shoes in the photo (heels, flats, etc.). Ask about customs related to shoes: *Can young girls wear heels? Is it OK to show bare toes in every country?* Expand this to discuss customs regarding clothing: *What are some rules about clothing in different countries?* For example, in Italy women can't wear sleeveless clothes in churches.

2 CHECK, page 414   5 min.
1. b   2. a   3. d   4. c   5. e

3 DISCOVER, page 414   5 min.

A 1. can wear, can't wear
   2. cannot parachute
   3. can't drive

B c

- **Tip:** In Unit 11, students learned that *can/can't* is used to express ability. Show the difference between ability and permission. On the board, write: *I can swim. I can't speak Italian. I can't use my phone in class. We can't speed in a school zone.* For each statement, ask, *Is this ability, or is it a rule or law?*

LEARN

Chart 13.3, page 415   10 min.
- **Notes 1 & 4:** Traditionally, *may* was used to ask for permission. However, most people use *can* now.
- **Note 5:** It is grammatically correct to say, *Yes, you may* or *Yes, you can* to respond to requests for permission, but it is not common and sounds very formal. Students may notice that we teach questions with *may,* but not statements. This is because it is uncommon to use *may* for permission in a statement. (See Unit 14, Lesson 3 for the use of *may* and *might* in statements about possibility.)
- **Tip:** For higher-level students, teach an additional way to ask permission: *Is it OK if I/we . . . ?*

REAL ENGLISH, page 415
Give additional prompts for students to practice such as *borrow your book, use your eraser, talk to you after class.*

4 page 416 5 min.

1. You can't drive
2. people can change
3. people can vote
4. You can't travel
5. people can bring
6. You can't park
7. You can't take
8. We can drink coffee

5 page 416 5 min.

1. May I sit
2. Can my brother come
3. Can I have
4. Can I bring
5. When can we eat
6. Can I take
7. Where can we park
8. Why can't we go

- **Tip:** Have students practice the conversations in exercise **5**.
- **Expansion Tip:** Give students prompts to use in short requests for permission: *leave class now, use my cell phone in class, go home early today, go to the restroom*. Have them work in pairs to ask and respond.

Chart 13.4, page 417 10 min.

- **Note 1:** Students sometimes don't hear *has to* and *have to* because the stress is usually on the main verb. Model pronunciation of the example sentences.
- **Note 2:** *Have to* is sometimes called a *semi-modal* or a *phrasal modal* because it changes form and is followed by *to* + verb. However, it is a modal in the sense that it adds meaning to the main verb.
- **Notes 3 & 5:** Students who have studied British English may have learned the negation of *have* as *haven't* (*I haven't any cash.*). If so, they may want to say *I haven't to work on Sunday*. Point out that this is incorrect. *I don't have to work on Sunday* is correct and expresses lack of necessity.
- Students may ask about the use of *have got to*. It has the same meaning as *have to*. The contraction is often used (e.g., *I've got to leave now. They've got to hurry*). It is not used in the negative and is lower frequency than *have to* in questions.

REAL ENGLISH, page 417

Point out that it is not common to use *must* in spoken English unless someone is stating a law or rule. For example, on airplanes, flight attendants say, *Passengers must fasten their seat belts for takeoff and landing. Cell phones must be in airplane mode.*

- **Tip:** For higher-level students, explain that *must* is more common in the passive voice. (e.g., *Carry-on bags must be stowed securely.*) Elicit additional examples.

6 page 417 5 min.

1. have to hurry
2. have to catch
3. have to work
4. has to come
5. don't have to pay
6. don't have to make
7. have to study
8. have to get up

7 WRITE & SPEAK, page 417 5 min.

- **Tip:** As you listen to students speak, help them put the stress on the important words in their sentences: *I have to go to the doctor. I don't have to cook tonight.*

Chart 13.5, page 418 10 min.

- Use a nonverbal cue such as your fingers showing a small word and switching positions over your other hand to show the use of an auxiliary verb in question formation.
- **Tip:** Give students short prompts and ask them to make a *yes/no* question with *Do you have to...*, for example, *study tonight, cook dinner tonight, do homework every night*.
- **Expansion Tip:** Write *parents* and *children* on the board. Have students help you write a list of the differences in their responsibilities, e.g., *go to work, do homework, clean the house, go to school, pay bills, study*, etc. Then have students ask each other *Yes/No* questions. (E.g., *Do parents have to go to work? Yes, they do. Do children have to go to work? No, they don't.*)

8 page 418 10 min.

1. Why does he have to wear a suit?
2. When does Nasir have to leave?
3. Do I have to ask my manager?
4. Where does she have to go next week?
5. Do you have to study tonight?
6. Do we have to bring our books to class?
7. What do we have to bring to the exam?
8. Who do you have to call after class?
9. Does Lily have to give her presentation today?
10. What does Rosa have to do tomorrow?

9 SPEAK, page 419 — 10 min.

- **Tip:** Give students time to write notes for this activity before they practice. After they finish, ask a couple of students, *What does [your partner] have to do tonight?* Listen for the *-s* ending on *has to*.

PRACTICE

10 page 419 — 10 min.

1. can't
2. have to
3. don't have to
4. can
5. Can
6. have to
7. has to
8. doesn't have to
9. has to
10. has to

11 EDIT, WRITE & SPEAK, page 420 — 25 min.

A Can my bride make all the decisions about our wedding, or does she ~~has~~ **have** to think about my ideas, too? My fiance, Sally, wants to get married on a beach in Hawaii. My mother is very unhappy about this. My mother says, "You **can't** ~~to get~~ married on a beach! The wedding can't be in Hawaii. You ~~has~~ **have** to get married close to home. Sally ~~haves~~ **has** to think about our family, too." Sally says, "A wedding can be anywhere. It **doesn't have** to be indoors. It's my wedding, so I **should** ~~to~~ decide. My opinion should be the most important."

B *Answers will vary. Possible answers:*

Jeff's Mother's Opinions	Sally's Opinions
A wedding can't be on a beach. The wedding can't be in Hawaii. You have to get married close to home. Sally has to think about our family, too.	A wedding can be anywhere. It doesn't have to be indoors. I can decide. My opinion is the most important.

12 LISTEN & SPEAK, page 420 — 25 min.

A 1. b   3. c
     2. d   4. a

B 1. have to wait
     2. doesn't have to do
     3. doesn't have to wear
     4. have to exchange
     5. has to put
     6. have to walk

13 APPLY, page 421 — 25 min.

- **Tip:** If your students are from different countries, put them in groups to discuss wedding customs.
- **Expansion Tip:** Watch the wedding scene of a movie. (Possible movies include *27 Dresses*, *My Big Fat Greek Wedding*, or *Four Weddings and a Funeral*.) Use the scene to review simple past and past progressive as well as modals.
- **Expansion Tip:** Assign each student a country to research for wedding customs. Have students present their information to a group or the class.

LESSON 3 | Can/Could/Would: Polite Requests and Offers

Student Learning Outcomes	• **Read** a conversation between a professor and a student about cultural differences disappearing. • **Make** polite requests using *can you, could you,* and *would you.* • **Make** polite offers using *can I, could I,* and *would you like.* • **Complete** conversations using polite requests or offers. • **Rewrite** conversations that are too direct with more appropriate language. • **Read** situations and **role-play** conversations with requests and offers.
Lesson Vocabulary	(n.) attraction (adj.) cultural (v.) disappear (v.) recommend (n.) contact (adv.) definitely (n.) lecture (adj.) remote

EXPLORE

1 READ, page 422   15 min.

- Explain that the men in the photos are from different *tribes* in Vanuatu, an island nation in the South Pacific. They are performing traditional dances for tourists. Ask, *Do you think they still do these traditional dances when tourists are not watching?*

Be the Expert

- Professors at colleges and universities usually have doctorate degrees. Students usually call them Professor, but they can also be addressed as Doctor. In the USA, most high school teachers do not have doctorate degrees. Their students address them by their last names with *Mr.* or *Ms.* They do not call their teachers "Teacher."

- Vanuatu is an island nation in the South Pacific. Most of the 83 islands are very mountainous because they were formed by volcanoes. This means there are many areas that are difficult to reach, and tribes in remote areas developed their own customs and traditions. In fact, there are over 120 different languages spoken. Many tribes in Vanuatu offer cultural village experiences where tourists can see demonstrations of ancient ways of life and traditional dances.

- **Expansion Tip:** Have students find photos or videos of cultural tours offered to tourists by searching online for *Vanuatu travel cultural tours*. Then discuss the impact of tourism on traditional culture, e.g., *What are the advantages and disadvantages of tourism for remote villages? Would you like to visit Vanuatu? Why, or why not?*

2 CHECK, page 423   5 min.

    1. a   2. a   3. b   4. a   5. b

- **Tip:** Ask, *Do students sometimes talk to their teacher after a class? How are their conversations similar or different from this conversation?*

3 DISCOVER, page 423   5 min.

    1. T   2. F   3. T

- **Tip:** *Could* is sometimes used to discuss possibility, but in this conversation, *can* and *could* are used to make a polite request. Point out that the student never used *please* in the conversation and go through the notes in Chart 13.6.

LEARN

Chart 13.6, page 424   5 min.

- **Notes 1 & 2:** The use of modals *can* and *could* to express ability was introduced in Unit 11, so students will be familiar with the forms of statements and questions.

- **Note 3:** Explain that the past form *could* is more polite than *can,* but the use of *please* adds a degree of politeness to a request with *can.* If students ask, explain that we use *would* when the request is not unexpected by the person we are asking. For example, *Could you help me with my suitcase?* is appropriate for a stranger on an airplane. *Would you help me with my suitcase?* is appropriate for a friend or family member who might be expected to help.

- **Note 4:** Responses to an affirmative request are usually short, e.g., *Sure./Of course./No problem.* Negative responses require an apology or an explanation. Without this, a negative response sounds rude.

> **REAL ENGLISH, page 424**
>
> Model a request and a negative response followed by *Thanks anyway*. This usually follows a negative response when someone apologizes or seems sorry for not having been able to accommodate the request.

4 page 424   10 min.

Answers will vary. Possible answers:

1. Could you give me some ideas for my project?
2. Could you explain the answer, please?
3. Could you tell me about the article?
4. Could you repeat the question?
5. Can you please show me that website?
6. Would you help me with the assignment?
7. Could you do some research for me?
8. Could you recommend some books about your country?

5 page 425   5 min.

- **Tip:** Remind students to use *Thanks, anyway* when someone has refused their request.

Chart 13.7, page 425   5 min.

- **Tip:** Pantomime situations for students to make offers, e.g., carrying a heavy bag, having trouble opening the window.

6 page 425   5 min.

1. Can I help
2. Can I make
3. Would you like
4. Can I help
5. Would you like
6. Can I get
7. Would you like
8. Can I give

- **Alternative Speaking & Writing:** Put the offers and responses on small pieces of paper and give one to each student. The students with offers walk around saying them until they find the student with the response. Then they write the conversation on the board.

7 SPEAK, page 425   5 min.

PRACTICE

8 page 426   10 min.

1. b	3. f	5. a	7. c
2. d	4. h	6. g	8. e

9 SPEAK, page 426   10 min.

- **Expansion Tip:** After students practice the conversations from exercise **8**, have them make up their own answers for Speaker B.

10 WRITE, LISTEN & SPEAK, page 426   10 min.

1. **Jessie:** You always tell me such interesting things about Panama. I'd like to go there some time. <u>Give me</u> some suggestions about places to see.

   Felipe: Oh. <u>What do you want</u>? The names of my favorite places?

   Jessie: Yes. <u>Tell me</u> the name of a hotel, too.

   Felipe: Sure. <u>Let me know</u> if you have any other questions.

   Jessie: Great. Thanks, Felipe!

2. **Agent:** Hello. Adventure Travel Company. <u>Do you want help</u>?

   Hans: Yes, <u>I want</u> some information about tours to the South Pacific.

   Agent: <u>Hold on</u> for a minute.

   Hans: OK.

   Agent: Hello, I'm back. Now, <u>give me your name.</u>

B *Answers will vary. Possible answers:*

1. Could you give me some suggestions for places to see? Would you like the names of my favorite places? Could you tell me the name of a hotel, too?

2. Can I help you? Yes, I'd like some information about tours to the South Pacific. Could you hold on for a minute, please? Now, could you please give me your name?

- **Alternative:** Ask, *What are some typical situations when you need to make requests?* Have students think of two situations and write short dialogs.

11 APPLY, page 427   10 min.

- **Alternative Writing & Speaking:** Set up "stations" in different parts of the classroom with short situations for students to read. Have students write the appropriate request and offer for each.

Review the Grammar UNIT 13

1 page 428   15 min.

Answers will vary. Possible answers:

1. Would
2. Can/Could
3. have to
4. can/could
5. Can/Could
6. should
7. can't/shouldn't
8. Can/Could

- **Expansion Tip:** Have students write conversations in a hotel, taxi, or tourist information center that include the functions in this unit: asking for advice, expressing necessity or lack of necessity, requests, and offers.

2 EDIT, page 428   10 min.

Hi Patricia,

After you told me about your trip to Papua New Guinea, I decided to plan a trip there, too! Could you ~~to~~ give me some tips? Here are some questions:

- ~~Have I to~~ Do I have to get a visa?
- Where should I ~~should~~ stay?
- What about clothing? Can women wear shorts?

Thanks for any suggestions!

Best,

Donna

Hi Donna,

That's exciting! Papua New Guinea is amazing. ~~Could~~ Would you like to have lunch next week? I have a lot of information for you. Yes, you have to get a visa. I went with a tour group. I think you should ~~to~~ go with a tour group, too. On a tour, you ~~haven't~~ don't have to worry about hotels or transportation. Also, ~~would like you to~~ would you like to borrow some guide books? I have a few really good ones. See you soon!

3 LISTEN, WRITE & SPEAK, page 429   25 min.

A
1. F
2. T
3. F
4. F
5. T

B
1. don't have to
2. have to
3. can't
4. should
5. don't have to
6. can't
7. have to
8. don't have to

C *Answers will vary.*

- **Expansion Tip:** Have students research and prepare a presentation about a challenge for indigenous or remote cultures, e.g., vanishing languages, changes in traditional lifestyle, changes in homeland, lack of political power, or health.

Connect the Grammar to Writing

1 READ AND NOTICE THE GRAMMAR, page 430   15 min.

B Dear Ms. Glenn,

I have to take my daughter to her school, so I can't meet with you this morning. I'm very sorry. <u>Could you meet with me</u> after class tomorrow?

I'm having trouble with questions, especially questions with *who*. <u>Can you help me</u> with this? I'm also having trouble with the present progressive. <u>Would you please show me</u> some more examples?

Thank you.

C

Requests
Could you meet with me after class tomorrow?
Can you help me with this?
Would you please show me some more examples?

2 BEFORE YOU WRITE, page 431   15 min.

- **Alternative Writing:** Have students write e-mail messages to an advice columnist. In the e-mails, they should describe a problem and ask for advice, including a request. Have students respond to each other's writing with advice.

3 WRITE, page 431   20 min.

> **WRITING FOCUS, page 403**
>
> Show students an e-mail similar to the example below that is extremely direct. Have them rewrite it to be more appropriate. Show examples of how students revised the e-mail to the class and vote on the most appropriate one.

Teacher,

Here is my paragraph. Correct it.

Also, I need an appointment to talk with you on Monday morning.

Michael

UNIT 14 Education and Learning

The Future

Unit Opener

Photo: Ask students to read the caption. Ask, *What is on the wall? Do you think the boy can see? Why or why not?*

Location: The Roosevelt Memorial in Washington, DC, displays many achievements of Franklin D. Roosevelt. This wall allows people with visual disabilities to read about the president and the people he helped during his presidency. Roosevelt himself was disabled by polio.

Theme: Students will read about different types of learning experiences, including study abroad and online learning.

Page	Lesson	Grammar	Examples
434	1	Future with *Be Going To* and Present Progressive	I'm **going to study** in Japan next year. What **are** they **going to do** tomorrow? I'm **leaving** tomorrow. **Is** she **coming** tonight?
443	2	Future with *Will*; Possibility with *May/Might*	In five years, I'**ll be** 30. Who **will be** there? I **may/might go** to the game tonight.
452	3	*If* Clauses; Future Time Clauses	You'll get a good grade **if you study hard**. **If I have time before class,** I usually go to the library. **After I finish my homework,** I'm going to go to the gym. **When we graduate,** we'll have a party.
460	Review the Grammar		
462	Connect the Grammar to Writing		

Unit Grammar Terms

conditional: a structure used to talk about an activity or event that depends on something else.
> *If the weather is nice on Sunday,* we'll go to the beach.

future: a verb form that expresses an action or situation that has not happened yet. *Will, be going to,* the present progressive, and the simple present are used to express the future.
> *We're going to go* to the movies tomorrow.
> *I'm taking* French next semester.

time clause: a clause that tells when an action or event happened or will happen. Time clauses are introduced by conjunctions such as *when, after, before,* and *while.*
> *I'm going to call my parents after I eat dinner.*
> *I called my parents when I got home.*

LESSON 1 — Future with *Be Going To* and Present Progressive

Student Learning Outcomes
- **Read** about an unusual school.
- **Ask** *Yes/No* and information questions using *be going to* and the present progressive for future.
- **Listen** and **discriminate** between present and future.
- **Find** and **edit** errors with *be going to* and the present progressive for future.
- **Listen** and **discuss** graduates' future plans.
- **Write** questions and opinions about future plans.

Lesson Vocabulary
| (adj.) abroad | (n.) clinic | (n.) experience | (v.) register |
| (n.) cancellation | (n.) community service | (n.) major | (n.) semester |

EXPLORE

1 READ, page 434 — 10 min.
- Direct students to the photo. Ask, *How are a sailboat and a health clinic connected to education? What do you think the "unusual college experience" is going to be?*
- **Tip:** After reading, ask, *What is/was your major? Can/Could you study it on a boat? Is community service common for people in your country/culture?*

Be the Expert
- About 250,000 college students in the United States study abroad, either for a semester or for a year, and get academic credit for their courses. Although the number has tripled over the past twenty years,* this is less than 10 percent of college students in the United States. More than half study in Europe. About 15 percent study in Latin America, and approximately 12 percent study in Asia. The most popular places to study abroad are the United Kingdom, Italy, and Spain.
- It is not very common to study on a boat, but several programs do exist. Most are sailboats, but one program is on a 590-foot cruise ship that goes all over the world.

- **Expansion Tip:** Search *study abroad academic programs at sea* to find photos and blogs about programs.
- **Expansion Tip:** View and discuss as a class infographic data on international students from the Institute of International Education website.

*The Institute of International Education. (Nov. 11, 2013). *Open Doors,* 2013. Retrieved May 10, 2014, from http://www.iie.org/en/Research-and-Publications/Open-Doors/Data

2 CHECK, page 435 — 5 min.
Yes: 3, 4, 5
No: 1, 2, 6

3 DISCOVER, page 435 — 5 min.

A
1. Are, going to take
2. 'm not going to be
3. 'm spending
4. 'm going to do
5. 'm going to do
6. are, going to do

B c

- **Tip:** With higher-level students, say, *Tell me about Hannah. What are her plans?* (*She's going to study on a boat. She's spending a semester on a boat.*) Say that in English we use several different forms to talk about the future, including *be going to* and the present progressive. Have students look at Chart 14.1 to examine the use of *be going to*.

LEARN

Chart 14.1, page 436
- **Tip:** To illustrate *be going to* in predictions, ask, *What's the weather prediction for today/tomorrow/next week?* Students respond. (e.g., *It's going to be nice. I think it's going to rain.*)

REAL ENGLISH, page 436
Give additional examples with *be going to,* stressing the information after *be going to*: *I'm gonna **go now**. She's gonna **come** with **us**.* Tell students that the reduction happens naturally because these words do not have stress in the sentence. Point out how strange it sounds to stress *gonna*: *My professor is not . . . **gonna** . . . give us a test tomorrow.*

4 page 436 — 5 min.

1. is going to have
2. 's going to be
3. 's going to study
4. are going to take
5. 're going to travel
6. 'm going to do
7. 's not going to be
8. 're going to graduate in

5 SPEAK, page 436 — 5 min.

- **Tip:** After students discuss, have them share information about their partners with the class, e.g., *Clara isn't going to take another English course.*

Chart 14.2, page 437

- **Note 1:** Use a nonverbal cue to illustrate the movement of the helping verb *be* before the subject in questions.
- **Tip:** Ask questions to practice, e.g., *Are we going to have a test tomorrow? No, we aren't. Are you going to do your homework tonight? Yes, I am. / Yes, we are.*

6 page 437 — 10 min.

1. What are they going to do?
2. Are you going to be on campus tomorrow?
3. What is she going to study next semester?
4. Are you going to take French next semester?
5. How are you going to get there?
6. Is our teacher going to give us a test tomorrow?
7. When is this course going to end?
8. What are you going to do tonight?
9. When are you going to go on vacation?
10. Is it going to rain tonight?

7 SPEAK, page 438 — 5 min.

- **Tip:** Have students think of one additional question to ask each other.
- **Expansion Tip:** Imagine a special $50,000 prize has been awarded to your students. Have students brainstorm ideas on what they are going to do with it. They can tell a partner, or you can do a circle memory game where each student says the previous student's plan and adds his or her own, e.g., *Gail is going to study art in Italy. I'm going to give my money to poor people.*

Chart 14.3, page 438

- **Note 1:** After you present the note, say, *These verbs are often used with present progressive for future because they're related to travel or visits, and they are often arranged ahead of time.*
- **Note 2:** Elicit or explain that the *context* is the situation or setting.

> **REAL ENGLISH, page 438**
>
> Give an additional example such as *My favorite TV show is on at 9:00 tomorrow night.* Then give cues for students to say more examples:
>
> *Tomorrow/class/begin. . .*
>
> *Next quarter/classes/start. . .*

8 page 438 — 10 min.

1. isn't taking; next semester
2. 're starting; next week
3. are coming; in a couple of weeks
4. 's not starting; this year
5. 'm studying; next year
6. isn't offering; next semester
7. 's graduating; in June
8. 're not going; tomorrow night

9 page 439 — 10 min.

1. Are you taking
2. When is Pedro giving
3. Are we starting
4. Who is teaching
5. Where is she studying
6. Is she arriving
7. Why is he leaving
8. How are you getting

10 SPEAK, page 439 — 5 min.

- **Tip:** Remind students that they should talk about plans they have already made arrangements for. Otherwise, they would use *be going to*.

PRACTICE

11 page 439   10 min.
Present: 2, 3, 8, 10
Future: 1, 4, 5, 6, 7, 9

12 EDIT, page 440   10 min.

Our college ~~having~~ **is going to have** a new program next fall. Five students are going to go to Scotland in September. They **are** going to study at the University of Edinburgh. They **are going to** stay in dormitories on campus. Everyone is very excited about this new program.

We are not ~~send~~ **sending / going to send** students to study in Turkey this year. We only received one application for the program. However, we **are going to** offer it again next year.

We **are** moving to the new Student Union Building on August 1, so the office **is** not going to be open from July 30 until August 1.

13 page 440   10 min.

1. Are you going to take / Are you taking
2. I'm going to take
3. are you going to do / are you doing
4. I'm going to study
5. You're going to love
6. It's going to rain
7. I'm going to go / I'm going
8. I'm going to meet / I'm meeting
9. We're going to go / We're going
10. are you going to see

14 SPEAK, page 441   10 min.

- **Tip:** Put students in two lines, so they face each other to have these conversations. After a few minutes, move the person from the head of one line to the end so that everyone has a new partner. After three different partners, have everyone sit down again. Ask each person to report on the plans of the last person he or she spoke to.

15 LISTEN, WRITE & SPEAK, page 441   10 min.

A

	Sonya	Trey	Mylo
1.		✓	
2.	✓		
3.			✓
4.			✓
5.	✓		

B
1. What is Trey going to do next year?
2. When are they going to graduate? / When are they graduating?
3. Where is Trey going to study?
4. Is Sonya going to go to college next year? / Is Sonya going to college next year?
5. Who is going to work?
6. Why is Mylo going to visit India?
7. What is Sonya going to teach in Kenya?
8. What is Sonya going to do in Nairobi?
9. Where is Sonya going to live in Kenya?
10. Are Mylo and Sonya going to go to college?

16 APPLY, page 442

- **Tip:** Have someone from each group report on the group's opinions.
- **Alternative Speaking & Writing:** Give students ten minutes to plan a six- to ten-week activity that includes a course of some kind and also community service. Ask, *Where are you going to go? What are you going to do?* Have students report to the class. If necessary, provide a model to get them started (e.g., *Here is my plan. I am going to go to . . . and . . . Then I'm going to . . .*).

LESSON 2	Future with *Will*; Possibility with *May/Might*
Student Learning Outcomes	• **Read** about the impact that online learning may have on education. • **Complete** sentences with *will* and *won't* to make predictions, offers, and promises. • **Ask** and **answer** questions about the future with *will*. • **Discuss** possibility with *may* and *might*. • **Find** and **edit** errors with *will*, *won't*, *may*, *maybe*, and *might*. • **Listen** to people discuss opinions about online courses. • **Discuss** opinions on and experiences with online learning.
Lesson Vocabulary	(n.) access (n.) concept (n.) expert (n.) population (adj.) basic (v.) direct (n.) hybrid (n.) role

EXPLORE

1 READ, page 443   15 min.

Be the Expert

- Although the popularity of MOOCs (Massive Open Online Courses) has decreased a bit, online learning is still growing quickly. In 2013, 4.6 out of every 10 college students were taking an online course. This is expected to double by 2020. The money spent on e-learning worldwide is also expected to double from its current $56 billion.

- **Tip:** Ask, *Do you take any online courses? Did you in the past?* Discuss any online learning opportunities associated with your course.
- To reinforce the meaning, ask, *Do we have* **access** *to computers in class? Do you have access at home?*
- **Tip:** Stop the audio at the question, *"What do you think?"* and ask students the questions that follow. Take a class vote.

2 CHECK, page 444   5 min.

1. d   2. b   3. a   4. c   5. e

3 DISCOVER, page 444   5 min.

A 1. will be   3. may not be
    2. may change   4. might not need; might learn

B 1. F   2. T

- **Tip:** With higher-level students, show the reading in Lesson 1 about Hannah's plans. Ask, *Why do we use* be going to *and present progressive here, but not in the article about online learning? What do we use* will *for? Are* may *and* might *as definite as* will *and* won't? Move on to Note 2 in Chart 14.4 to show when we use *will* and *won't*.

LEARN

Chart 14.4, page 445

- **Tip:** Write *Modals* above this list on the board: *can, could, should*. Ask, *What form of the verb follows a modal?* (the base form) *And the base form follows* will, *too*. Write *will* at the end of the list. Ask, *What's the negative of will?* (will not/won't)

- **Tip:** Because students' languages may have one way to talk about the future instead of many, they may be tempted to use *will* to talk about plans. Reiterate that we don't use *will* to talk about plans (except if we use *probably*, which is the Real English note).

REAL ENGLISH, page 445

Explain that the future is rarely 100 percent certain so we hedge by saying *probably*. Give additional examples: *I'll probably live until I'm 80 or 90. I probably won't live until I'm 100.* Tell students they can use *I'll probably. . .* to talk about possible plans, but for definite plans, they will say, *I'm going to go. . .* or *I'm going. . .*

4 page 445   5 min.

1. will take   7. 'll help
2. will be   8. won't know
3. 'll send   9. will tell
4. will make   10. won't be
5. won't teach   11. 'll call
6. will send   12. 'll get

5 page 446 — 5 min.
1. I'll see
2. there will be
3. I'll drive
4. It'll make
5. I'll be
6. I'll call
7. You won't remember
8. It'll help
9. I'll do
10. I'll e-mail

6 SPEAK, page 446 — 5 min.
- **Tip:** If students use *will* for plans, remind them to use *be going to* instead, or to add *probably*.

Chart 14.5, page 447 — 5 min.
- **Note 2:** Point out that we often also ask a short question, *Why not?* following negative statements in various tenses, for example, **A:** *I won't be in class tomorrow.* **B:** *Why not?*

7 page 447 — 10 min.
1. Will we be late?
2. Will the teacher be there at 9:00?
3. When will we get our tests back?
4. Will the test be difficult?
5. Will you help me?
6. Who will they talk to?
7. Who will take notes?
8. Where will the lecture be?
9. Will you be absent tomorrow?
10. Will there be a final exam?

8 SPEAK, page 448 — 10 min.

Chart 14.6, page 448 — 10 min.
- **Note 1:** Explain that the distinction between present and future with *may* and *might* is clear from the context. There is no difference in form.
- **Note 2:** Explain that we use *might* more than *may*, especially in conversation. *May* is more formal.

9 page 449 — 5 min.
1. may study
2. may not come
3. may have
4. may rain
5. might be
6. might not be
7. might not go
8. might take

10 page 449 — 5 min.
1. a 2. b 3. a 4. b 5. a 6. a 7. b 8. a

11 SPEAK, page 449 — 5 min.

PRACTICE

12 page 450 — 20 min.
A
1. will
2. will this
3. will
4. won't
5. may
6. save
7. won't
8. may be
9. review
10. may be

B
1. When will online classes start?
2. Will the change help the college?
3. Who won't need to come to campus?
4. When will the college review the online program?
5. Will the college spend less on classes?
6. Will classes be more expensive?
7. Will the college need more instructors?
8. Will more students take online classes?

- **Alternative Speaking & Writing:** Have pairs write an announcement about an imaginary change in policies at your program; for example, free tuition or shorter/longer class periods. As they read their announcements aloud, have classmates ask questions about the changes and their impact.

13 EDIT, page 450 — 10 min.

Kerry: Hey, did you hear the news? Next year a lot of our courses will be online.

Justin: Really? That's great! It'll be easier for me. I ~~mightn't~~ might not need to come to campus as often. Will many first-year courses be online?

Kerry: Yes, they ~~'ll~~ will. We won't ~~has~~ have those huge lecture classes anymore, the ones with 600 students. Students will ~~listening~~ listen online. In a few years, all classes ~~maybe~~ may be online.

Justin: Online classes, that's intererresting. Everyone might ~~has~~ have more free time.

Kerry: That's true. ~~May be~~ Maybe I won't have any 8:30 classes!

14 LISTEN & SPEAK, page 451 — 25 min.
A 1. a 2. b
B 1. won't learn as much 3. may/might lose
2. won't need as many

15 APPLY, page 451 — 15 min.
- **Expansion Tip:** Ask, *Do you agree or disagree with these statements? Online language courses will replace face-to-face courses. In ten years, most college courses will be online.*

UNIT 14 LESSON 2 **145**

LESSON 3 | *If* Clauses; Future Time Clauses

Student Learning Outcomes
- **Read** a conversation about the effect of color on test scores.
- **Use** *if* clauses to present conditions and results related to facts, habits, and future events.
- **Use** time clauses with *before, after,* and *when* to discuss facts, habits, and future events.
- **Talk** about future plans.
- **Listen** to complete information about plans.
- **Discuss** opinions using conditional and time clauses.
- **Write** reasons to support a recommendation for a change in a program.

Lesson Vocabulary

(n.) booklet	(n.) entrance exam	(v.) focus	(n.) reward
(n.) effort	(adj.) final	(adv.) on one's own	(n.) score

EXPLORE

1 READ, page 452 — 15 min.

- **Tip:** Before reading, try an experiment. Give half the class a quiz using red font or with a red cover. Give the other half the same quiz using black font or a white cover. See if there is any difference in their scores.
- To introduce the topic, ask, *Does the color red mean anything special to you? Is it positive or negative?*

Be the Expert

- Andrew Elliot, a psychology professor at the University of Rochester in New York State, has researched the impact of color on intellectual performance. The research showed that people associate red with failure. This, in turn, leads them to avoid taking risks and to make mistakes. These studies were done in the United States, where teachers traditionally use red ink to mark mistakes.
- **Expansion Tip:** Have students research and report on the impact of different colors on people and/or test performance. Search online using the keywords *color psychology* or *the effects of color*.

2 CHECK, page 453 — 5 min.

1. F   2. T   3. F   4. F   5. F

- **Tip:** Ask students to correct the false statements.

3 DISCOVER, page 453 — 5 min.

A 1. have   3. change
      2. see   4. see

B 1. b   2. a   3. a

- **Tip:** For a higher-level class, ask, *Do you agree or disagree with the research? Why, or why not?* Move to Chart 14.7 when students have trouble using *if* clauses.

LEARN

Chart 14.7, page 454 — 5 min.

- **Tip:** For a higher-level class, show examples of other modals in the main clause. Write one condition and many possible results: *If you get a bad grade on the next test, . . . you might fail the course / you should study harder / you're going to be unhappy.*

4 page 454 — 5 min.

1. If I have breakfast, I'll be late for my exam.
2. Don't wear that red shirt <u>if you have an exam</u>.
3. <u>If he has a test</u>, he studies hard.
4. <u>If you study hard</u>, you'll get a good grade.
5. You can borrow a pencil <u>if you don't have one</u>.
6. <u>If I don't understand the assignment</u>, I'll call you.
7. <u>If they have questions</u>, they should ask the professor.
8. <u>If the weather is nice</u>, we walk to class.

5 page 454 — 5 min.

1. don't have   5. studies
2. finishes   6. don't take
3. don't understand 7. 're / are
4. get   8. don't leave

6 SPEAK, page 455 — 10 min.

- **Tip:** Give an affirmative condition and ask students to say a result. Then change the condition to the negative (e.g. *If I'm happy . . ., / If I'm not happy . . . / If I go out tonight. . . . , / If I don't go out tonight. . .*).

Chart 14.8, page 455 — 5 min.

- **Note 2:** Point out the use of the present in the time clause even when it is talking about the future.
- **Tip:** For a higher-level class, do exercise **9** next and assign exercises **7** and **8** for homework.

7 page 456 — 5 min.

1. a (add comma)
2. b
3. a (add comma)
4. b
5. b
6. b (add comma)
7. b
8. a (add comma)

8 page 456 — 5 min.

1. When
2. After
3. When
4. before
5. after
6. When
7. after
8. before

9 SPEAK, page 456 — 10 min.

- **Expansion Tip:** Write a story with a sequence of activities using pronouns and time clauses to refer to previous activities. Put each sentence on a strip of paper. Put students in groups and give each student a strip of paper with a sentence to memorize. Students listen to each other to decide on the order of the sentences. The first group to get it correct retells the story to the class.

PRACTICE

10 page 457 — 5 min.

1. h
2. e
3. g
4. c
5. f
6. d
7. a
8. b

11 page 457 — 10 min.

- **Tip:** Before beginning this exercise, ask, *When you were a child, did your parents reward you for good grades?*

A
1. receive
2. Will they study
3. get
4. get
5. will give
6. I'll get
7. gets
8. gets
9. doesn't get
10. get
11. are going to get
12. works

B Answers will vary.

Items 1, 3, 6, and 7 require a comma.

- **Expansion Tip:** Ask, *When you have children, will you give them rewards? If you give rewards, will they get better grades? What if your child has a learning disability? Will you still give rewards for good grades?* Have students discuss in groups.

12 LISTEN & SPEAK, page 458 — 25 min.

- **Tip:** Before beginning exercise **12**, ask, *Did you ever take a test preparation course?*

A 1. a 2. a

B
1. you need it
2. I take
3. If I don't get, I won't get
4. you'll do well; you're not smart,
5. you take a test prep course,
6. I start college,
7. After I finish school,
8. I don't work

- **Alternative Writing & Speaking:** If your students have different opinions on this topic, set up a debate. First, have each side prepare their arguments. Each side gets a presentation, rebuttal, and questions.

13 APPLY, page 459 — 20 min.

- **Tip:** If students are from different countries, have each country/student work individually to come up with ideas for changes and reasons. Then have them share.
- **Expansion Tip:** Have students write their suggestions and reasons in an e-mail to someone in the administration.

Review the Grammar UNIT 14

1 page 460 10 min.
1. will learn
2. arrive
3. will have
4. will also learn
5. start
6. will learn
7. will hike and camp
8. will be
9. spend
10. will return
11. are never going to forget

- **Expansion Tip:** Have students brainstorm unusual ways to learn English. Then have them write advertisements for the programs they design.

2 EDIT, page 460 10 min.

Hal: Hi, Adam. What are you doing?
Adam: Hey, Hal. I'm ~~make~~ making a packing list.
Hal: Where ~~you are~~ are you going?
Adam: I'm going to the Andes Mountains next month.
Hal: Wow. Are you going there for vacation?
Adam: No, I'm going to study Spanish.
Hal: Really? Are you going to stay with a family?
Adam: No. I'm ~~go~~ going with this unusual language program I found online. It combines hiking and camping trips with Spanish classes. After I ~~will~~ get there, I'll meet the other students in the program and the guides. Then we're going to go on a two-week camping trip. The guides are Spanish teachers, too.
Hal: That sounds amazing! I'm sure you're going to have a great time and learn a lot.

3 LISTEN, WRITE & SPEAK, page 461 25 min.

A

	Sure	Not Sure
1. Take more English courses	✓	
2. Study English for eight more months		✓
3. Take the English test in May	✓	
4. Go to university next September		✓
5. Get married	✓	

B Long-Term Goal: Be a math teacher

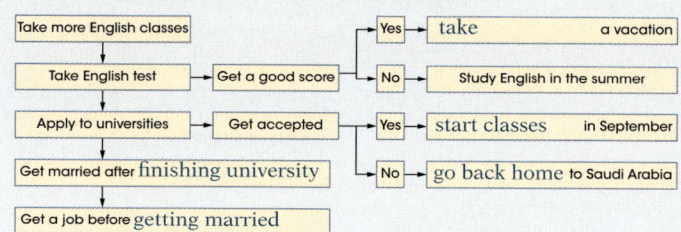

C *Answers will vary. Possible answers:*
1. When Ali finishes his English course, he'll take a test.
2. If he doesn't get a high score, he'll study English again.
3. If he gets a high score, he'll take a vacation.
4. If he gets accepted, he'll start classes.
5. If he doesn't get accepted, he'll go home to Saudi Arabia.
6. After he finishes at the university, he'll go home.
7. Before he gets married, Ali will get a job.

4 SPEAK, page 461

- **Alternative Writing:** Have students write about their plans for the future using *if* clauses and time clauses.

Connect the Grammar to Writing

1 READ AND NOTICE THE GRAMMAR, page 462 15 min.

B Right now, I'm a student at a community college. <u>I'm going to be</u> a nurse. Next semester, <u>I'm starting</u> a nursing program. When I finish it, <u>I'm going to take</u> a test to get my nursing license. If I pass, <u>I'll apply</u> for a job in a hospital. If I don't pass the test, <u>I'll take</u> a test preparation course and <u>take</u> the test again.

After I work for a couple of years, I <u>might take</u> more nursing courses and <u>get</u> a four-year degree. If I do that, <u>I'll be able to get</u> better nursing jobs. I think this is a good career plan because there <u>will always be</u> jobs for nurses.

C **Binh's long-term goal:** Be a nurse

Reasons for goal: There will always be jobs for nurses.

Plans:

1. start a nursing program
2. take a test
3. apply for a job or take a test preparation course
4. work for a few years
5. take more nursing courses and get a four-year degree

2 BEFORE YOU WRITE, page 463 15 min.

3 WRITE, page 463 20 min.

> **WRITING FOCUS, page 463**
>
> Give students the following notes. Have them compete to see how many different sentences they can write using clauses with *if, when, before,* or *after*. There are many possibilities.
>
> Dream: Get a college degree
>   1. Apply to college, apply for a scholarship
>   2. Get accepted?
>   Yes – apply for a scholarship
>   No – apply to a different school
>   3. Get a scholarship?
>   Yes – go to college
>   No – work and save money
>   4. have the money, start school
>   5. study hard, get good grades
>   6. graduate, be very happy!
>
> *I'm going to apply to college.*
>
> *If I get accepted, I'll go to college.*
>
> *If I don't get accepted, I'll apply to a different school.*
>
> *When I apply, I'm going to apply for a scholarship, too.*
>
> *If I . . .*

- **Alternative Writing:** Have students interview each other about their plans and write about their partner's plans.

AUDIO SCRIPTS

UNIT 1

LESSON 1

1 READ, page 4 — CD1–Track 2

8, page 8 — CD1–Track 3

1.
A: Hi. My name's Ali. I'm from Saudi Arabia.
B: Hi, Ali. It's nice to meet you. I'm Maria.

2.
A: Hello. I'm Ted.
B: Nice to meet you. My name's Chris. I'm from Vancouver.
A: Oh, you're Canadian! I'm from Canada, too. Toronto's my hometown.

3.
A: Hello. We're in the same English class.
B: Hi. You're Ricardo, right? I'm Martin.
A: That's right. You're from Germany.
B: Yes, I am. How about you?
A: I'm from Mexico.

11A, page 9 — CD1–Track 4

Adele: Hello. My name's Adele Silva.
Registration person: Silva . . . Let me see if I can find you. Yes, here you are. Oh, you're from Brazil!
Adele: Yes, I'm from Recife.
Registration person: Right. I see you here, and here's your name card. Well, I hope you enjoy Boston, Adele.
Adele: Thank you.
Lucas: Adele? Adele, over here!
Adele: Hey, Lucas!
Lucas: Everyone, this is Adele. We're from the same city in Brazil. Adele, this is Anna. She's from Italy.
Adele: Nice to meet you. Where are you from in Italy?
Anna: I'm from Rome. Have you been there? . . . Oh, this is my friend, Nick Clark.
Adele: Hi, how are you?
Nick: Good! How are you?
Adele: You don't sound like you're an international student.
Nick: No, you're right. I'm from here. Boston's my hometown.
Adele: Oh, really?

LESSON 2

1 READ, page 11 — CD1–Track 5

7 PRONUNCIATION — CD1–Track 6

7A and B, page 15 — CD1–Track 7

12B and C, pages 19–20 — CD1–Track 8

1.
Jeff: Hey Beth, this is my friend Larissa.
Beth: Nice to meet you, Larissa.
Larissa: You, too.
Jeff: Larissa is from Salvador.
Beth: That's in Brazil, right?
Larissa: Yes.
Beth: So, Larissa, are you a student?
Larissa: No, I'm visiting my sister. She's a student here at the university. I'm a doctor back in Salvador.
Beth: Oh, interesting. Well, enjoy your visit. Nice to meet you.
Larissa: Thanks. You, too.

2. — CD1–Track 9
Matt: Hey, the Green Lights are in town.
Dave: Who?
Matt: The Green Lights—Liz Stanford and Jude Wilson—they're musicians. Their band is called the Green Lights.
Dave: Oh, yeah? What kind of music do they play?
Matt: Pop. They're great! I love their music!
Dave: Really? Where are they from?
Matt: England. They're from London. They're very popular over there. They both play guitar, and Liz Stanford is the lead singer. They're really amazing.
Dave: Sounds good. Let's go see them tonight.
Matt: OK, great!

3. — CD1–Track 10
Carla: So, how do you like your history class?
Steve: With Professor Liu?
Carla: Yeah, I want to take it next semester.
Steve: It's really interesting, and Professor Liu is a great professor. I like him a lot.
Carla: Really? That's good . . . Where is he from?
Steve: From China, but he lives in the United States now.
Carla: Interesting. Does he give a lot of homework?
Steve: Yeah, actually he does. And his exams are really *hard*, but I'm learning a lot.
Carla: Hmm . . . I'll think about it.

LESSON 3

1 READ, page 21   CD1–Track 11

8B, page 26   CD1–Track 12

    Hi. My name's Kevin Kennedy. So . . . about your ad, well, let's see . . . um, I'm a high school student . . . I'm studying Japanese . . . and I need some help with conversation, too. Um, I'm funny . . . and my teachers say I'm smart. Anyway, my number is 555-8817. OK, thanks. Bye.

    CD1–Track 13

    Hi. This message is for Keiko. Keiko, my name is Liz Brown, and I'm calling about your ad for a conversation partner. Just a little information about me. . . . I'm an artist, and I love languages. I speak German, Spanish, and a little French . . . but not Japanese . . . I'm hardworking and patient. Again, my name is Liz Brown, and my number is 555-2173. Thanks. Bye.

    CD1–Track 14

    Yes, hello! My name is Jane Reed. It's Wednesday morning—about eleven o'clock. I'm calling about your advertisement for a conversation partner. I don't work now . . . I'm retired. In fact, I'm actually a retired *English* teacher! . . . I'm very patient and I really like to help people. I have a lot of free time now, and I really enjoy teaching. So, my number is 555-4285. Again, my name is Jane Reed . . . Goodbye.

LESSON 4

1 READ, page 28   CD1–Track 15

10A, page 34   CD1–Track 16

    The Malms are another unusual family. Doug and Phil Malm are brothers, and they're identical twins. Their wives Jill and Jena are identical twins, too. Jena is Phil's wife, and Tim is their son. Jill is married to Doug. Rylie is their daughter. This family of six lives in the same house. They're a very interesting family!

REVIEW THE GRAMMAR

2, page 35   CD1–Track 17

1. I'm a teacher.
2. He's my brother.
3. It isn't an easy job.
4. My friend's name is Jim.
5. Our parents aren't happy.
6. She's a serious person.
7. Your new shoes are nice.
8. Our homework isn't difficult.

8A and B, page 37   CD1–Track 18

    Sheng Ling is from China. He's an acrobat. He's married. His wife isn't an acrobat, but his two children are. In fact, Sheng and his son Li are in a show together. Sheng's daughter's name is Min. She's only eight, but she's already an acrobat, too. She's a student at a special school for acrobats.

    Wu is Sheng's father. He's a teacher. In fact, he's a teacher at Min's school. And the owner of the school? . . . Can you guess? . . . It's Jing, Sheng's grandmother. You see, acrobatics is the family business for the Ling family.

UNIT 2

LESSON 1

1 READ, page 42   CD1–Track 19

8, page 47   CD1–Track 20

1. **A:** It's noisy. Are you at a party?
   B: No, I'm not. I'm at a wedding.
   A: Is it fun?
   B: Yes, it is! It's a lot of fun!
2. **A:** Is our meeting at nine o'clock?
   B: Yes, it is. Are we late?
   A: No, we aren't. We're early. It's only 8:45.
3. **A:** Hi. Are you at home?
   B: No, I'm not. I'm at school. Carol and Ann say hello.
   A: Oh, are they with you?
   B: Yes, they are.

10A, page 47   CD1–Track 21

    One special celebration is called a *quinceañera*. *Quinceañera* is a Spanish word. It's a celebration for a girl when she is 15. It's a popular celebration in Latin America. Isabel is the name of a girl in Miami, Florida. Her family is from Cuba. Today, Isabel is 15, and she's very happy. It's her *quinceañera*! Her family and friends are at her house for a big party. For a *quinceañera*, the girl's dress is very beautiful. Isabel's dress is long, and it's pink. A *quinceañera* party is a lot of fun. People dance, eat, and celebrate!

LESSON 2

1 READ, page 50   CD1–Track 22

9A, page 56   CD1–Track 23

    Welcome to our walking tour of the French Quarter . . . Today we're going to see many interesting places in the French Quarter. As you all know, the French Quarter is a very old part of New Orleans. We're standing in front of the Cabildo Museum. Next to the Cabildo Museum is the beautiful Cathedral. The big, green area in front of us is Jackson Square. Now, look left and look right. These two big brick buildings are the Pontalba Buildings, the first apartment buildings in the United States. Stores and restaurants are on the first floor of the Pontalba Buildings, and people live in apartments above the stores and restaurants. The Pontalba Building on St. Ann is actually a museum.

AUDIO SCRIPTS

As you see, we're very near to the Mississippi River here. Let's walk through the square. Here in the middle of the square is a statue of a man on a horse . . . The man is Andrew Jackson, a president of the United States . . . Let's continue to Decatur Street. Across Decatur Street is the world-famous Café du Monde. This is a great place to get coffee and a special New Orleans treat, *beignets*.

LESSON 3

1 READ, page 58   CD1–Track 24

12, page 64   CD1–Track 25

1.
A: What time is it?
B: It's one o'clock.
A: Oh no! Are we late for the meeting?
B: No, it's at two o'clock.

2.
A: Hi, Peter. How's the weather in Miami today?
B: It's warm and sunny.
A: You're lucky! It's cold and rainy here in Toronto.

3.
A: Hmmm. What's the date today?
B: It's July 9th.
A: Thank you.

4.
A: When's the game?
B: It's on Saturday.
A: Is it in the morning?
B: No, it's in the afternoon. It's at three o'clock.

14A and B, page 65   CD1–Track 26

It's 7:00 a.m.! Good morning, New Yorkers! It's Wednesday, February 14th. It's Valentine's Day. It's windy and cold. Stay warm and have a happy Valentine's Day!

LESSON 4

1 READ, page 66   CD1–Track 27

7, page 70   CD1–Track 28

1. Is this your phone?
2. Are these Marc's books?
3. Is that their house?
4. Is this Room 311?
5. Are these computers new?
6. Are those students in your class?
7. Is that your car?
8. Is that an interesting book?

REVIEW THE GRAMMAR

1, page 73   CD1–Track 29

1. Is she from Brazil?
2. Are they in India?
3. Are those your glasses?
4. When is your meeting?
5. What time is it?
6. Where is our class?
7. What are these?
8. How's the weather?

UNIT 3

LESSON 1

1 READ, page 80   CD1–Track 30

9, page 85   CD1–Track 31

Bush Pilots

Bush pilots have interesting jobs. They fly special planes to Alaska's bush country. (This is a wild area, far away from cities with airports.) Bush pilots carry people or supplies in their bush planes. They also help rescue people.

Paul Claus is a famous bush pilot. He has a lot of experience, and he is an excellent pilot. Paul also owns a hotel in Alaska. He flies customers to his hotel and takes them on adventures. He goes to interesting places with them. It's an exciting job!

11, page 85   CD1–Track 32

11A, page 86   CD1–Track 33

12A, page 86   CD1–Track 34

Alvaro: Hi, my name's Alvaro.
Galina: Nice to meet you. My name's Galina. This is a nice party, isn't it?
Alvaro: Yeah, it is. The food's delicious.
Galina: I know. So, Alvaro, are you new here?
Alvaro: Well, yes, my cousin lives here, and I'm on vacation. I live in Quito.
Galina: Oh, in Ecuador. Interesting. So, you're on vacation. That's nice.
Alvaro: Yes, I'm a professor. I teach biology at a university in Quito.
Galina: Oh! I'm a biology teacher, too.
Alvaro: Really? Where?
Galina: At a high school.
Alvaro: Here in Chicago?
Galina: No, I live in Russia—in Moscow, but I visit my sister here once a year.

Alvaro: Interesting . . . So what's your job like in a Russian high school? I mean, I'm sure it's different from a university job.

Galina: Oh, well, I just *love* biology. And I love teaching, too . . . though it's not always easy.

Alvaro: True. What's your schedule like there?

Galina: Well, I teach from eight in the morning until two in the afternoon, so I get up very early, but I usually go home at about three. What about you? A university schedule is nice, huh?

Alvaro: Yeah, it's pretty nice. I have classes from ten to five most days. Then sometimes I meet with students after class, so I usually go home at about six o'clock.

Galina: Six o'clock. Wow, that's late. What about Saturday?

Alvaro: I just relax on Saturday! It's my day off! How about you?

Galina: Me, too! No classes on Saturday! I like to relax on weekends.

LESSON 2

1 READ, page 88 — CD1–Track 35

14, page 95 — CD1–Track 36

Ted: Hi, Jana!

Jana: Hey, Ted! How about coffee sometime? I'm free in the morning on Thursday.

Ted: I have class in the morning. How about at 2:00?

Jana: Sorry. I'm not free then. I have soccer practice from two to four. How about Saturday?

Ted: I'm sorry. I work on Saturday from nine to five. How about Sunday afternoon?

Jana: Sure. That sounds good. How about at two?

Ted: Great. See you then!

16A, page 96 — CD1–Track 37

Workweeks around the World

People all over the world are busy working, but the workweek isn't the same in every country. Workdays and weekends are different around the world. In many countries, such as the United States, Canada, and Thailand, people work from Monday to Friday. They don't work on Saturday and Sunday. This is their weekend. In Austria, people work from Monday to Friday, but they don't work all day on Friday. They only work a half day—from nine to twelve.

In other countries, the workweek is completely different. For example, in Saudi Arabia and the United Arab Emirates, people work from Sunday to Thursday. They don't work on Friday or Saturday. That's their weekend. In Japan, people work from Monday to Friday and sometimes Saturday. And in India, Sunday is the only day off work for many workers.

LESSON 3

1 READ, page 97 — CD1–Track 38

10A and B, page 102 — CD1–Track 39

1. Most people don't want a job like Kelly Arnold's. Kelly tastes animal food. That's right! She works for a pet food company. She tastes the animal food and tells the company, "Yes, this tastes good," or "No, this isn't very good." Luckily, she doesn't need to eat the animal food. She only tastes it. Kelly doesn't like her job very much, but the company pays her very well because it's not easy to find someone to do this job.

2. Tim has an interesting job. He's a golf-ball diver. A lot of people hit golf balls into the water by mistake. Every week, Tim puts on his scuba gear, goes into the lake, and looks for golf balls. A store pays him money for each golf ball he finds. Then the store sells the used golf balls. He likes his job, except for one thing. An alligator lives in the lake. Tim watches the alligator carefully.

3. Max and Jackson live in Australia. They work for the government. They catch crocodiles. Max and Jackson don't kill the crocodiles. They move them to special crocodile parks. Most people are afraid of crocodiles. Max and Jackson aren't afraid, but they are very, very careful.

LESSON 4

1 READ, page 104 — CD1–Track 40

12A, page 110 — CD1–Track 41

So, you want to be an underwater photographer. It's a fun and interesting job, but there are some important things you need to know. Here's some advice from experts:

- Swim a lot. As an underwater photographer, you need to be comfortable in the water, so learn to swim and swim a lot.
- Learn about the ocean and about the creatures that live in the ocean. It's helpful to know about the fish or other animals you want to take photos of.
- Don't try to catch fish or other animals in the ocean. They might be dangerous, or you might hurt them.
- Choose the right camera. Then practice in a swimming pool before you take photos in the ocean. Swimming pools are safe and calm.
- Don't jump into the water with your camera. And don't leave your camera in the sun. Be careful with it.
- When you are finally in the ocean, be patient. Good photos take time and practice.
- And most of all, remember to have fun. The ocean is an amazing place, so enjoy it!

AUDIO SCRIPTS

REVIEW THE GRAMMAR

4, page 112   CD1–Track 42

A Dangerous Job

    Chris Hansen works in Alaska in the winter. He has a job on a crab boat. He fishes for crabs from October to January. Chris and the other fishermen drop heavy crab pots in the ocean and pull them back onto the boat a day later. Chris doesn't like his job. It is very dangerous on the ocean. Even in bad weather, the work doesn't stop. The days are very short in the winter. The sun doesn't rise until about 10:00 a.m., and it goes down at around 4:00 p.m. Chris's mother worries about him. She says, "Be careful, Chris! Don't fall off the boat!" He says, "Don't worry, Mom!"

6A and B, page 113   CD1–Track 43

1.
Tom has a new job. It starts on Monday. He's very happy about the job, but he has one problem. He doesn't have a car.

2.   CD1–Track 44
Sue has a problem. She has an important meeting today, but she feels terrible. She has a bad headache.

3.   CD1–Track 45
Jay and Bill have a test tomorrow in the morning, but their best friend is 20 today. Everyone's invited to a big birthday party. It starts at ten o'clock. It probably won't end until one or two in the morning.

4.   CD1–Track 46
Ann and Jim have a new baby boy. He's five months old. The baby doesn't feel very well. He has a bad cold. It's ten o'clock at night. Ann wants to take him to the emergency room at the hospital right now. Jim doesn't want to go to the hospital.

UNIT 4

LESSON 1

1 READ, page 118   CD1–Track 47

8A, page 122   CD1–Track 48

Nora: Lucia, hi! How are you? Do you like Miami?

Lucia: Yes, I do. I love the university and the people, but the American lifestyle is so different from my lifestyle at home.

Nora: Really? Do you miss Italy?

Lucia: Yes, I do. I miss my family and friends—and the food.

Nora: Do you like the food here?

Lucia: No, I don't. American food is terrible!

Nora: Well, I like it. Do you eat different food in Italy?

Lucia: Yes, I do. I don't eat fast food, and I eat fresh vegetables from our garden every day. We have a huge vegetable garden.

Nora: Well, that sounds healthy. Do you help with the garden?

Lucia: Yes, I do. It's a lot of work, but I enjoy it.

Nora: Do your parents speak English?

Lucia: No, they don't. They only speak Italian and German.

Nora: Do you have a big family?

Lucia: Yes, I do. I have four brothers and three sisters.

Nora: Wow! That *is* a big family! Do you all live in one house?

Lucia: Yes, we do. My grandparents live with us, too. It's noisy, but I love it!

10A, page 124   CD1–Track 49

Rena: New York City is so fast, Kate. Everything moves so quickly. People, taxis, cars. The people here even *talk* fast!

Kate: That's true. I am always in a hurry. But I like this lifestyle here. Do you come from a small town in Greece?

Rena: Yeah. I'm from Ikaria. It's a small Greek island. Life there is peaceful and slow . . . It's very nice.

Kate: Hmmm . . . That does sound nice. My life here is so stressful. I work all the time. It's really hard. Do you work?

Rena: Yes, I do . . . Well, it's just a part-time job. My family owns a restaurant by the sea. I help out there a couple of days a week. I also have a lot of work at home. My parents and my two aunts live with us—that is with my husband and our three children. I cook for the family every day! Do you cook, Kate?

Kate: Oh, no, I don't. I don't have time. I usually get some fast food, or I eat at a restaurant. I don't eat all that much during the day. I don't have time, but I drink *a lot* of coffee. I'm *always* tired.

Rena: That's too bad. You need more sleep. At home, in Greece we have a midday nap. We call it *ores koinis isixias*.

Kate: Really? Is it like a *siesta*?

Rena: Yeah. Everyone in Ikaria rests between about 3:00 and 6:00 in the afternoon. Most shops are closed, too. We close our restaurant at three, and open it again for dinner at seven, so we get a rest during the day. I think you need *ores koinis isixias* in New York!

Kate: Ha! In New York? Now that *would* be amazing! I never nap, not even on the weekend, and usually only sleep for four or five hours a night.

Rena: Oh no! Kate—that's not healthy.

Kate: I know. I know. It isn't healthy. I probably need a vacation in Ikaria.

Rena: Well, you're always welcome!

LESSON 2

1 READ, page 125   CD1–Track 50

9A, page 129   CD1–Track 51

Inside Thailand by Tom Hill

I often travel for work. I go to Asia about twice a year. In Thailand, I almost always go to the floating markets. At a floating market, people sell things from their boats. They usually have colorful umbrellas and wear large hats.

The Amphawa floating market is my favorite market, so I often go there. It's open every weekend from around 4:00 p.m. to about 8:00 p.m. I try a different snack every time. The Damnoen Saduak floating market is open every day from 7:00 a.m. to 11:00 a.m. I almost never go there because it's usually very crowded.

10, page 130   CD1–Track 52

Amy: Hi, Sophie!
Sophie: Amy! Wow! It's good to hear your voice!
Amy: How's France?
Sophie: Oh, it's great! I love Paris! I'm so glad we get to live here this year!
Amy: So . . . are you enjoying the French food?
Sophie: Oh . . . Yes, I am! . . . And the markets, too! You know, in Canada, I almost never cook. I rarely go to the grocery store there! . . . But here, I walk to a market every morning, and I buy bread or pastries twice a day at a wonderful bakery next to our apartment!
Amy: Wow! That sounds great, Sophie.
Sophie: Oh, it is . . . And I cook dinner every night. Peter loves it.
Amy: I'm sure he does. So how *is* Peter? Does he like his job there?
Sophie: Yeah, it's interesting . . .

LESSON 3

1 READ, page 131   CD1–Track 53

8A, page 135   CD1–Track 54

Scott: Hello. Excuse me. Do you have time to answer some questions for a short survey?
Camila: Um . . . Yeah, OK.
Scott: Great! So, here's the first question. Where do you live?
Camila: Here in Mexico. I'm from Puebla.
Scott: OK, thanks. Who do you live with?
Camila: My family—my husband and our two daughters. My mother lives with us, too.
Scott: Do you work?
Camila: Yeah, I do. I'm a nurse.
Scott: Where do you work?
Camila: At the Hospital Betania in Puebla.
Scott: How do you get to work?
Camila: Well, I usually drive, but sometimes I take the bus.
Scott: When do you start work?
Camila: Early. I usually start work at seven o'clock in the morning.
Scott: Wow! That *is* early! What do you do for fun?
Camila: Well, I shop, and I listen to music.
Scott: Really? Who's your favorite musician?
Camila: Hmmm. Carla Morrison.
Scott: I like her music, too. Next question: How often do you take a vacation?
Camila: Twice a year.
Scott: Thanks. Where do you usually go on vacation?
Camila: Well, we usually go to the beach, but this year we want to see the mountains.
Scott: Nice! Why do you like the beach?
Camila: I love the sun and water! Who doesn't love the beach?
Scott: Well, those are all of my survey questions. Thank you very much!
Camila: No problem. Good luck with your survey!

9, page 136   CD1–Track 55

1. When do you have class?
2. What does *cap* mean?
3. Where do you live?
4. Who speaks French?
5. Why are you late?
6. How often do you eat at a restaurant?
7. What do you usually have for lunch?
8. How do you get to work?

12A, page 138   CD1–Track 56

Max: My wife Sara and I live in a suburb near the city. We're retired, so we don't go to work anymore . . . So, what do we do all day? Well, we exercise in the morning. After lunch, we work in the garden, and in the afternoon we take care of our grandchildren after school. In the evenings, we usually do things with our friends . . . It's fun.

CD1–Track 57

Kai: I live in Hawaii. I sell surfboards and clothes at a store. Actually, it's a surf shop! What do I do in my free time? Well, I like to surf. I surf every day after work and on my days off. Oh yeah, sometimes I teach surfing. And I like to take photographs . . . of other surfers, of course. It's great.

CD1–Track 58

Julie: I live in New York City. I write books for children. I work all day at home at my desk. I usually go out for a walk in the late afternoon . . . Most of my friends have families, so I don't see them too much. But my sister lives in New York too, so we often have dinner together, and we go to a play or a movie about once a week . . . I love New York.

AUDIO SCRIPTS

REVIEW THE GRAMMAR

2, page 139 CD1–Track 59

1. How often do you visit your parents?
2. Do you play soccer?
3. What does *huge* mean?
4. Why do you ride your bike to work?
5. Does she have a big family?
6. Who takes the subway to class?
7. Where do they usually go on vacation?
8. When do you usually go shopping?
9. How does Sonia get to work?
10. Who do you live with?

4A and B, pages 140–141 CD1–Track 60

Angela: Hi, Lena. Did you read my e-mail?
Lena: No, sorry.
Angela: Really? I sent it yesterday.
Lena: I know, sorry. I'm really busy, and I don't read my personal e-mail every day.
Angela: You don't? How often do you read it?
Lena: Oh . . . about three times a week.
Angela: Three times a week!? That's all!? Wow! I check my e-mail every hour.
Lena: Well, I don't have a smartphone, and I'm really busy during the week, so I usually read e-mails on weekends.
Angela: Huh. Do you belong to any social networking sites?
Lena: Yeah, one. I go on it about once a week—not often.
Angela: I can't imagine that. I'm online all of the time. What about banking? Do you bank online?
Lena: No, never.
Angela: Really? Why not? It's so easy . . . and fast.
Lena: I know, but I like to talk to a real *person*.
Angela: Ha! You're like my *grandmother*, Lena.
Lena: Oh, stop it, Angela! I am *not*. I shop online sometimes, right?
Angela: True. Do you read the news online?
Lena: No, I read the newspaper.
Angela: You *are* like my grandmother.

UNIT 5

LESSON 1

1 READ, page 146 CD2–Track 2

13A, B, and C, pages 152–153 CD2–Track 3

Conversation 1
Hotel Clerk: Hello. Front desk. May I help you?
Guest: Yes, I need help. I have a problem with the TV in my room. It only gets two channels.
Hotel Clerk: I'm sorry to hear that, sir. I'll send someone right away.
Guest: OK. Thank you.

Conversation 2 CD2–Track 4
Woman: Good afternoon. Welcome to the Philadelphia airport. Would you like a map of the city?
Traveler: Yes, I would. Thanks. I'd also like information about trains into the city.
Woman: Sure. No problem. It's really easy to take a train downtown. It leaves every 30 minutes. Just follow the signs to the station.
Traveler: Thanks!

Conversation 3 CD2–Track 5
Mike: Hello! This is Mike Jones on WLKY Radio! Do you drive to work? Well, don't get stuck in traffic! Listen to our traffic reports every morning. Mary?
Mary: Thanks, Mike. Right now, traffic is very slow on all of our roads. The drive into the city from the airport is now 45 minutes.

CD2–Track 6
Karen: Hey, sorry. I'm still at the office. I have about an hour of work here. Can we change our dinner to tomorrow night?
Berta: Working late again? I think you need a new job!
Karen: No, I really like my job. I need to finish a report for my boss.
Berta: OK. Let's meet tomorrow then. 6:30?
Karen: Uh . . . How about 7:30 instead?
Berta: OK . . . 7:30. See you then.

LESSON 2

1 READ, page 154 CD2–Track 7

9, pages 158–159 CD2–Track 8

1.
Server: Are you ready to order?
Customer: Yes, I'd like a glass of lemonade.
Server: I'm sorry. We don't have any lemonade. Would you like some iced tea or juice?
Customer: Hm. No, thank you. I'd just like a glass of water.
Server: Would you like something to eat?
Customer: Yes, I'd like a bowl of tomato soup.

2.
Dalia: You look great, Mila. What's your secret?
Mila: Thanks. I just eat healthy food. I don't eat any meat, and I eat a lot of vegetables. I also have about six pieces of fruit each day.
Dalia: Wow! Do you eat any bread or sweets?

Mila: I don't eat sweets, but every morning I have a slice of bread with some butter on it! I *love* butter!

3.

Andy: Do you have any easy recipes for dinner?

Tasha: Sure. I have a very easy recipe for spaghetti. For four people, you need a box of pasta, a jar of pasta sauce, and some cheese.

Andy: Great! Thank you!

11A and B, page 160   CD2–Track 9

Arlene: Hey, Jack. Let's make potato pancakes for dinner.

Jack: Yum! . . . Good idea! . . . Do we have all the ingredients?

Arlene: Let's see . . . We have a large bag of potatoes.

Jack: Good . . . We definitely need *potatoes*!

Arlene: We have a carton of eggs. How many do we need?

Jack: We only need two, so we're all set. We don't need to buy any more.

Arlene: OK, onions . . . Do we have any onions?

Jack: Um . . . No, we don't. How many do we need?

Arlene: Just one.

Jack: OK, let me write that down. One . . . onion. All right, what else?

Arlene: Um . . . We need two tablespoons of flour and some salt.

Jack: We have a lot of of flour and salt.

Arlene: OK, good . . . We also need two cups of oil.

Jack: Hmmm . . . We don't have any oil.

Arlene: OK, then let's add that to the list, too.

LESSON 3

1 READ, page 163   CD2–Track 10

11A, page 170   CD2–Track 11

Henry: Hey, Sunil, I was just reading about the Mediterranean diet. Do you know much about it?

Sunil: Yeah, you mean a diet with a lot of grains and fruit and vegetables?

Henry: Yeah. It's supposed to help you live a long time.

Sunil: I think it's really similar to the way I eat. My family's from India, so we eat a lot of rice and vegetables. I don't eat any beef.

Henry: You don't eat beef?

Sunil: No, never . . . and I think I'm pretty healthy. I mean, I don't eat a lot of sweets, and I eat a lot of fruit, especially mangos. I love mangos.

Henry: Good for you. I'm just the opposite. We're Irish, so we eat potatoes at almost every meal.

Sunil: Potatoes are a big part of the Mediterranean diet, though, so they're probably pretty healthy, right?

Henry: Well, yes, I guess so, but probably not with all the butter I put on them! . . . I also eat a lot of beef, and I don't like vegetables.

Sunil: Really, you don't like vegetables? C'mon Henry. They're good for you. What about fruit? Do you each much fruit?

Henry: Yeah, I have a little fruit now and then, but not every day . . . Oh, and I eat a lot of ice cream. That's my favorite food—ice cream . . . ice cream with chocolate sauce and whipped cream. Mm-mm-mm!

Sunil: That doesn't sound very healthy, Henry.

Henry: I know. I think my diet is just the opposite of the Mediterranean diet, but I follow the Mediterranean lifestyle! I spend a lot of time with my family, and I exercise every day.

Sunil: Me, too.

REVIEW THE GRAMMAR

2A, page 171   CD2–Track 12

In some countries, coffee is an important, but quick part of the day. People usually only spend ten or fifteen minutes with their morning coffee. Not in Ethiopia. In Ethiopia, a special coffee ceremony takes a few hours. The ceremony starts with coffee beans. First, they wash and dry some green coffee beans. Next, they roast the beans over a fire and watch them carefully, so they don't burn. The beans change color from green to dark brown. The open door of a house is an invitation to others to come in and have coffee. Usually family members and a few neighbors enter the house when they smell the coffee. The woman making the coffee puts the beans into a basket to cool. Everyone enjoys the wonderful smell of the roasted coffee beans. Next, she grinds the beans into a powder and boils the powder with water for a few minutes. When the coffee is ready, she pours the coffee into cups and everyone enjoys it. People often have a few peanuts or other salty snacks with the coffee. Then, it's time for another cup of coffee, and the process begins again. They usually enjoy three cups of coffee. It's a relaxing time to enjoy good coffee and talk with friends and family.

4A and B, pages 172–173   CD2–Track 13

Woman: Hey, we need to get food for our barbecue.

Man: You're right. Let's make a list.

Woman: OK, how about steak?

Man: That's kind of expensive for eight people. How about hamburgers?

Woman: OK, so put hamburger meat on the list. Now . . . do we have tomatoes?

Man: No, we need to buy tomatoes . . . and onions, too. A lot of people like onions on their hamburgers. Let's get a few tomatoes and some onions.

Woman: OK, and what about a vegetable? Some broccoli maybe? Or some green beans?

Man: I don't know . . . Hey, how about corn? Everybody likes corn.

Woman: Good idea! How many pieces of corn do we need?

Man: Hmmm . . . Two per person?

Woman: That sounds about right . . . OK, so do we have any butter?

AUDIO SCRIPTS

Man: Yes, we're all set. We have two sticks of butter. OK, . . . so . . . now what about dessert? How about an apple pie?
Woman: Good . . . And let's get some vanilla ice cream to go on top.
Man: Great idea!
Woman: Oh, wait! Don't forget rolls for the hamburgers.
Man: Right. Thanks!

UNIT 6

LESSON 1

1 READ, page 178 CD2–Track 14

11A, page 184 CD2–Track 15

12A and B, page 186 CD2–Track 16

I'm from Vancouver, Canada. I really like it here. There's a lot to do, lots of fun activities, I mean clubs and restaurants, the theater . . . There's a lot going on. The only problem is that all those things are expensive and I don't have a lot of money. It's a big city, and it's pretty crowded, but there's still a lot of open space. We have a lot of beautiful parks, and on any nice day, you can see people out enjoying themselves. There are beautiful mountains all around, and there's a lot of water everywhere you look. The scenery is gorgeous! The only thing I don't like is that we have so much rain . . . In the summer, we don't get much rain, but in the winter we get a lot. In the winter, we don't get much snow in the city, but there's always snow in the mountains, and I like that because I really like to ski . . . OK, let me think. Is there anything else I don't like? . . . Oh, I know. There's no big highway downtown in Vancouver, and that's a good thing, but there's a lot of traffic. Basically, though, it's a great place to live!

LESSON 2

1 READ, page 187 CD2–Track 17

6A and B, page 190 CD2–Track 18

1. There isn't enough furniture in the room.
2. There's not enough empty space.
3. We have enough chairs.
4. There are enough books for everyone.
5. We don't have enough money.
6. There's enough time.
7. We have enough food for dinner.
8. There isn't enough light in the kitchen.

8A and B, page 191 CD2–Track 19

Woman: That was a fun evening, wasn't it? Jennifer is a wonderful cook.
Man: She really is . . . but this neighborhood! Next time we get together for dinner with Dino and Jennifer, let's go to a *restaurant* where there's parking, OK? There's no place to park in this neighborhood.
Woman: Yeah, but it's a great neighborhood, isn't it? Look at all those restaurants!
Man: Gosh, it's busy. And it's so noisy. Are those *restaurants*? . . . No, they're *night clubs*. I bet it's really noisy late at night with all these clubs. It looks like there are five or six just on this block . . . Hmmm . . . Where did we park?
Woman: Over there . . . I see our car.
Man: Oh, good.
Woman: I like Dino and Jennifer's apartment building, but not all of those stairs . . . and they're on the *fourth* floor, too.
Man: That's a good thing about their apartment, isn't it? They get their daily exercise with all of those stairs.
Woman: Oh, I don't know. It's too many stairs to climb with groceries . . . or in high-heel shoes. I think they need an elevator in their building, . . . but I love all the windows. They get a lot of sunlight, and they have a great view from every room.
Man: Yeah, and it makes it seem bigger . . . They don't have much space.
Woman: I know. Their apartment is really small! There's hardly any space at all . . . It's amazing the way they cook in that tiny kitchen.
Man: I know. All of that furniture makes it look even smaller, too. There's no space for anything! And all those little "thingies" all over the place.
Woman: What do you mean, "thingies"? That's not a word.
Man: You know what I mean. They have all those little things all over the place. Books, little bowls of candy . . . Every single table has stuff on it. It's way too crowded.
Woman: Yeah, but that makes it cozy. It has a happy feel.
Man: Oh, you mean all those flowers everywhere? Flowered couch, flowered chairs, flowers on the wall. Flowers everywhere.
Woman: Oh, come on. There aren't that many flowers! Well, maybe there are, but I love the flowers! They're so pretty and colorful . . . What do you want? All solid colors? Black and white furniture?
Man: Yes! Exactly. Simple, clean lines. Basic colors. No flowers.
Woman: Like a hotel . . . or your office!? Here we are . . . OK next time we go to a restaurant.
Man: Good.

1 READ, page 193 CD2–Track 20

9A and B, page 199 CD2–Track 21

Zoe: What does everyone want to do for vacation? Does anyone want to go camping?
Kathy: Not me. To me, there's nothing relaxing about camping. It's just a lot of work. On vacation, I don't want to do anything. I want to relax and do nothing.
Mary: Yeah, and I never get enough sleep when I go camping. Cold tent. Sleeping bag. Hard ground. Rocks. No thanks.
Zoe: Well, how about *glamping*?

Mary: Glamping? What's that?

Zoe: It's glamour camping—luxury camping. They have tents with real beds and nice blankets. You don't do any work or anything. Someone else does everything for you. Seriously! Someone else gets the wood for the fire. Someone even gets the food for you to cook over the fire . . . I mean, someone even cooks for you, if you want!

Kathy: Wow—really?

Zoe: Yeah. Really?

Mary: I bet it's expensive.

Zoe: Well, yeah, probably. Nothing good is ever free, right?

Kathy: Well, let's check out the prices. I like this idea!

10, page 200   *CD2–Track 22*

Alex: Hey, everyone! Let's talk about our camping trip. First, everyone needs to bring a sleeping bag.

Matt: Right. We also need a tent or something to put over our sleeping bags. Does anyone have one?

Jim: I have a tent.

Alex: Great. Next, it gets cold at night. Does everyone have warm clothes?

Matt: No. I don't have anything warm to wear. Does someone have an extra jacket or something?

Jim: Yeah, I do. Now, how about food? We need eggs or something for breakfast. How about pancakes? They're easy to make.

Alex: Sure. That's fine. There's a store near the campground. It sells everything: food, maps, bug spray . . .

Jim: Great. Let's go there tomorrow.

REVIEW THE GRAMMAR

1, page 201   *CD2–Track 23*

Luisa: I'm so excited about our little beach house. Let's go this weekend and figure out the furniture.

Carmen: We don't need much furniture. There isn't much space.

Rosa: True. We don't want to have too much furniture. What do we need?

Luisa: Well, we need something to sit on, so we need some chairs.

Rosa: There are a few chairs in my garage. Let's use those.

Carmen: OK, good. Does anyone have a small table?

Luisa: I do. There's one in my bedroom at home.

Rosa: Great! Is there space for a sofa?

Luisa: Yes, there's space for a small one.

Carmen: How about the kitchen?

Rosa: It's really small. It doesn't have much space. There aren't many cabinets or shelves.

Luisa: That's OK. Do you want to cook on vacation? I don't!

Carmen: Me neither. Nobody wants to cook on vacation.

Rosa: True! After all, it is a vacation house.

3A, page 202   *CD2–Track 24*

Mark: Hey, does anyone know about any apartments for rent? I'm looking for a new place to live.

Tammy: I do. Someone's moving, so there's one available in my building.

Mark: There is?

Tammy: Uh huh. I think it's on the eighth floor, but there's an elevator, of course.

Mark: How many bedrooms does it have?

Tammy: I think there are two bedrooms. Yeah, it has to be two.

Mark: Does it have a washer and dryer?

Tammy: Well, there isn't a washer and dryer in the apartment, but there's a laundry room in the basement.

Mark: How many units are there in the building?

Tammy: Well, it's a large apartment complex. I think there are probably about 150.

Mark: Wow, that's a lot. Are they all in one building?

Tammy: No, there are three buildings.

Mark: But, there's only *one* laundry room?

Tammy: Well, yeah, there's one laundry room in each building.

Mark: That doesn't seem like enough.

Tammy: No, it's fine.

Mark: Well, that's good. Is there an exercise room?

Tammy: No, there isn't.

Mark: How about a swimming pool? Does it have a swimming pool?

Tammy: No, no swimming pool . . .

Mark: Hmmm . . . Not too many extras, that's for sure! How much is the rent?

Tammy: Oh, you know, I'm not sure about that, but I don't think it's a lot.

Mark: OK. Well, I'll probably come and see it. Is anyone in the apartment now?

Tammy: I don't think so. If you want, I can ask someone.

Mark: OK. Great. Thanks for letting me know.

Tammy: Sure.

UNIT 7

LESSON 1

1 READ, page 208   *CD2–Track 25*

10, pages 213–214   *CD2–Track 26*

1. The ice climber is using special equipment.
2. She's wearing special boots.
3. The kiteboarder is jumping in the air.
4. He's standing on his kiteboard.

AUDIO SCRIPTS

5. The skier is trying to win the race.
6. She's going very fast.
7. The hang glider is flying over the valley.
8. He's looking at the camera.
9. These people are doing interesting things.
10. They're having fun.

LESSON 2

1 READ, page 218 — CD2–Track 27

12, page 224 — CD2–Track 28

1. What's he doing?
2. Is he working with other people?
3. Where are they hiking?
4. Who's speaking right now?
5. Why aren't you watching the movie?
6. What are you studying?
7. Where's she living?
8. Is Erica sleeping?

14A, page 226 — CD2–Track 29

Tay: Hello?
Jake: Hi. Tay, it's Jake.
Tay: Oh, hi Jake. How are you doing?
Jake: Great. Hey, do you want to climb in Logan Canyon this afternoon?
Tay: You know, I'd like to, but I'm in the middle of something. I'm working on a project, and I need to finish it.
Jake: How about Evan? Is he busy?
Tay: He's not living at home anymore.
Jake: Oh, really? I didn't know that.
Tay: Yeah, he has a new job. You know he really likes to climb, right? Well, he's climbing now as a job. Can you believe that? He's climbing and making money at the same time.
Jake: Somebody's paying him to climb? Is he working as a guide or something?
Tay: Sort of . . . You know all those huge wind turbines? Somebody has to fix them sometimes, so they use people like Evan.
Jake: Really? That's interesting.
Tay: Yeah, and he's traveling all over the world for his job. He's working in Greece this month.
Jake: Are you joking?
Tay: No, I'm not kidding. I'm serious. And he's making a lot of money, too.
Jake: Wow! I want a job like that!

LESSON 3

1 READ, page 228 — CD2–Track 30

11A, page 234 — CD2–Track 31

Alvaro: We're talking now with our news reporter, Maria Lopez. She's on the coast. This storm is just beginning, but the wind ahead of the hurricane is already causing a lot of damage.
Maria: It sure is, Alvaro. Do you see the waves? They're huge.
Alvaro: Yes, I do. I hear the wind, too.
Maria: Yes, the wind is blowing more than 75 miles per hour already. And it's getting stronger. Already, the waves are hitting the houses on the beach.
Alvaro: Are any people still in those houses, Maria?
Maria: Yes, some people don't want to leave their homes. The police are asking everyone to leave, but some people are staying in their homes.
Alvaro: Maria, I see smoke behind you. What's going on back there?
Maria: Further down the beach there are fires in some of the houses. Unfortunately, there's nothing anyone can do about the fires right now. The firefighters can't reach them, so the houses are still burning.
Alvaro: And where are you exactly? Do you feel safe?
Maria: Well, yes. I feel OK here. I'm standing outside a big hotel, and it seems pretty safe.
Alvaro: OK, well we'll check back with you soon, Maria. Stay safe!
Maria: Thanks, Alvaro. Back to you.

REVIEW THE GRAMMAR

1, page 235 — CD2–Track 32

1. Who's taking the photo?
2. What are you doing?
3. Who are you talking to?
4. Where are they living now?
5. Why are people standing there?
6. Why aren't you skiing?
7. What are you reading?
8. Are they eating lunch now?

3, page 236 — CD2–Track 33

Alex: Hello, everyone. Our visitor today is Isabel Lee. Isabel, how are you doing?
Isabel: I'm doing great, Alex.
Alex: So, are you training for a new event now?
Isabel: Yes, I'm training for a triathlon competition.
Alex: Really? Wow. What do you like about triathlons?
Isabel: I enjoy the challenge. Triathlons are very difficult! Also, triathlons include three sports: biking, swimming, and running, and I like all of them a lot!

Alex: Interesting. How many bicycles do you own?

Isabel: I have three. I need all of them because bicycles often break.

Alex: Well, good luck in your next triathlon!

Isabel: Thank you.

4A, page 236   CD2–Track 34

Joe: Wow, look at this photograph!

Beth: Oh my gosh! Where is that guy?

Joe: In Norway.

Beth: Wow. That looks really scary.

Joe: Yeah, I know. I guess he enjoys the thrill.

Beth: It looks really dangerous. I mean, he's just holding onto that plane with his hands. He's not attached to anything. He's just *hanging* from the plane! What's he doing?

Joe: I don't know. I think he's looking for a place on the ground to land. He needs to find someplace safe.

Beth: Why's he wearing a backpack?

Joe: I think that's a parachute.

Beth: Oh, he has a parachute! OK, that makes sense. I thought he was just riding on the wing of the plane.

Joe: No, no. He's jumping from the plane.

Beth: Wow! That's still pretty brave. When I fly, I like to stay *inside* the plane.

UNIT 8

LESSON 1

1 READ, page 242   CD2–Track 35

7, page 246   CD2–Track 36

1. I was in Thailand.
2. It's a beautiful country.
3. The weather was really hot yesterday.
4. The mountains aren't very high.
5. The hike yesterday afternoon wasn't difficult.
6. He's an excellent guide.
7. He was very helpful.
8. They weren't very happy last night.

11A and B, pages 247–248   CD2–Track 37

Selena: Our camping trip in Yosemite last month was so much fun. Let's do it again next year.

Nick: Are you serious? No way!

Selena: Why not?

Nick: Don't you remember? First of all, the weather was horrible. It was cold and wet.

Selena: No, it wasn't. There was a little rain on Friday night. Big deal.

Nick: Yes, and all our stuff was wet the rest of the trip. My backpack was so heavy.

Selena: It wasn't that bad. It was beautiful on Saturday and Sunday! . . . Sunny and warm.

Nick: And the insects! The mosquitoes, especially—they were terrible!

Selena: No, they weren't. There weren't very many insects. I didn't get any mosquito bites.

Nick: And that hike up to Glacier Point was really difficult.

Selena: It wasn't difficult! We were at the top in two hours. It wasn't that bad. It was easy.

Nick: Well, I was really tired.

Selena: What about seeing that bear? And the scenery? That was incredible!

Nick: Yeah, that *was* pretty amazing.

Selena: So, let's do something fun this weekend.

Nick: How about dinner and a movie?

Selena: Sounds good.

LESSON 2

1 READ, page 249   CD2–Track 38

8, page 253   CD2–Track 39

1. Where were you?
2. When were you in India?
3. Was it a good trip?
4. How was your trip?
5. Why weren't your friends on the tour?
6. Were the people on the tour friendly?
7. Who were you with?
8. Where was your hotel?
9. What was her name?
10. How was the weather?

9, page 254   CD2–Track 40

Ann: Hi, Beth. Where were you last week? Were you in California again on business?

Beth: No, I wasn't. I was in Africa.

Ann: Africa? Why were you in Africa?

Beth: I was on vacation.

Ann: Where were you in Africa?

Beth: I was in South Africa, Botswana, and Zambia.

Ann: Were you on a safari?

Beth: Yes, I was. It was amazing. We saw a lot of zebras, some giraffes, . . . and a few lions, too.

Ann: Lions? Wow! Were you afraid?

Beth: No, I wasn't. It was fun and really interesting.

11A, page 255   CD2–Track 41

Neeta: How was your summer, Jackie?

Jackie: It was OK. I just stayed here in Springfield and worked at my uncle's restaurant. Most of my friends were away all summer, so it was kind of boring. How about you?

Neeta: My summer was great. I was away in June, and worked in July and August.

AUDIO SCRIPTS

Jackie: Where were you?
Neeta: I was in India.
Jackie: Really! Why were you in India?
Neeta: I was there for my cousin's wedding? Do you remember my cousin Usha? She was here last summer.
Jackie: Oh yeah, I do . . . So, was the wedding fun?
Neeta: Yeah, it was. All of my relatives from India were there. It was a huge wedding. Everyone was really happy, especially Usha and her husband. His name's Anil. He's really nice . . . and the food was delicious!
Jackie: Yum! I love Indian food! . . . How was the weather?
Neeta: It was *hot*.
Jackie: Wow. The weather was nice here. That was one good thing about my summer.
Neeta: Oh. Hey, do you want to go somewhere and get a cup of coffee or something?
Jackie: Sure. I want to hear more about the wedding. There's a nice little café nearby on Green Street.
Neeta: Great. Let's go there.

LESSON 3

1 READ, page 256   CD2–Track 42

6 PRONUNCIATION, page 260   CD2–Track 43

6A, page 260   CD2–Track 44
1. My friend Tony and I wanted an adventure.
2. We discussed the trip.
3. We decided to go to Mexico.
4. We looked at a lot of travel websites.
5. We discussed the trip.
6. I reserved the hotel rooms online.
7. We packed our suitcases.
8. We called a taxi. It was time to go!

10A and B, page 262   CD2–Track 45
1. We went on a trip.
2. She came on Monday.
3. He travels a lot for his job.
4. You stayed at a nice hotel.
5. They always make their hotel reservations online.
6. I left my camera at the hotel.
7. I really want to go to Italy.
8. She really enjoyed her vacation last summer.

13A and B, page 264   CD2–Track 46
Ana: I always wanted to go to Machu Picchu. My sister Sudie wanted to go too, so we went together. We went with a tour group. Everyone on the tour was really nice. We arrived in Cusco three days early because Cusco is very high up in the mountains. At first, we were kind of tired, but we felt better after a couple of days. So, we stayed in Cusco for three nights and walked around a lot in the area. There were a lot of trails nearby. It was really interesting. Then, we joined our group and started our hike up to Machu Picchu. We had a guide, and it was great because we hiked the Inca Trail for four days! We stayed in a tent at night. Finally, we saw Machu Picchu. It was so exciting! We stayed there for a couple of days and had a wonderful time. We had a great trip—just amazing.

   CD2–Track 47

Don: I went to Machu Picchu last year. I always wanted to go, but nobody else wanted to come with me. So finally, I just decided to go by myself. So, I arrived in Cusco at night, and the next day, I went to Machu Picchu. It wasn't a long trip, only four hours because I went by train and then took a bus at the end. I stayed in a hotel at Machu Picchu, but I got really sick. I think it was because it was so high up in the mountains. I left early. I mean, I only stayed one night! It was really too bad. I'm glad I saw Machu Picchu, but it was a terrible trip overall.

LESSON 4

1 READ, page 265   CD2–Track 48

12A and B, page 271   CD2–Track 49
  Lee took a trip to Alaska last summer. On one day of his trip, he went on a group tour to a park. The guide told everyone, "Stay with the group. Don't go off alone." Lee didn't listen. He didn't stay with the group. Instead, he walked along a different path by himself. All of a sudden, he saw a big black bear and two cubs. The big bear looked at him. Lee didn't make any noise. He didn't turn around. Instead, he walked slowly backwards. In a few minutes, the bears went in the other direction. Lee turned around and ran back to join the tour group. They were sorry they didn't see any bears. Lee didn't feel very happy then, but later he had a great story to tell. He was sorry about one thing. He didn't take any photos.

REVIEW THE GRAMMAR

3A and B, page 273   CD2–Track 50
  In 1994, Jason Lewis and Steve Smith left England on an unusual journey. They wanted to go around the world on human power—no wind, no fuel—just their own two legs and feet. When they left England, they planned to spend three and a half years on the trip, but their journey was difficult and slow. It took a lot longer than three and a half years. After five years, Smith decided to stop. He left the journey in Hawaii, and Lewis continued alone. Eight years later, Lewis was still only in Australia, about half way in his trip around the world.
  Lewis didn't know it, but he wasn't the only person with this idea. In Canada, Colin Angus also wanted to go around the world on human power. In 2002, he started to plan his trip. He wanted to finish his journey around the world before

Lewis, so he didn't want Lewis to know anything about it. He didn't say to everyone, "I'm going to go around the world." He kept his plans secret.

In 2004, Angus, his fiancée, Julie Wafaei, and a man named Tim Harvey left Vancouver, Canada, on bicycles. They went north to Alaska. From Alaska, Angus and Harvey rowed in a small boat across to Russia. In Russia, Harvey left the journey, but Wafaei joined Angus and traveled with him for the rest of the trip. They rowed across the Atlantic. They planned to reach Miami, Florida, but a hurricane carried them south to Costa Rica. From there, they rode their bicycles all the way back to Vancouver, Canada. They completed their trip in 2006 after 720 days of travel. However, a question remains. Did Angus really go all the way around the world? Some people say no because he didn't cross the Equator.

In 2007, after 13 years, Jason Lewis finished his trip and arrived back in England. Angus finished his journey first, but Lewis crossed the Equator.

UNIT 9

LESSON 1

1 READ, page 278   CD3–Track 2

12, page 285   CD3–Track 3
1. Where did he live?
2. When did he move to Kenya?
3. How did you feel about that?
4. Who helped you with the research?
5. What happened?
6. Did she answer your question?
7. Why did she move to Paris?
8. When did you leave work?

13, page 285   CD3–Track 4
Interviewer: OK so, Mr. Nash, where were you born?
Nash: In Jamaica.
Interviewer: Why did you move to London?
Nash: I knew a lot of people there.
Interviewer: Did you always want to be a writer?
Nash: No, I really wanted to be a football player!
Interviewer: Really? What happened?
Nash: I broke my ankle and had other injuries.
Interviewer: Were you a good player?
Nash: No, I really wasn't very good.
Interviewer: Who taught you to write?
Nash: My teachers.
Interviewer: When did you write your first book?
Nash: Ten years ago. No one liked it.
Interviewer: How did you feel about that?
Nash: I felt terrible, of course.
Interviewer: Why didn't people like it?
Nash: It really wasn't very good. It was horrible, in fact.
Interviewer: Did you want to give up?
Nash: Yes, but I continued to write, and now I'm glad I did.

17A and B, page 287   CD3–Track 5
Wong How-Man was born in Hong Kong in 1949. He grew up in Hong Kong. He went to college in the United States. In 1974, he got a job as a journalist in China. He is an excellent photographer. He led six expeditions in China for *National Geographic* in the 1980s. During his travels he explored several rivers, including the Mekong River and the Yellow River. He took photographs and wrote articles about these trips for the magazine. Wong How-Man also led two expeditions—one in 1985 and one in 2005—to find the source of the Yangtze River. In 1986, he started the China Exploration and Research Society.

LESSON 2

1 READ, page 288   CD3–Track 6

9, page 293   CD3–Track 7
Jacques Cousteau
Jacques Cousteau was a famous ocean explorer. He was born in France in 1910. He learned to swim when he was four. When he was thirteen, he bought his first movie camera. After he finished school, he joined the navy. When he was 23, Cousteau was in a bad car accident. He almost died. After his accident, he went swimming every day in the Mediterranean Sea. When the salt water hurt his eyes, he started to wear goggles. This changed his life. Before he used goggles, he never saw anything underwater. With goggles, he saw a lot of interesting things in the sea. After this, he wanted to dive deeper and deeper.

10A and B, page 294   CD3–Track 8
Jacques Cousteau was an interesting man. He loved to explore the ocean. He also liked mechanical things. When he was a teenager, he bought a movie camera and took it apart because he wanted to learn how it worked.

In 1937, Cousteau married a French woman named Simone. She also loved to explore the ocean. After he got married, his father-in-law introduced him to a man named Emile Gagnan. Gagnan was an inventor. Together, Cousteau and Gagnan designed the first aqua lung. The aqua lung gave divers a way to swim deep under water and stay there for long periods of time. It was the first scuba-diving equipment. After that, Cousteau also helped design an underwater camera because he wanted to film fish and other animals in the sea.

In 1950, Cousteau bought a ship and named it the *Calypso*. He wanted to explore the ocean, but he didn't have very much money at that time, so he wrote a book called *The Silent World*. The book became a film and made Cousteau famous. After that, Cousteau started to lead expeditions to study the ocean. Cousteau continued to design and improve

AUDIO SCRIPTS

scuba-diving equipment, and, in 1959, he designed a very small submarine called a diving saucer. Cousteau had a TV show in the 1960s and became very famous. He traveled around the world on the *Calypso*, and taught people about the ocean and about the fish and other animals that live in it.

12A, page 295   CD3–Track 9

Conversation 1

Rachel: That was a great presentation, Max! Good job!

Max: Oh, thanks, Rachel. I was really nervous before I started. Did you see my hands shaking? And my face was red. But after I started to talk, I didn't feel nervous.

Rachel: I didn't notice that at all. You looked fine. Did you practice a lot before your presentation?

Max: Yeah, I did. I gave my presentation to my dog . . . five times.

Rachel: To your dog?

Max: Yep! And each time he fell asleep before I finished.

Rachel: That's funny.

Conversation 2   CD3–Track 10

Angela: Hey, Sidney, how was your game?

Sidney: Oh, it was terrible.

Angela: Really? Why?

Sidney: Well, just before the game started, I began to feel sick to my stomach. And then when we started to play, my stomach hurt a lot. I asked for a substitute and left the game before halftime.

Angela: How do you feel now? Did you go back in and play later?

Sidney: No, I feel fine now, but I felt sick the whole time. I'm not sure. I think I was just really nervous.

Angela: That's too bad. Did your team win?

Sidney: Yes, actually, it was a great game. They won two to nothing. They scored the first goal just after I left the game.

LESSON 3

1 READ, page 297   CD3–Track 11

8A, page 301   CD3–Track 12

The year was 1912. The *Titanic* was a brand new ship. It was the largest ship on the ocean. It was going on its first voyage from Southampton in England to New York in the United States. More than 2000 people were on the ship. The ship had space for 64 lifeboats, but it was only carrying 20.

The ship left England on the night of April 10, 1912. Four nights later, other ships ahead of the *Titanic* sent reports about icebergs. Unfortunately, those warnings didn't reach the captain. He was having dinner with the guests on the ship.

The ship was going at full speed, and at 11:40 p.m., the *Titanic* hit an iceberg. The ship started to fill with water. The 20 lifeboats left the ship, but some weren't full. At first, people didn't believe that the *Titanic* was sinking. When they understood the danger, it was too late. The 20 lifeboats were gone.

At 2:30 a.m., the *Titanic* sank to the bottom of the ocean. More than 1500 people died. Only about 700 people survived.

REVIEW THE GRAMMAR

2A, page 303   CD3–Track 13

Exploration of the Arctic and the Antarctic

The early 20th century was a time of great exploration. Expeditions from several countries were trying to reach the North and South Poles. Voyages to the Arctic and Antarctic took several years and were very dangerous. Many explorers died when they were traveling. The weather was very cold. Sometimes the temperature was only -20 degrees Fahrenheit (-29 degrees Celsius).

In 1910, several explorers wanted to reach the North Pole. A Norwegian, Roald Amundsen, was one of the explorers, but when he was preparing for his voyage, two explorers from the United States reached the North Pole. This was bad news for Amundsen because he wanted to be first.

After the challenge of the North Pole ended, the race for the South Pole began. In fact, in 1910, explorers from Germany, France, Japan, Norway, and the United States all were planning new expeditions to the South Pole. The explorers all had the same goal: They wanted to be the first expedition to reach the South Pole.

4A, B, and C, pages 304–305   CD3–Track 14

Dana: Wow, Allen! Hi! It's nice to see you!

Allen: You, too! Are you back here, I mean, are you living here in Oklahoma?

Dana: No, I live in New York.

Allen: Oh yeah, I remember. You went to Columbia University.

Dana: That's right. You have a good memory! Do you still live here?

Allen: Yes, I'm still here in Tulsa. I took over my father's business. Remember, I worked for him when I was in high school?

Dana: Yeah, I do.

Allen: Did you come back here after college? I remember I saw you once at a party or something.

Dana: That's right. I came back for a while after I graduated, but just for a visit before I started my job. I was here when we had the tornado.

Allen: Oh, yeah. Did it hit your parents' house?

Dana: No, we were lucky. There wasn't any damage to their house. How about you?

Allen: Yes, it took the roof off the house. Luckily, it happened during the daytime. We saw it coming, so we ran downstairs. Fortunately, no one got hurt. That was just before our daughter was born.

Dana: Oh, when did you get married?

Allen: I got married when I was still in college. I married Sally Martin. Do you remember Sally?

Dana: Of course I remember Sally! . . . So you have a daughter?
Allen: Well, actually we have two daughters, . . . and our first grandchild was just born.
Dana: Allen, we're not old enough to have grandchildren!
Allen: Oh, yes we are! How about you? Are you married? Do you have any children?
Dana: Mmhm. I'm married. I've been married for oh, 15 years now . . . and we have a daughter. She's only 12, so I'm not ready for grandchildren yet!

UNIT 10

LESSON 1

1 READ, page 310   CD3–Track 15

13A and B, page 318   CD3–Track 16

Most people get out of the ocean when they see a shark fin. Not Brian Skerry! He quickly puts on his scuba suit and jumps into the water. Skerry was recently on a work assignment in the Bahamas. The water there is very clear. Skerry saw a shark fin next to the boat. He jumped into the water and started taking photos. The huge shark swam right next to Skerry. It was an oceanic whitetip shark. Skerry was happy because there aren't many of them. This kind of shark is very rare. He was also careful because oceanic whitetip sharks can be dangerous. Skerry got very close to the shark and took some amazing photos. His job as an underwater photographer is very dangerous, but he enjoys it. It's an exciting job.

LESSON 2

1 READ, page 320   CD3–Track 17

13A and B, page 327   CD3–Track 18

Jersey is an island between France and England. At the Durrell Wildlife Park, which was once the Jersey Zoo, the gorillas live in a large area. This area is big enough for the gorillas to wander freely. One day, a five-year-old boy was visiting the wildlife park with his family. He was very excited about seeing the gorillas. He climbed up on the fence to see the gorillas up close, but he got too close to the top of the fence, and he suddenly fell into the gorilla area. He hit his head hard and was unconscious.

A 400-pound gorilla named Jambo walked slowly over to the child. Everyone was very frightened, but Jambo touched the boy gently on the back. Then the huge gorilla sat quietly near the boy.

All of a sudden, the boy woke up. Everyone yelled loudly, "Don't move! Stay still!" The boy started to cry. Jambo seemed scared of the noise. He got up quietly and slowly walked away from the boy. When he left, the zookeepers quickly climbed down into the gorilla area and rescued the boy.

LESSON 3

1 READ, page 329   CD3–Track 19

9, page 333   CD3–Track 20

Ethan: Look. This is very interesting. There's a new exhibit at the zoo.
Emma: I don't like to go to zoos. I feel very sad when I see the animals in those little cages.
Ethan: Me, too. The areas for the animals aren't big enough, especially for the large animals such as lions and tigers.
Emma: Yeah, I agree with you, but zoos want to show the animals. When the exhibits are too large, sometimes people don't see any animals. The animals usually don't stay close enough to the windows of the exhibit, so it's difficult to see them.
Ethan: You're right. That's very true. The animals are often too far from the windows for anyone to see them.
Emma: My friends and I want to go on a safari someday. In Africa, animal parks are big enough for the animals. The animal parks help protect the animals.
Ethan: I know, but safaris are very expensive.
Emma: That's true. They're too expensive for me right now. Maybe someday!

11A and B, pages 334–335   CD3–Track 21

Conversation 1

Mindy: Hey, we're having a picnic at the zoo. Do you want to come with us?
Eduardo: A picnic, today? Isn't it too windy and cold? The wind is blowing too hard to eat outside.
Mindy: No, it isn't. It's definitely warm enough to eat outside.
Eduardo: Well, OK. I love the zoo.
Mindy: Me, too.

Conversation 2   CD3–Track 22

Sam: Did you see that new exhibit at the zoo, the one with all the night animals? There were some really cool animals such as bats and slender lorises. It's a beautiful exhibit. It's very interesting.
Liz: I know. I saw it, but I didn't like it. It was too dark.
Sam: Well, of course it was dark. The animals are active at night, not in the daytime. It has to be dark enough for the animals. They're nocturnal. When it's light, they go to sleep.
Liz: I know, but it was also too crowded, and it was hot! Ugh! . . . And there were too many people, and everyone was walking way too slowly. I was so happy to get outside again into some fresh air and sunlight! I didn't like it at all!

Conversation 3   CD3–Track 23

Marta: Oh, look at that bear? Isn't it cute?
David: Cute? It's not cute. It's a grizzly bear. Grizzly bears are too big to be cute.
Marta: This exhibit isn't very big, is it? It doesn't look like it's big enough for a huge bear like that.

AUDIO SCRIPTS

David: You're right. It's too small, but I heard they're building a new area for all the bears.

Marta: Oh, that's good.

REVIEW THE GRAMMAR

3A and B, page 337   CD3–Track 24

Dugongs are very gentle animals, but unfortunately, they are endangered. This means there are not many dugongs left in the world. Their numbers are decreasing quickly. There are four main reasons for this.

First, there is a problem with the dugong's food supply. Dugongs eat a lot of seagrass, but the supply of seagrass is not large enough to feed all of them. Seagrass grows very slowly, and some of the changes in the ocean kill large areas of seagrass.

Second, dugongs are protected in many countries, but in others they are not. In some countries, people hunt and kill them. Dugongs swim very slowly and come to the surface often, so hunters are able to catch and kill them easily.

Fishing boats are another reason why dugongs are endangered. Large fishing boats sometimes kill dugongs accidentally. The fishing boats use large nets to catch fish. Dugongs aren't fast enough to swim out of the nets, so they often get caught in the nets and can't get out. Unfortunately, this kind of accident happens very frequently.

And finally, dugongs don't have a lot of babies. A female dugong only has one baby every one to five years. This means the number of dugongs does not grow very quickly. Many people are worried about the future of dugongs. How much longer will these beautiful, gentle animals exist?

UNIT 11

LESSON 1

1 READ, page 342   CD3–Track 25

5 PRONUNCIATION, page 345   CD3–Track 26

5A, page 345   CD3–Track 27

1. I can't hear you very well. Please speak up.
2. She can speak three languages.
3. I can't swim.
4. He can't come with us.
5. My sister can't drive.
6. They can run very fast.
7. She can't write very well.
8. I can't understand you.
9. He can't remember my name.
10. You can speak English.

12A and B, pages 350–351   CD3–Track 28

Is there a flying car in your future? Three companies are trying to sell them. Here are your choices. One car is called the Transition. This flying car looks like a real plane in the sky, but on the ground, the wings fold. You can drive it to an airport to fly it. It can fly 115 miles per hour (185 kilometers per hour), and you can fly as far as 490 miles (787 kilometers) before you need to get more fuel.

The PAL-V is short for Personal Air and Land Vehicle. This flying car flies like a tiny helicopter. It can go 110 miles per hour (177 kilometers per hour), and fly for 350 miles (563 kilometers). On the ground, it's a bit like a motorcycle with three wheels. It's very fun to drive!

The SkyRunner is very unusual. It uses a parasail to fly! It can take off from a beach or any other flat area. It can take off when it's going 45 miles per hour on the ground, but it can fly 55 miles per hour (88 kilometers per hour) in the air. You can fly it for 200 miles (321 kilometers).

All three cars can carry two passengers, but they're very small, and they can't carry very much luggage. And don't worry about flying lessons. The companies will make sure that you know how to fly their cars!

LESSON 2

1 READ, page 352   CD3–Track 29

12A and B, page 358   CD3–Track 30

It wasn't easy for women to get an education in science or medicine before the 1900s. In the 1700s, in Paris, a young girl named Sophie Germain wanted to study math, but she had a big problem. Her parents told her, "No, Sophie. Young women don't study mathematics!" But that didn't stop Sophie. Late at night, when her parents were asleep, Sophie taught herself math. She continued to study in secret.

A few years later, a new science and math college opened in Paris. Sophie wanted to go to that college to study math, but the college was for men only. Sophie soon learned about a student named Antoine-August Le Blanc. Le Blanc wasn't a very good student, and he was terrible at math. He quit the college and left Paris, but he didn't tell the college. This was great for Sophie. She wrote a letter to le Blanc's math professor at the college, and she signed it with the other student's name, Monsieur Le Blanc. She asked the professor for the homework assignments. He sent them to her, and she sent the completed homework assignments back to the professor.

The professor didn't know Monsieur Le Blanc was a woman. He graded Sophie's homework assignments and answered the questions in her letters, so Sophie was able to learn a lot about math! In fact, the professor was very surprised because Monsieur Le Blanc had such bad grades in math before, but now he seemed like a very good student. The professor sent a letter and asked the student to visit his office. Sophie couldn't say no. She went to visit the professor. When he saw her, he was very surprised. He couldn't believe it! Monsieur Le Blanc was a woman!

The professor continued to work with Sophie, and she continued to study and share her ideas about math. She didn't become a teacher or get a job, but she worked hard to solve difficult math problems. In fact, she solved some math problems that many other people weren't able to do. Later, Sophie Germain became interested in physics. One of her ideas in that field made it possible for people to build tall buildings such as the Eiffel Tower. She never graduated from college, but her ideas were very important.

LESSON 3

1 READ, page 359   CD3–Track 31

11, page 364   CD3–Track 32

Conversation 1

Andres: I really want to play in the game tomorrow, but I can't.

Jill: Why not?

Andres: Well, I was practicing yesterday, and I hurt my foot.

Jill: That's too bad. Ted is sick, so he can't play either.

Conversation 2

Yuri: Terry won the bike race yesterday, so we're having a party for her. Are you free on Friday night?

Liam: That's great, but I have plans for dinner with my parents. What time is the party?

Yuri: The party's at eight, and it's at Carol's house.

Liam: Oh, well, we usually eat dinner at six, and Carol lives near me, so I can go to the party after dinner.

Conversation 3

Jason: It's noon, and I'm thinking about lunch. Do you want to join me?

Ed: Sorry. I just finished breakfast, so I'm not hungry.

Jason: Hi, Mark. Ed isn't hungry, but I am. How about lunch?

Mark: Oh, I'm sorry. That sounds good, but I have a lot of work today.

13A, page 365   CD3–Track 33

Section 1

Everyone knows the name Walt Disney. Walt Disney was the man who started the famous film studio and amusement parks. He created Mickey Mouse. He became a very successful artist and businessperson, but most people don't know about his life when he was young. His family was poor, so he got a job to help when he was still a boy. He wasn't a good student, and he left high school after just one year. He started a company, but it didn't do well. When he was 22 years old, Disney left his hometown for California with only $40. But finally, in California, he and his brother started another company, and it was a great success.

Section 2

Bruce Hall was born with a lot of eye problems. In fact, he was almost completely blind. This makes him very unusual. He's a photographer, but he can't see! When Hall was a child, he heard people talk about the stars at night, but he couldn't see them. Then one night when he was visiting a friend, he looked through a telescope. He was able to see stars for the first time! After that, he started to use a camera to see things. He also learned how to scuba dive, so he takes photos underwater, too. His photos are very interesting, and they've been in exhibits all over the world.

Section 3   CD3–Track 35

Ludwig van Beethoven was a very famous musical composer. He was a great musician, and he started to write music when he was only 12 years old. He became famous and wrote many very beautiful symphonies and other works of music, but when he was about 26, he began to lose his hearing. A few years later, he was almost completely deaf. He wasn't able to hear his own music, but even after he became deaf, he still continued to write music. In fact, he composed some of his most famous music, including the Ninth Symphony, in the last years of his life.

REVIEW THE GRAMMAR

4A and 4B, page 369   CD3–Track 36

Ned: Look, here's a book by Tami Oldham Ashcraft.

Patty: Who's she?

Ned: Oh, she's the woman who had that terrible experience on a sailboat in a hurricane. Don't you remember? There was a guy on the boat with her, but he died.

Patty: No, I don't remember that at all. Tell me about it.

Ned: OK, so Tami was pretty young, about 23 years old, and she wanted to see the world, so she helped other people sail their boats around the world. You know, when they needed another person on the boat to go across the ocean or something . . . And then sometimes she sailed boats from one place to another for other people. So, anyway, she was in Tahiti, in the South Pacific, and she and this guy, Robert, . . . no Richard, Sharp—he was her fiancé—they had a job to sail a boat from Tahiti all the way across the Pacific to the US, California. . . . Anyway, they left Tahiti, and everything was fine. Nice boat, good weather, . . . But then, they heard about a hurricane coming across the Pacific. They couldn't believe it, really, because it wasn't hurricane season. So they changed direction and went a different way to try to get out of the hurricane's way, but the hurricane changed direction too, . . . and it was a terrible hurricane—a category four, with really huge waves. Tami was inside the boat and Richard was outside, you know, at the wheel steering the boat, and all of a sudden, a huge wave picked the boat up and turned it completely upside down. The boat turned all the way over and then it was right side up again!

Patty: Yikes. Scary!

Ned: Oh, yeah, can you imagine? Anyway, Tami was hurt pretty badly. She was unconscious. This happened at one in the afternoon, and she didn't wake up until four the next day. When she woke up, the ocean was completely calm, no waves, nothing, but everything in the boat was a complete wreck. There was water in the boat, and everything was all over the

AUDIO SCRIPTS

place. It was a mess! Anyway, Tami went up onto the deck of the boat and called for Richard, but he wasn't there.

Patty: Oh my gosh! How terrible!

Ned: Yeah, she kept looking for him, but she couldn't find him. He got washed off the boat by that huge wave I guess. So she was all alone.

Patty: Wow! So what did she do?

Ned: Well, she couldn't do much. The boat was very badly damaged, so she couldn't sail it, and there was no electricity. The radio was gone too, so she couldn't call for help.

Patty: How about the engine? Did *that* work?

Ned: No, there was too much water in the engine, so she couldn't use it. She just steered the boat and tried to move toward Hawaii.

Patty: How did she know where to go? I mean, she didn't have any electricity, so she couldn't use GPS or anything.

Ned: No, but luckily, she knew how to use the sun to figure out her location. So finally, she got to Hawaii. It took her 41 days. That's almost *six* weeks. Can you imagine?

Patty: No, I really can't imagine that at all.

Ned: And another amazing thing. After that, she went back to Tahiti, and then she got on another sailboat! She sailed to Fiji, and she still sails. Isn't that amazing?

Patty: It sure is. Wow. That's an incredible story! Now I want to read the book!

UNIT 12

LESSON 1

1 READ, page 374   CD3–Track 37

14B, page 382   CD3–Track 38

Phuket

Phuket is an island in Thailand. It has tropical beaches, beautiful mountains, and jungles to explore. The best weather is from December to April, when it is drier than it is during the rest of the year. The rest of the year is quite rainy. In fact, the average rainfall is 62 inches (160 centimeters) a year. The weather is very warm there. In fact, from February to April, the average high temperature is 92 degrees Fahrenheit (33 degrees Celsius).

There are about 500,000 residents on the island, and about 5.3 million visitors every year. They come to enjoy the beaches, go scuba diving, go swimming, and even to go on safaris into the jungle where they can see elephants and other animals. It's a very popular tourist destination.

Prague   CD3–Track 39

Prague is a city in the Czech Republic with a population of over 1.2 million. It's a beautiful city with lots of interesting historic places to visit, like the Old Town Square, the Prague Castle, and the Charles Bridge. Most of the approximately 5 million tourists come in the summer months, and they enjoy the attractions as well as the beautiful museums, cafés, and parks.

In the summer, the average high temperature is 70 degrees Fahrenheit (21 degrees Celsius). Many people visit in the off-season, but the city does get snow in the winter. The yearly average rainfall each year is 20 inches (50 centimeters), and the rainiest months are in the summer. From May to August, the city gets a lot of rain.

LESSON 2

1 READ, page 383   CD3–Track 40

12A and B, page 389   CD3–Track 41

Conversation 1

Dennis: What city in Europe has the most museums? I want to figure out how much time to spend in the cities we're going to visit.

Annecy: The most museums or the best museums?

Dennis: Both, I guess.

Annecy: Well, that's really hard to say. Maybe Berlin? Or London? Of course, Paris has the Louvre, the most famous museum in the world. My favorite is St. Petersburg in Russia. It has a lot of museums, but the best is the Hermitage. It's one of the biggest museums in the world, and it's a really interesting place. But Berlin has some of the best museums in the world, too. Hmmm. I don't really know.

Dennis: Well, maybe we'll just allow an extra day in each big city to visit museums.

Annecy: That's a good idea.

Conversation 2   CD3–Track 42

Gabi: How about lunch? Do you want to go to the place on Main Street?

Sharon: Oh, thanks. I brought a sandwich today. I'm trying to save money for a trip.

Gabi: Oh, yeah? Where to?

Sharon: The Galápagos.

Gabi: The Galápagos! Cool. Are you going on a tour to see wildlife?

Sharon: Well, you don't exactly go there to go shopping! Yeah, I'm going on an eight-day tour. I can't wait. You know the Galápagos Islands have some of the most unusual wildlife in the world.

Gabi: Wow! That sounds like a wonderful trip. Have fun.

Sharon: Thanks.

Conversation 3   CD3–Track 43

Amy: Look at this Top 10 list. It has the most expensive streets to shop on . . . There's one in Zurich, Switzerland. I can't pronounce it. And then Rodeo Drive in California. It's also one of the most expensive places to shop.

Barb: What about that area in Tokyo? The Ginza? Is that on the list?

Amy: Yes, it's number four, after a street in Reykjavik, Iceland.

Barb: You know, I don't know why they make a list like that. Who has the money to shop at the most expensive places in the world?

Amy: Obviously, the richest people in the world! Most people just go there to look, you know, window shop.

Barb: Well, that's definitely all I could afford to do!

LESSON 3

1 READ, page 391   CD3–Track 44

11A, page 397   CD3–Track 45

1. The architect of this building is a woman named, Zaha Hadid. The building is in Montpelier, France. It's very large. In fact, it has a sports center, a library, and a place for government archives in it. The shape of this building is traditional, but it has smooth lines and an interesting, flowing design.

2. Two architects, Jacques Herzog and Pierre de Meuron, worked with other architects in their company to design this building. It is a library at the Brandenburg University of Technology in Cottbus, Germany. The shape of their building is unusual. It doesn't have any straight lines, and many people can't tell the front from the back because they look almost the same. The outside of the building has letters from many different alphabets all over it.

3. Frank Gehry, an architect, is well known for his unusual designs. This building is very interesting. Its design is definitely not traditional with its mix of colors and shapes. It has some straight lines, but the walls go in different directions. This building is a technology center on the campus at a university in the United States, MIT, the Massachusetts Institute of Technology.

REVIEW THE GRAMMAR

3A and B, page 400   CD3–Track 46

Woman: I really want to go to visit Mesa Verde when we're in Colorado.

Man: Me, too.

Woman: So I looked up ways to visit the park.

Man: Oh, good. What did you find out?

Woman: OK, so first, we can drive, or we can take a tour.

Man: OK.

Woman: So the bus tour is a half day. It starts at eight, and it lasts for four hours. You stop at different places to see the cliff dwellings and other stuff. It's on a big tour bus. Air-conditioned.

Man: How much does it cost?

Woman: Around $50 each.

Man: Hm. That's expensive.

Woman: Well, yes, but they give you a lot of information along the way. I mean, you learn a lot on the drive, and it's cheaper than a couple of other options.

Man: Oh, yeah?

Woman: Mhmm . . . There's another option. It's a full-day tour. Leaves at eight and gets back at five. Lunch is part of this one. It costs $145. It's a smaller group. You ride in vans, not a big bus.

Man: I wonder why it takes so long.

Woman: Well, there's a lot to see at the park. I mean, they recommend that you spend two days visiting.

Man: OK. So are there any more options?

Woman: Yeah, there's also a jeep tour.

Man: Oh, that sounds like fun. I like that idea.

Woman: Yeah, but it might be hot in a jeep. We're going in August, you know.

Man: Good point, but how much does it cost?

Woman: About $100 a person. So, anyway, the last idea is to drive ourselves and just go to each place on our own. We could rent a car for about $75.

Man: Hmmm . . . Does the park offer any tours?

Woman: Yes, they do. They cost $3 a person.

Man: Really? That's all?

Woman: Uh huh.

Man: OK, so we need to rent a car anyway, right?

Woman: Right . . .

UNIT 13

LESSON 1

1 READ, page 406   CD4–Track 2

7, page 410   CD4–Track 3

Sidney: Do you know much about German culture? I'm going to Berlin on a business trip next month.

Darcy: I know one thing. You shouldn't be late! Germans are very punctual.

Sidney: That's right. I should be on time for my meetings. Should I take gifts with me?

Darcy: That's a good question. I don't know. You should ask Greta. She's from Germany.

Sidney: You're right! In fact, if I'm not mistaken, I think she's from Berlin! What else should I ask her?

Darcy: Well, should you wear formal clothes, or is it OK to dress informally?

Sidney: Good idea. Also, should I call people by their first names? I know in some countries it's better to use Mr. and Ms.

Darcy: Right. That's important. You should look for information about German business customs online. You can probably find a lot of helpful information there.

Sidney: That's true. Thanks. Maybe I should buy a guidebook, too. Well, we should hurry. It's time for our meeting with the director.

AUDIO SCRIPTS

9A, page 411   CD4-Track 4

When you do business in another country, you should try to learn about some of the customs before you go. For example, in most countries, you should be on time for meetings, but in some countries, such as the United States, you should try to arrive a few minutes early for a meeting. You definitely shouldn't be late.

In South Africa, you should take some time at the beginning of a meeting to talk about topics such as health or family. You shouldn't "talk business" immmediately. Also, you shouldn't put someone's business card in your pocket. You should put it in a business-card holder. It's also polite to make a comment about the card. Non-verbal customs are also important to know. In many countries, for example, in Thailand, you shouldn't use your left hand to give someone something. For example, you should never present your business card with your left hand. And, speaking of parts of the body, in Thailand, it's not appropriate to touch someone on the head, or to pass something over someone's head. And it's rude to show anyone the bottom of your foot.

LESSON 2

1 READ, page 413   CD4-Track 5

10, page 419   CD4-Track 6

Wedding Customs around the World

Customs for marriage are different around the world. For example, in some countries, arranged marriages are common. In an arranged marriage, young people can't choose their own husbands or wives. They have to marry the person their family chooses. In other societies, young people don't have to get their parents' approval before they marry. They can make their own decisions. What is the custom in your country? Can you choose your husband or wife, or are arranged marriages common?

Wedding ceremonies are also different around the world. For example, in China, couples have to do research to decide on a lucky day for their wedding. A wedding has to begin on the half hour because the hands on the clock are moving up. The bride has a choice for the color of her dress; she doesn't have to wear red, but red is a lucky color for weddings. In some countries, such as Panama, the groom has to give the bride 13 coins. In Sweden, the bride has to put a gold coin from her mother in one shoe and a silver coin from her father in the other shoe.

12A and B, pages 420–421   CD4-Track 7

In India, there are a lot of different traditions surrounding weddings. There are a lot of different cultures and traditions in India, so let me tell you about my tradition. First, before the wedding, the bride has a special event called a "mehndi." This is when the women in the wedding party put beautiful designs on their skin with henna. Henna is a dye. It colors the skin. You have to be careful with it. After you put henna on, you can't wash it off your skin. You have to wait for it to wear off. There's a nice tradition related to this—after the wedding, the bride doesn't have to do any housework until the henna wears off!

Next, let me tell you about the wedding clothes. A bride doesn't have to wear red, but *most* brides wear red or red and white. They have to wear a *sari*, traditional clothing for women. The groom also wears special traditional clothes.

The groom usually arrives with his family and friends at the wedding. When the groom arrives, the bride and groom have to exchange garlands. These are ropes of flowers that they wear. The groom has to put a red mark on the bride's forehead. This is a special sign that she is now a married woman.

A traditional wedding ceremony takes place under a canopy by a special fire on the ground. The bride and groom have to walk around the fire, and they have to make seven promises to each other.

LESSON 3

1 READ, page 422   CD4-Track 8

10B, page 427   CD4-Track 9

Conversation 1

Jessie: You always tell me such interesting things about Panama. I'd like to go there sometime. Could you give me some suggestions for places to see?

Felipe: Oh. Would you like the names of my favorite places?

Jessie: Yes. Could you tell me the name of a hotel, too?

Felipe: Sure. Let me know if you have any other questions.

Jessie: Great. Thanks, Felipe!

Conversation 2

Agent: Hello. Adventure Travel Company. Can I help you?

Hans: Yes, I'd like some information about tours to the South Pacific.

Agent: Could you hold on for a minute, please?

Hans: OK.

Agent: Hello, I'm back. Now, could you please give me your name?

REVIEW THE GRAMMAR

3A and B, page 429   CD4-Track 10

Sandra: When we go to Papua New Guinea, I'd like to visit the Huli tribe. I'm really interested in their culture.

Armando: The Huli?

Sandra: Yeah. They have an interesting tradition. The Huli men grow their hair long and then make it into wigs. A good wig is important. It shows that they are strong, so the young men work hard to grow their hair. They have to eat special food, and they water their hair several times a day.

Armando: Wow! Really?

Sandra: Yeah. Also, there are some interesting rules for Huli boys. They can't run, and they can't get close to fires.

Armando: Really? Why not?

Sandra: Because they have to be careful of their hair. Then, when their hair is long enough, they make it into a wig.

Armando: That's interesting! Can we see them?

Sandra: Yes, they like to show people their culture. We should give them some money when we visit, of course, but they welcome visitors. They put on their wigs and wear traditional clothes and do traditional dances for visitors.

Armando: So, they don't wear these wigs all the time?

Sandra: No, the wigs are for special occasions.

Armando: How about the women? Do they wear wigs, too?

Sandra: No, just the men wear them. It's interesting. The women and men live in separate houses. The women have to do most of the work. They do the farming, and they take care of the children. There are special buildings for men, and the women can't go inside them.

Armando: Interesting. So the men don't have to work?

Sandra: I don't think so.

Armando: Do we have to go with a group, or can we go on our own?

Sandra: I don't know. I need to do some more research.

Armando: Can I help you?

Sandra: Sure. That would be great.

UNIT 14

LESSON 1

1 READ, page 434 CD4–Track 11

11, page 439 CD4–Track 12

1. I'm going to talk to the teacher this afternoon.
2. She's studying in the library now.
3. Marcel isn't studying on campus this year.
4. A lot of courses are going to be online next year.
5. My sister is staying with me next week.
6. I'm going to get a job next summer.
7. She's leaving tonight.
8. She's taking English classes this semester.
9. We're graduating next month.
10. She's calling her mother.

15A, page 441 CD4–Track 13

Trey: Hi, Sonya. How are you?

Sonya: Oh, hi Trey! I'm good. How are you doing?

Trey: Great! Just one more month, and we graduate!

Sonya: I know. So, what are you going to do next year?

Trey: I'm going to Central State College. How about you?

Sonya: Well, I'm not going to go to college right away. I'm going to take a year off.

Trey: Oh, really? That's what my cousin wants to do. Do you remember Mylo?

Sonya: Sure. I remember him.

Trey: He wants to travel for a year. Well, first he needs to work and save some money. And then he wants to go to India.

Sonya: Really? Wow! That's interesting. What made him choose India?

Trey: His best friend's family is from India. They're going back to India, and they invited him to visit their home in Jodhpur.

Sonya: Jodhpur? Where's that?

Trey: It's in the state of Rajasthan. And how about you? What are you going to do?

Sonya: I'm going to go to Africa and do community service in Kenya. First, I'm going to teach at a school in a village near Nairobi, the capital. That starts in August.

Trey: Wow! That's really interesting. What are you going to teach?

Sonya: Science and math. I'm just going to be helping another teacher.

Trey: What are you going to do after that?

Sonya: I'm going to work in a medical clinic in Nairobi, just helping out again. I don't know much about it yet.

Trey: And where are you going to live?

Sonya: With families in their homes. I'm really excited about that.

Trey: I bet. It sounds really interesting. You're going to learn a lot about Kenyan culture! So, are you going to be a teacher or a doctor?

Sonya: I have no idea. I think it's going to be an interesting year, though.

Trey: Are you going to go to college after that?

Sonya: I hope so. I'm going to apply next year. I don't know where yet.

Trey: Well, keep in touch!

Sonya: You, too.

LESSON 2

1 READ, page 443 CD4–Track 14

5, page 446 CD4–Track 15

1.

Berta: Bye! I'll see you in class tomorrow.

Jess: OK. It's raining, and I think there'll be a lot of traffic on your way home, so be careful.

Berta: OK, I'll drive slowly.

2.

Tasha: Your cold sounds terrible. Have some hot tea with lemon. It'll make you feel better.

Kim: Please don't worry about me. I'll be fine.

Tasha: OK, but get some sleep and feel better!

Kim: OK. Thanks. I'll call you tomorrow.

3.

Cory: Why are you studying now for next week's vocabulary test? You won't remember all the words next week.

Sid: There are a lot of words on the list. I'm studying a few each day. It'll help me remember them.

AUDIO SCRIPTS

Cory: Well, I guess I'll do the same thing, but I don't have a list of all of the words.
Sid: I'll e-mail you my list.
Cory: OK. Thanks!

14A and B, page 451   CD4–Track 16

Keesha: Hi, Craig. Do you know what you're teaching next fall yet?
Craig: Oh, hi Keesha! Yeah, I'm teaching Spanish 203 and a literature course. How about you?
Keesha: I'm teaching Spanish 101 and 103, and I'm going to teach them both online.
Craig: Oh, really? You're going to teach *Spanish online*?
Keesha: Uh-huh. Why?
Craig: Well, I mean, how will students practice? How will they learn pronunciation? They won't learn as much as they do in a classroom.
Keesha: Well, that's not what the research shows. Students actually do fine in online courses. In fact, their grades might even be higher than students in traditional classrooms.
Craig: I don't believe that. You know what I'm worried about, though? That the college won't need as many teachers with all these online classes. Some of us may lose our jobs.
Keesha: OK, well, yeah, that might be true, but I like teaching online. I can do it from anywhere. I might even work from my beach house next year.
Craig: Sounds like a great plan, but not for me. I'll never teach online.
Keesha: You never know, Craig! You might like it!

LESSON 3

1 READ, page 452   CD4–Track 17

12A and B, page 458   CD4–Track 18

Martha: So what are you going to do for vacation?
David: Unfortunately, I'm not going to have a vacation this summer. I'm going to be studying.
Martha: Really? That's too bad! What are you studying for?
David: Well, I'm taking a test preparation course.
Martha: What for?
David: The college entrance exam.
Martha: But we still have two years of high school. You don't have to take the exam for another year! Why are you taking the course before you need it?
David: Well, I'm taking a course now . . . Then, I'm going to take another course before I take the exam. So I'm going to take two courses. I mean, this exam is really important. If I don't get a good score on the entrance exam, I won't get into a good university, and then I won't get a good job.
Martha: But do you think those test prep courses make a difference? I don't think they really help. I mean, if you're smart, you'll do well on the test. If you're not smart, you won't.
David: Oh, no. I think these courses really make a difference. If you take a test prep course, you can do a lot better.
Martha: Hmm . . . Well, I hope so. Do you already know what you want to study in college?
David: No, not yet. When I start college, I'll figure it out. How about you? What are you going to study?
Martha: I'm going to study business. After I finish school, I'm going to work in my family's store.
David: You're so lucky you already know you have a job.
Martha: Well, I don't really have a choice. If I don't work for my father, everyone will be upset.

REVIEW THE GRAMMAR

3A and B, page 461   CD4–Track 19

Teacher: So, Ali. What are your plans after you finish this course?
Ali: Well, my long-term goal is to be a math teacher.
Teacher: Great.
Ali: Yes, and I want to get my degree at a university here, so I'm going to take some more English courses.
Teacher: That sounds like a good idea.
Ali: I think I'll probably study English for another eight months, until June . . . Actually, it depends on my test scores. I'm going to take the English test in May . . . If I don't get a good score on the test in May, I'll have to study English in the summer and take the test again in the fall . . . If I get a good score, I'm going to take a vacation!
Teacher: And what about after that?
Ali: Well, I'm not sure. I'm applying to several universities for next September. So, if I get accepted, I'll start classes then. If I don't get accepted, I'll probably go back home to Saudi Arabia.
Teacher: And are you going to get married?
Ali: Oh, sure. Sometime . . . I'll probably get married after I finish university, but I have to get a job before I get married.
Teacher: Well, keep in touch, OK?
Ali: Definitely! I'll e-mail you when I have some news. Thank you for teaching me. I really enjoyed your class.
Teacher: Oh, I'm glad. You're welcome.